Prayer:
The
Global
Experience

Prayer:
The
Global
Experience

Francis A. Eigo, O.S.A.
Editor

The Villanova University Press

Copyright © 1997 by Francis A. Eigo, O.S.A.
The Villanova University Press
Villanova, Pennsylvania 19085
Library of Congress Cataloging-in-Publication Data
Prayer: the global experience / Francis A. Eigo, editor.

    p.   cm.
  Includes index.
  ISBN 0-87723-090-0
  1. Prayer—Comparative studies. 2. Christianity and other
  religions. I. Eigo, Francis A.
BL560.P68 1997   97-14146
291.4'3—dc21   CIP

à

D C C B

Félicitations

et

Bonne Chance,

Monsieur le Président!

Contents

Contributors

WILLIAM CENKNER, a member of the faculty of The Catholic University of America, has published in scholarly journals and books. He is the author of *Creative Moral Protest: The Teaching of Mohandas K. Gandhi* and *The Hindu Personality in Education: Tagore, Gandhi, Aurobindo*; he has coauthored and edited *The Religious Quest* as well as edited several books, including *Multicultural Experience in U.S. Church and Theology* and *Evil and the Response of World Religions*.

CAROL JOY GALLAGHER, an ordained priest of the Episcopal church, married and the mother of three daughters, a Ph.D. Candidate at Princeton Theological Seminary, a Native American of Cherokee heritage, is a member of the faculty of Villanova University and Rector of Saint Anne's Episcopal Church, in Middletown, Delaware. Her professional experience includes the field of ministry development for which she has written articles and led workshops that focus on women's roles and Native issues; Christian education for which she has designed and implemented curricula for preschool through adult education; and pastoral experience which involves designing and leading cross cultural and intergenerational dialogues and workshops.

DOLORES LEE GREELEY, R.S.M., a member of the faculty of Saint Louis University, a recipient of numerous awards and grants, has presented papers before professional societies and has published in scholarly journals and books. She is the author of *The Church as "Body of Christ" according to the Teaching of St. John Chrysostom*.

MARY JO MEADOW, Director of the Religious Studies Program at Mankato State University, has contributed chapters to a number of books, has published a series of cassette tapes, and has written numerous articles for scholarly journals. Her most recent books include *Gentling the Heart: Buddhist Loving Kindness Practice for Christians, Purifying the Heart: Buddhist Insight Meditation for Christians* (with Kevin Culligan and Daniel Chowning), and *Through a Glass Darkly: A Spiritual Psychology of Faith*.

GERARD STEPHEN SLOYAN, Adjunct Professor at The Catholic University of America, has a rich and varied professional background that includes prestigious positions held, awards received, and eighteen popular books and some two hundred articles published. Among his most recent books authored he includes *Jesus Redeemer and Divine Word, What Are They Saying about John?, The Crucifixion of Jesus: History, Myth, Faith,* and *Walking in the Truth.*

JANE IDLEMAN SMITH, Professor at Hartford Seminary, has engaged in wide ranging professional activities that include articles published in professional journals, chapters contributed to a number of books, and professional papers and lectures delivered both at home and abroad. She has recently coauthored with Yvonne Yazbeck Haddad *Muslim Communities in America* and *Mission to America: Five Islamic Sectarian Movements in the United States.*

Introduction

This second of two volumes on the topic of prayer considers Christians and the global experience of prayer. After Dolores Greeley's introductory essay on the theme, William Cenkner looks at Christians and the Hindu experience of prayer, followed by Gerard Sloyan's essay on Christians and the Jewish experience, Mary Jo Meadow's Christians and the Buddhist experience, Jane Smith's Christians and the Islamic experience, and, finally, Carol Gallagher's the Native American Christian experience.

Once again, my appreciation is due the ever faithful Theology Institute Committee composed of Walter Conn, Bernard A. Lazor, O.S.A., Lee Makowski, O.S.A., Gaile Pohlhaus, and Arlene Swidler; the presiders (Edward Enright, O.S.A., B. A. Lazor, Gaile Pohlhaus); the Coordinator, Gaile Pohlhaus, especially for her special assistance in an emergency; my assistant, Patricia Fry; the essayists, and, by no means least, the Administrators of Villanova University who consistently provide unstinting support in our endeavors.

Francis A. Eigo, O.S.A.,
Editor

Christians and the Global Experience of Prayer

Dolores Lee Greeley, R.S.M.

INTRODUCTION

A Starting Point for Prayer

At Georgetown University, we read these words, etched in marble, of the famous Jesuit paleontologist, Teilhard de Chardin:

> The Age of Nations is Past.
> It remains for us now,
> If we do not wish to perish,
> To set aside the ancient prejudice
> And build the earth.

Writing in the early to mid 1900s, this complex and brilliant thinker held views on creation and evolution highly suspect for the early decades of the twentieth century; yet, most of his thinking and writing had to do with the future — the future of humankind and of society. He approached the intricate and cosmic system of the universe from both a scientific and a Christian point of view. He expressed and extended in his vision and spirituality great insights of philosophical and religious leaders of the past, described later by Karl Jaspers in his work, *The Origin and Goal of History*.

Jaspers had described the change in consciousness that occurred around five hundred B.C.E., a shift from thinking of persons with identity coexisting only with their social group and merging at death into the cosmos, to a realization of, and dialogue about, each person's separate, individualized identity in life and continuing in some fashion after death. Great spiritual leaders, teachers, and prophets of this time included Confucius and Lao-Tze in China, Siddhartha Gautama who became the Buddha in

1

India, Zoroaster in Persia, and in Israel the Hebrew prophets: Amos, Hosea, Isaiah, and Jeremiah. In Greece came Socrates, Plato, and Aristotle. All the great religious traditions, with their teachings, practices, rituals, prayers, and values, came to be at this time. Jaspers wrote: "In this age were born the fundamental categories within which we still think today, and the beginnings of the world religions, by which human beings still live, were created."[1] Teilhard saw that we are indeed individual persons before our Triune God, but also that we belong to an earth, created by, evolving, and, with ever greater consciousness, returning to oneness in God.

In our own time, we seem to have expressed the limit of individuality of persons and nations. We have lived, as it were, under the aegis of individual rights and nationalism. Nations have looked to their own interests, legitimizing war with other countries, occupying them, building an empire with armies, navies, and, more recently, nuclear arsenals. We honored heroes who died for their country, advancing or defending its existence. A memorial plaque at the University of Notre Dame is inscribed with the names of young graduates who died with countless others: FOR GOD, FOR COUNTRY, FOR NOTRE DAME.

A New Age

The twenty-first century, still in embryo, is forcing new ways of thinking about who is our neighbor. There are a new theology, *Planetary Theology*,[2] and new forms of prayer, *Planetary Prayers*,[3] a new ethic, *Global Responsibility: In Search of a New World Ethic*,[4] *Liberation Theologies: The Global Pursuit of Justice*.[5] There is a search for a new answer to the question, "What does it mean to be human in the universe as it is now understood?"[6] All the signs of the times point to the fact that we have no other choice but to broaden our horizons, to enter into dialogue and bond across borders. Communications and information encircle our world. More than two thousand satellites and space objects are circling the earth, sending information and messages constantly back to planet earth. In every living room and out to the most farflung hut in the desert of Baluchistan, the whole world is linked by telephone, postal systems, radio, television, E-Mail, and the Internet. All of us stand today in a relationship of interdependence economically, politically, and socially, whether facing a crisis together, striving for peace, or succumbing to chemical or nuclear death. This is the most pressing need for us today — the recognition of our common humanity, our common jeopardy, our common possibilities and destiny. We have, as of now, little experience in planetary thinking. We are just beginning.

An awareness of a "Global Age," we hope a Golden Age, took a sudden leap, burst into consciousness when, in 1969, we saw for the first time, like an incredible Christmas ornament of the universe, planet earth from space. We were filled with a sense of togetherness, bondedness, unity, oneness, wholeness, connectedness. It was a profound experience that had a deep effect on all of humankind. It allowed for the first time for many of us a global experience of prayer, as words of praise, awe, and wonder deepened profoundly the song of the psalmist in exaltation: "O Lord, Our Lord, how awesome is your name through all the earth!" (Ps. 8). For Edgar Mitchell, the sixth man to walk on the moon, it was an experience of instant global consciousness. "When you're up there you are no longer an American citizen, or a Russian citizen. Suddenly all those boundaries disappear. You are a planetary citizen."[7] Russell Schweikart, of the Apollo 9 flight crew, expressed the same sentiment while on a mission to the moon: "From out here there are no limits, no frames, no boundaries; from here the earth is a whole."[8] How powerfully these reflections call us to transcend ourselves and to pray with a fellow world citizen:

> We call upon the power which sustains the planets in their orbits, that wheels our Milky Way in its 200-million-year spiral, to imbue our personalities and our relationships with harmony, endurance and joy. Fill us with a sense of immense time so that our brief, flickering lives may truly reflect the work of vast ages past and also the millions of years of evolution whose potential lies in our trembling hands.[9]

For the first time in history, human beings can have a sense of the earth as a whole, not merely of our limited, earth bound horizons, but of a single organic unit. This new image of the earth is the symbol of the emerging global consciousness of our time. Such pictures as these are the icons of our time, spiritual symbols of wholeness, of oneness, which elicit reflections on issues of concern for all of humankind. We realize the connectedness of the ecological system of the planet. We understand a little the complexities of the issues of peace and economic justice toward developing countries and the importance of setting a global agenda as women did in Beijing, China, last summer. Walbert Buhlmann tells it plainly, "Despite all obstacles and difficulties, the world, for the first time in history is not only called to unity but downright condemned to it."[10]

Crossing Over

The radical transformation to a global consciousness today makes us aware of our connectedness to the whole of the material universe and of the encompassing of the whole of humankind on the planet in the entirety of its human experience. This unity is simply a fact. But, if we are to do more than survive, we must link mentally and spiritually. We must embark as a human community on a spiritual journey. The image of the earth moving peacefully through space is a symbol of our common spiritual journey. People seek their spiritual roots in their own tradition as well as in the ancient wisdom of the Orient. The spiritual journey can take many paths. One path is to "pass-over" from one's own belief system to that of another culture or religion and then to return to one's own enriched reality stretched by the insights achieved. To undertake such a spiritual journey, to "pass-over" to the Hindu faith, for example, we must look at the world through Hindu eyes. It helps to familiarize ourselves with Hindu writings, Hindu beliefs, the Hindu way of life, the caste system. Yet, the faith of the Hindu does not lie in data, not even in the heart, but in the gut. The data serve the Hindu by inducing in him or her a certain orientation to the world. To appreciate the world view of the Hindu, to critique, for example, the caste system, we must search to find what the tradition, what the universe mean to the Hindu in the light of the tradition. We might ask, "What has the *Gita* been doing to people these thousands of years as under its influence they have gone about their daily tasks?"[11] Diana L. Eck asked these questions. In her book, *Encountering God*, she describes her spiritual journey from Bozeman, a small town in Montana, to Banaras, India, where she encountered a multitude of gods and "met dedicated, socially concerned, spiritually alive Hindus who worshipped them."[12] Such an encounter was a real challenge to her own faith as a Christian: "How can we Christians articulate our own faith fully aware of the depth and breadth of the faith of others? How is a Christian worldview, challenged and changed when we take seriously the fact that we are not alone as religious people, when we recognize as truly religious the traditions, the lives, and the pilgrimages of our neighbors of other faiths? What is Banaras to a Christian?"[13] Or again, to "pass-over" to the Hindu or Buddhist tradition, a Christian may come to appreciate the spiritual values of what it means to be fully in the present moment. As an Indian Jesuit, Anthony de Mello had access to both the Hindu and the Christian spiritual traditions of prayer. "After all," he said, "my family was baptized four hundred years ago, but then I've got five thousand years of Hinduism to contend with! That's the way it is with so many of the Christians in India, you scratch the surface and you find the Hindu." He saw himself as the fulcrum, uniting the best of both cultures. The priest came often to St. Louis University to share his perspectives on prayer in retreats, seminars, and workshops. His book, *Sadhana: A Way to God*, is considered by some to be a masterpiece in the art of learning the way to pray. Is there a how-to for prayer? De Mello told the story of the disciple who asks, "Master, what can I do to attain God?" The master responds with a question, "What can you do to make the sun rise?" The disciple is indignant, "Then why are you giving us all these methods of prayer?" And the master replies, "To make sure you're awake when the sun rises." That is what de Mello tried to do: to give us methods for being awake and watchful. He tried to make us aware of ourselves, rather than focus on God where a lot of theological constructs can get in the way. He writes:

> The head is not a very good place for prayer. It is not a bad place for *starting* your prayer. But if your prayer stays there too long and doesn't move into the heart it will gradually dry up and prove tiresome and frustrating. You must learn to move out of the area of thinking and talking and move into the area of feeling, sensing, loving, intuiting. That is the area where contemplation is born and prayer becomes a transforming power and a source of never-ending delight and peace.[14]

No one really knows who or what God is. Anthony de Mello writes, "Suspect the image you have formed of God."[15] In a similar vein, Tagore reminds us to contemplate "the inscrutable without name and form."[16] Diana Eck realized that, whatever we may think of God, "the referent of that word, that symbol, is a mystery. God is finally beyond our grasp."[17] But, if we would become aware of ourselves, perhaps we would be much less selfish, greedy, unloving, and less hateful. When we become aware, hatred goes out, sin goes out. Peace, contentment, happiness come in, and love comes in. When you are aware, you are present. Maybe that is a good definition of prayer: to be fully in the present moment, to be awake and watchful. Life, God, happiness, and love are all in the present. To fully experience them, we must have the capacity to be in the present. This "passing-over," therefore, is a journey which results in the expansion of our own empathetic understanding. After such an experience one is never the same.

In this volume, we are beginning a voyage in space and time and eternity. We will travel to distant places, remote times, immerse ourselves in reflections, the themes of which are beyond space and time. The vocabulary may be unknown to us, images and concepts unfamiliar as we encounter Jewish, Muslim, Hindu, Buddhists, Indigenous peoples' experiences of prayer. But, we believe and hope that our experiences of prayer can be deepened and enhanced by them. With this enrichment, we are assured "consciousness can expand its horizons to encompass the entire human community with its accumulated heritage of spirituality in a new interrelated, global consciousness."[18]

Journeying Together

Thomas Berry,[19] another modern day prophet, follows closely in the footsteps of Pierre Teilhard de Chardin whose vision stretched beyond the community of humankind building the earth to the "planetisation of humanity."[20] What he saw in his prophetic vision, based on his study of the history of evolution, along with his own personal insights, is actually occurring before our very eyes in the exploration of the solar system. We are no longer rocking over the billows in separate boats; we are shooting through space in the same capsule, our planet earth capsule, all of us heading for the same fate as the rest of us. So, we must pool our efforts, Cosmonaut Valentina Tereshkova reminds us, "by seeing ourselves as the crew of one spaceship — planet earth. We need the collaborative efforts of all members of the crew to prevent us from straying off course or meeting with an accident."[21] We are focused not only on planet earth, so small, fragile, and defenseless, but also outward to the boundless space that surrounds us. Edward Hays in his book, *Prayers for a Planetary Pilgrim,* invites us to get on board the space vessel Earth and become a part of a cosmic traveling colony. We will travel with the other planets of our solar system, moving outward into infinite space: "Our earth is a living spaceship, a conscious interlocking organism on a voyage."[22] As we venture through the Solar System in the footsteps of the latest voyages of exploration and discovery, we can pray:

> May we join you, cosmic congregation of galaxies,
> as you dance with delight before our God.
> You spin and leap with brilliant bursts of light,
> never tiring of your sacred circle-play.
>
> May we join you, star-children of countless constellations,
> in the worship of our common Creator
> in your rotating rituals of nuclear energy
> as you sing cosmic chants of divine fire.
>
> May we join you, so that our prayers
> may also spin with sparking splendor,
> spawning long rails of luminous devotion
> to carry our praise and adoration
> straight to the heart of our Beloved God.[23]

From such an experience we realize that we need prayers with new terms, a new vocabulary, and a new content. Karl Rahner framed the question for us ten years ago when he asked, "On the Feast of Christ the King, what am I to think of Christ's rule over the whole cosmos when at the same time I have to think of it as a universe of 20 milliard light-years?"[24] Planetary pilgrims might well ask, "How God is to be thought of if not enthroned in the 'heaven of heavens' but still at work millions of light-years away — if God there be."[25] What is God for planetary pilgrims, adrift on the small spaceship earth in an immense sea of interstellar space? We, two billion Christian pilgrims, look around and realize our fellow travelers are four billion other people who are not Christians. The thought crosses our mind: "Are we the center of it all?" Are we the only ones who have been "graced with the incarnate revelatory wisdom of a loving, self-giving God?"[26] Or, perhaps are there other incarnations, other Christs? Will we sing with the poet?:

> . . .In the eternities
> Doubtless we shall compare together, hear
> a million alien gospels, in what guise
> He trod the Pleiades, the Lyre, the Bear.
> O be prepared, my soul,
> To read the inconceivable, to scan
> The infinite forms of God those stars unroll
> When, in our turn, we show to them a man.[27]

And, what about the future of humans in space? Carl Sagan, the celebrated space scientist, suggests that the young among us may well be taking their first steps on near-Earth asteroids and Mars during their lifetime. To spread out to the moons of the Jovian planets and the Kuiper Comet Belt will take many generations more. Perhaps our descendants, tens or hundreds of generations removed from us, will live on other planetary systems. We will have changed — still human, but we will have adapted to different circumstances. Perhaps we will be more confident, farseeing, capable, and prudent, the sort of being we would want "to represent us in a universe that, for all we know, is filled with species much older, much more powerful, and very different."[28] Whatever the visionaries predict, there is a new recognition that the human future lies far beyond the earth.

What new terms, new images, will Christians living beyond the earth use when they pray at Easter time? How will they envision the resurrection? I want to share a prayer I found this spring. It is a prayer inspired by our time, "A Psalm of the Resurrection":

> From the blast of the birthing of ten thousand galaxies
> Jesus, son of Joseph and Mary and son of God,
> exploded outward from his tomb
> in radiant light and love
> to fill the earth and the whole cosmos
> with the fullness of divine life.

I look up into the Easter sky,
beyond the limits of this small galaxy—
far beyond the boundaries of my mind—
into the billions of galaxies that glow
like flaming Easter flowers
filling the garden of the universe.

Light travels 5,787 trillion miles a year;
and to cross, just once at the speed of light
this universe whose every starry body
contains the fullness of the Risen Christ
would take all of twenty billion years.[29]

CHRISTIAN PRAYER: A GLOBAL VISION

Scripture

A relationship to philosophical and religious beliefs, however complex or simple, has always shaped reflections on the glorious height and depth and breadth of the universe. So it has been with the prose and poetry just quoted. Let us consider, for a few moments, the beliefs of early Christians, as these formed the basis for their prayers.

God over All

Christians shared the Israelite belief that it is *Yahweh* who rules the world. With Hebrew poets, they sang: "Say among the nations, 'Yea, the world is established; it shall never be moved'" (Ps. 95). "The Lord reigns, let the people tremble. He sits enthroned upon the cherubim; let the earth quake!" (Ps. 99). "All the ends of the earth have seen the victory of our God" (Ps. 98). Always it is *Yahweh* who has created all and who has given dominion over creation to us. In Psalm 24 we pray: "The earth is the Lord's and its fullness; the world, *oikoumene*, and those who dwell in it." It is never earthly rulers or foreign gods, but *Yahweh* who is Lord of the *oikoumene*. It is *Yahweh* who rules in justice and peace and who makes his will known through the house of Israel. The *Qedushah* seder prayer sings out: "Holy, holy, holy *JHWH* of Hosts. The whole earth is full of his glory." And again, "*Yahweh*, you have formed the light and created the darkness; you make peace and create all things; in mercy you have given light to the earth and to all who dwell therein, and in your goodness you renewest the creation every day continually. Praised be your name forever."[30]

Jesus the Lord

As Galatians tells us, "Even scripture, foreseeing that God would justify the Gentiles by faith, preached the gospel beforehand to Abraham, saying, 'In you shall all the nations be blessed' " (Gal. 3:8).

Christianity not only continued the understanding of God's reign over all of creation, but it also brought a message of salvation for the whole of humanity. Early Christians knew their mission; they lived and died for it: to proclaim the Good News to all people: "Go, therefore, and make disciples of all nations, baptizing them in the name of the Father, and of the Son, and of the Holy Spirit" (Mt. 28:19-20).

Whenever Paul speaks of his "gospel," we are to understand it as proclaiming Jesus as the *Kyrios* who is the power of God for the salvation of all persons. In his letter to the Philippians, he tells the Christian community of Christ's equality with God, his obedient death on the cross, and concludes with his hymn:

> Because of this, God greatly exalted him
> and bestowed on him the name that is above every name,
> that at the name of Jesus every knee should bend,
> of those in heaven and on earth, and under the earth,
> and every tongue should confess that Jesus Christ is Lord (Phil. 2:9-11).

To "the saints and faithful brethren in Christ at Colossae," Paul also had written a hymn, really a cosmic rhapsody:

> He is the image of the invisible God
> the first-born of all creation;
> for in him all things were created,
> in heaven and on earth, visible and invisible,
> whether thrones or dominions or principalities
> or authorities — all things were created
> through him and for him.
> He is before all things, and in him all things hold together.
> He is the head of the body, the church;
> He is the beginning, the first-born from the dead,
> that in everything he might be pre-eminent (Col. 1:15-18).

The Holy Spirit

The New Testament reveals that, through the Holy Spirit, the Risen Christ remains actively present in the midst of his people: "And behold, I am with you always, until the end of the age" (Mt. 28:20). In the Paraclete sayings of John, the purpose of the coming is explicit: "When the Advocate comes whom I will send you from the Father, the Spirit of truth that proceeds from the

Father, he will testify to me" (John 15:26). The writings of Paul are filled with the significance of the Holy Spirit: To the Corinthians he preaches the risen Lord, a "life-giving Spirit" (1 Cor. 15:45); to the Romans he explains: If Christ is in you, you have life; if the Spirit is in you, you have life (Rom. 8:10, 11).

Luke describes succinctly, in Acts, chapter 2, the first Pentecost: the strong, violent wind, the tongues as of fire which appeared and rested on each one present; the experience of being filled with the Holy Spirit, and the astonishment of those outside the house who then heard the Good News proclaimed in their own language:

> Amazed and astonished, they asked, "Are not all these who are speaking Galileans? How is it that we hear, each of us, in our own native language? Parthians, Medes, Elamites, residents of Mesopotamia, Judea and Cappadocia, Pontus and Asia, Phrygia and Pamphylia, Egypt and parts of Libya belonging to Cyrene, and visitors from Rome, Cretans and Arabs." All were amazed and perplexed, saying to one another, "What does this mean?" (Acts 2:1-12).

The dramatic event of speaking in tongues clearly meant that the coming of the Holy Spirit was a gift for all people. After experiences of the Spirit, by Jew and Gentile believers alike, Paul successfully argued that baptized Gentiles should not be subject to Jewish religious and dietary prescriptions. As Karl Rahner demonstrates,[31] Christianity thus became eventually, through the Holy Spirit, not a Jewish cult, but a world religion, another way of Christ, of the triune God, being present among us. As the Risen Lord says in Acts: "You will receive power when the Holy Spirit has come upon you; and you yourself will be my witnesses in Jerusalem, in all Judea and Samaria, and to the ends of the earth" (Acts 1:8). [The end of the world at that time was considered to be Rome.]

The Spirit is the way in which Christ builds up his Body, the Church, by bringing people to faith in him, by uniting them in love, thereby empowering them to share in all that he is and has. It is the Spirit who is the source of the Church's unity (1 Cor. 12:9), and it is the Spirit who is the power by which the Christian community can carry out its mission (Mt. 28:19-20).

Finally, the salvation brought by Christ and given to us through the power of the Holy Spirit is seen in some texts to extend to the entire universe. It is by the Holy Spirit that Christ will transform the whole of creation, creation which "waits with eager longing for the revealing of the sons of God," creation which has been "groaning in travail together until now"; and, not only the creation, "but

we ourselves, who have the first fruits of the Spirit, groan inward-
ly as we wait for adoption as sons, the redemption of our bodies"
(Rom. 8:19-22). St. Paul's vision sums up God's plan:

> Then comes the end, when he delivers the kingdom to God the
> Father after destroying every rule and every authority and power.
> For he must reign until he has put all his enemies under his feet.
> The last enemy to be destroyed is death . . . When all things are sub-
> jected to him, then the Son himself will also be subjected to him
> who put all things under him, that God may be everything to every-
> one (1 Cor. 15:24-28).

The world, as the early Christians knew it, was confined, for the
most part, to the Mediterranean world within the boundaries of
the Roman Empire. We are, however, learning more today about
the Christian communities outside the areas of the Empire, in
Syria and Mesopotamia. Though it was a small world compared
with what we know today, there were a great variety of expression
in religious belief, Christian practices, rituals, and prayers. Previously, this diversity was thought not to exist. It has been assumed
sometimes that the early Church existed in only one form, beautiful and simple, and that over the years it became fragmented,
cluttered with cultural accretions. All we had to do to return to
pristine Christianity was to peel off the bark from the tree to find
the original. However, this unity was illusory, as the discovery of
such documents as the Nag Hammadi, the Dead Sea Scrolls, and
the Gospel of Thomas has shown us.

Scholars speak of at least three forms of Christianity in the early
Church. Each form corresponds to a specific language and to a
specific geographical area: a) The Roman or Latin form used the
Latin language and was found especially in Italy, Africa, Spain, and
France (or Gaul), with the center being in Rome.[32] b) The Greek
form used the Greek language and was found in Greece, Asia
Minor, and Alexandria, the center being in Ephesus.[33] c) The
Hebrew form used the Syriac language and was found in eastern
Syria and Mesopotamia, the center being Edessa.[34]

Early Traditions

The Syrian Tradition

We will now see the way these three forms of Christianity found
expression in prayer. The Syriac Tradition, chronologically the
first, offers a distinct and unique tradition of its own, quite different from that of the Greek and Latin traditions. Sebastian Brock
describes for us some of the prominent characteristics of the
Syriac tradition: In Semitic Christianity, we find the frequent use

of the imagery of fire, light, and heat as symbols of the Holy Spirit.[35] Early Syriac writers speak of the Holy Spirit as feminine. An example of this is in the *Ode of Solomon* 36:1-3, where Jesus refers to the Spirit as feminine:

> I rested on the Spirit of the Lord: and She raised me on high: and made me stand on my feet in the height of the Lord, before His perfection and His glory, while I was praising (Him) by the composition of His songs. She brought me forth before the face of the Lord: and although a son of man, I was named the illuminated one, the son of God.[36]

Syriac Christianity valued and held in high esteem the virtues of holiness, virginity, celibacy, and asceticism. These ascetical ideals were not derived from a dualistic world view and a negative attitude toward the body, but were biblical and positive towards the human person. Therefore, they attached great value to the sanctity of the body. The heart is the spiritual center of the human person. It is the focal point of the intellect as well as the feelings. The heart is where prayer should take place — the prayer of the heart. The following excerpt from a work by Simeon the Graceful will illustrate this aspect of interior prayer:

> Prayer in which the body does not toil by means of the heart, and the heart by means of the mind, together with the intellect and the intelligence, all gathered together in deep-felt groaning, but where instead prayer is just allowed to float across the heart, such prayer you should realize is just a miscarriage, for while you are praying, your mind is drawing you away to some other business that you are going to see to after praying. In such a case you have not yet managed to pray in a unified manner.[37]

The heart also has an interior liturgical role: it is the altar inside the sanctuary of the temple constituted by the body, and on this altar the interior offering of prayer should continuously be made. In the *Book of Steps*, the "altar of the heart" is central. Here, there is the idea of a threefold liturgy taking place all at once: in the visible Church on earth, in the church of the heart of the individual Christian, and in the heavenly Church.[38]

St. Ephrem is the greatest of the Syriac writers. He has been acclaimed as "the greatest poet/theologian of the patristic age." Ephrem's contemporaries called him "The Harp of the Spirit."[39] He speaks of the baptized person as being a harp played by the Holy Spirit.[40]

St. Ephrem was born about 306 around Nisibis, at that time on the easternmost edge of the Roman Empire. He died in 373 in Edessa, the capital of Eastern Syria, located just east of the Euphrates. He lived at a time before the Syriac speaking churches had undergone any extensive Hellenization. Ephrem is, therefore, one of the few surviving representatives of a truly Semitic Christianity. His poetry, theology, and prayers show us the characteristically Semitic love of parallelism and antithesis which enabled him to express so poignantly the various paradoxes of the Christian mysteries.[41] It is not that Ephrem is against intellectual expressions in prayers, but he believes, "It is in fact only the paradox that can begin to describe the indescribable."[42]

Prayers in the Syriac tradition are always the product of a "creative and fruitful meditation upon the Scripture" as it is found in the wording of the Syriac Bible.[43] In his tenth "Hymn on Faith," Ephrem uses the image of "fire" as a symbol of the Holy Spirit. Not only is the "fire" of the Holy Spirit given to us in baptism, but is also imparted to us in the Eucharist, thus continuing the process of sanctification. Ephrem prays:

> In your Bread there is hidden the Spirit who is not consumed,
> in your Wine there dwells the Fire that is not drunk;
>
> the Spirit is in your Bread, the Fire in your Wine,
> a manifold wonder, which our lips have received.
>
> When the Lord came down to earth to mortal men
> he created them again in a new creation, like angels,
> mingling Fire and Spirit with them,
> so that in a hidden manner they might be of Fire and Spirit.[44]

In many of Ephrem's prayers we find the use of the image of light. For example, he speaks of Eve and Mary as the two spiritual eyes of the world, and the Second Person of the Trinity as the light by which those eyes can function.[45] Whereas the eye of Eve has become darkened, Mary's eye has been preserved luminous and so, "She is the land which receives the source of light: through her it has illumined the whole world with its inhabitants which had grown dark through Eve."[46] This idea of luminosity is linked to the image of a mirror. At this time, since mirrors were made of metal and not glass, they had to be constantly kept highly polished if they were to be of any use. Ephrem uses this image in a prayer addressing Christ: "Let our prayer be a mirror, Lord, placed before Your face, then Your fair beauty will be imprinted on its luminous surface."[47] The more luminous this interior mirror is, the better it is able to behold God in whose image we are created.[48]

Finally, Mary plays an important role in early Syriac prayers. Syriac writers found many types of Mary in the Hebrew Scriptures. In their prayers Mary is always seen in relationship to Christ and never just as herself "in vacuo." Ephrem begins the prayer by pondering on the mystery of Mary:

No one quite knows, Lord, what to call
Your mother: should we call her "virgin"?
—but her giving birth is an established fact; or
"married woman"?
—but no man has known her. If your mother's case
is beyond comprehension, who can hope to understand Yours?

She alone is Your mother,
but she is Your sister with everyone else. She was Your mother,
she was Your sister, she was Your bride too
along with all chaste souls. You, who are Your mother's beauty,
Yourself adorned her with everything![49]

The Greek Tradition

As language is recognized as the most important development in the formation of human culture, so the way we express religious beliefs is most important as we construct a shared symbolic universe of ultimate meanings. For example, the Greek language is one of the most subtle of languages and is much more philosophical than Syriac or Latin. When Christianity emerged as a Gentile Church, its relationship to the philosophical tradition of the time, the culture and the literature demanded much study and response. The Greek Christians themselves thought of Christianity as a philosophy. Justin Martyr even defined Christianity as a school of Philosophy. Justin Martyr, Clement and Origen of Alexandria, Athanasius and Cyril of Alexandria and the Cappadocian Fathers: Basil, Gregory of Nyssa, and Gregory of Naziansus were some of the best known Greek writers who used philosophy to convey Christian truths. How is Jesus truly God — equal to the Father? How is Jesus truly human? Our Christian creeds and prayers to this day reflect early Hellenistic influences.

Justin Martyr, the most important of the Greek apologists of the second century, was very much influenced by Plato. This influence is evident in Justin's concept of God who, being without origin, must be nameless (*Apol.* 2, 6). The best name for him is Father, because, being the Creator, he is really the Father of all (*Dial.* 60). Justin thought of God as transcendent and beyond all human beings. God, who dwells in the regions above the sky, cannot leave his place and appear in the world. It is necessary, therefore, to bridge the abyss between God and human beings. This is done through the Logos. And, God reveals himself only through the Logos. The Logos leads us to God and instructs us. Originally, the Logos was a power in God, but, just before the creation of the world, he came forth from God and created the world. This idea of the Logos links pagan philosophy and Christianity. The Divine Logos appeared in his fullness only in Christ, yet "a seed of the

Logos" was scattered among the whole of humankind long before Christ. Every human being possesses in his reason a seed of the Logos. Those persons living before the coming of Christ, e.g., Abraham, Moses, the Hebrew prophets, the pagan philosophers, Socrates, Plato, and the poets, Homer and "Orpheus," carried a seed of the Logos in their souls. Justin writes:

> We have declared that Christ is the Logos, of whom every race of man were partakers, and those who lived according to the Logos are Christians, even though they have been thought atheists, as among the Greeks, Socrates and Heraclitus, and men like them (*Apol.* 1, 46).

Therefore, there can be no contradiction between Christianity and philosophy, for whatever anyone says that is right belongs to the Christians.

Clement of Alexandria went further than Justin. Writing at the end of the second century, he maintained, "philosophy as a preparation, paving the way for the one who is perfected in Christ," in short, "a tutor to bring the Hellenic mind to Christ" (*Stromata* 1.5). Both the Hebrew Scriptures and Greek philosophy were the tributaries of the great river of Christianity. Using another image, Clement describes all history as one, insofar as all truth is one: "There is one river of truth; but many streams fall into it on this side and that."[50] So, we find in the Greek form of Christianity "a coming together of the categories of Biblical and Hellenic thinking, a synthesis which leaves an indelible mark on subsequent theology,"[51] and Christian prayer.

The Latin Tradition

The Latin form of Christianity originated in northern Africa, in the city of Carthage. Two of the great writers of the Latin form came from Carthage: Tertullian and Augustine, both of whom were probably lawyers. The Latin language being especially suited for law, the Latin form of Christianity took on a legalistic and moralistic mentality. Note these tendencies in the excerpt from Tertullian; Tertullian declares:

> Christians look up with hands outstretched . . . with head uncovered . . . and pray without ceasing for all our emperors. We pray for long life for them, for security to the empire, for protection to the imperial house, for brave armies, a faithful senate, a virtuous people, the world at rest, whatever is desired by man or Caesar (*Apology* 30, 4).

Tertullian had a very negative attitude toward Greek philoso-
phies, Greek culture, and Greek literary figures. Although
Carthage and Alexandria are on the same continent, only a thousand miles of coastline separating the two Christian centers of
learning, Tertullian inhabited worlds different, spiritually and
intellectually, from his Greek counterparts, Clement and Origen
of Alexandria. In a famous passage of robust rhetoric, Tertullian
cries: "What has Athens to do with Jerusalem?" (*De Prescriptione* 7).
And, Tertullian himself responds:

> Away with those who put forward a Stoic, a Platonic, a dialectic sort
> of Christianity! We have no need for curious speculation, once we
> have accepted Christ Jesus, nor for inquiry after receiving the
> gospel. Once we believe, we desire no further belief.[52]

Thus, in two hundred years profound differences of outlook
were manifested in Christianity. In succeeding centuries, diver-
gent views centered on the nature of Christ and the identity of the
Spirit. Ecumenical Councils: Nicea, Ephesus, Constantinople,
Chalcedon, attempted to resolve these controversies. All of us
know the subsequent story: the absorption of Syriac Christianity,
and most of the Greek world, into Islam, the spread of Christianity
throughout the Holy Roman Empire, and the fateful split between
the Churches of Rome and Constantinople in 1054. The culture
of Western Christianity became a composite of its preceding and
diverse experiences: Hellenistic formulations of doctrine, creeds,
and rituals, and a Latin structure of organization, law, and
language.

The contribution of Thomas Aquinas in the thirteenth century
was a rediscovery of Aristotelian philosophy, as distinguished from
the Platonic thought used by the early Church Fathers, and its
incorporation into a new theological synthesis. Though challenged and discarded by churches of the Reformers in the sixteenth century, Greek thought and Latin structures remained
normative for the long period from the early centuries of the
Church until our own time, the period identified by Karl Rahner
as the second epoch of Christianity — "The period of the church
in a distinct cultural region, namely, that of Hellenism and of
European culture and civilization."[53] The extent to which the
Roman Catholic Church thought of itself as essentially a society
and essentially one can be seen in this statement from the encyclical, *Mystici Corporis*: "Those who are divided in faith and government cannot be living in one body such as this, and cannot be living the life of its one divine Spirit."[54] The Church's prayer was for
the return to the one true Church of Christ of those separated
from it.

VATICAN COUNCIL II: A NEW PENTECOST

The Inspiration

A New Pentecost! What better phrase could describe more adequately what Angelo Roncalli, Pope John XXIII, desired so ardently, prayed for so fervently, and lived to see realized so concretely. Could a more authentic prophet of the Holy Spirit be found than one who so manifested those fruits of the Spirit in his own life: love, joy, peace, gentleness, kindness, and understanding, which, like a huge magnet, drew all the world to him! Realizing the supreme duty that was given to him to fulfill, Pope John XXIII felt a grave responsibility to be open and attentively responsive to the inspirations and movings of the Spirit. Indeed, it seems this openness demanded constant response to the intense activity of the Holy Spirit.

Soon after the beginning of his papacy, John announced his desire to call a Council. He tells us the idea of the Council came to him suddenly, as an inspiration, shortly before he was to speak at St. Paul's without the Walls on January 25, 1959. It was the answer to his agonized prayer. At St. Paul's he was to conclude the week of prayer for unity; what could he, the Head of the Church, do for unity of the Christian churches and for world peace? Surely, he could do something. And, the inspiration had come — a Council.[55] After the services, Pope John and the Cardinals retired into the adjoining Monastery. John speaks: "Venerable Brethren and beloved sons! Trembling a little with emotion, but with firmness of purpose, we now tell you of a two-fold celebration: We propose to call a Diocesan Synod for Rome, and an Ecumenical Council for the Universal Church!"[56] In the years before the opening of the Council in 1962, John seemed to use the feasts of Pentecost to advance the preparatory work of the Second Vatican Council, thus showing how intimately associated were the two realities in his mind. "Indeed," John says, "it is in light of the teaching and the spirit of Pentecost that the great event of the ecumenical council takes on life and substance."[57] Unity and peace, these were the deepest aspirations of John, and already they had become part of his vision of the Council. If the Council could serve Christian unity and world peace, it would indeed "shake the heavens and the earth."[58]

In the convocation of the Council, December 25, 1961, Pope John takes the occasion to exhort all of the faithful Christians throughout the world to unite in fervent prayer, begging the Holy Spirit to come again as he came to the apostles gathered in Jerusalem so long ago. In Pope John's prayer, he asks the Holy

Spirit: "Renew your wonders in our time, as though for a new Pentecost, and grant that the holy Church, . . . preserving unanimous and continuous prayer, . . . may increase the reign of the Divine Savior, the reign of truth and justice, the reign of love and peace. Amen."[59] On the feast of Pentecost, 1962, Pope John concluded his homily with a very beautiful prayer to the Holy Spirit, begging the grace of interior renewal not only for his flock, but also for all of humankind:

> O, Holy Spirit, Paraclete, perfect in us the world begun by Jesus: enable us to continue to pray fervently in the name of the whole world: hasten in every one of us the growth of a profound interior life, give vigour to our apostolate so that it may reach all men and all peoples, all redeemed by the Blood of Christ. . . . May everything finally be according to your Spirit, O Holy Spirit of love, which the Father and the Son desired to be poured out over the Church, . . . over the souls of men and over nations. Amen, Alleluia![60]

October 11, 1962, the memorable day of the opening of Vatican Council II, had arrived! Addressing his fellow bishops assembled from the four corners of the world as well as representatives from other Christian Churches and men and women lay observers, Pope John reiterates once more the way the idea of holding a Council had originated. He said that the decision came to him in a sudden flash of inspiration. The response was immediate: "It was as though some ray of supernatural light had entered the minds of all present: it was reflected in their faces; it shone from their eyes. At once the world was swept by a wave of enthusiasm, and men everywhere began to wait eagerly for the celebration of this Council."[61] In the conclusion of the address, the Holy Father reminded the Council of the role which is theirs, i.e., "to show prompt obedience to the supernatural guidance of the Holy Spirit and to do your utmost to answer the needs and expectations of every nation on earth."[62]

Nine days after the opening of the Council, the assembled delegates presented an unscheduled document to the world. Pope John himself had sent it to the Assembly and desired that it be the first official act of the Council. The message was addressed to the whole world in the name of the Council Fathers and presented what would emerge as key themes of the future Council documents: Christ, the light of the world; hope in the power of the Holy Spirit; and the bishops as shepherds devoted to the service of the people. This reliance and hope in the Holy Spirit is evidenced in many passages of the message: "Under the guidance of the Holy Spirit, we intend in this assembly to seek the most effective ways of renewing ourselves and of becoming increasingly more faithful witnesses of the Gospel of Christ. We will strive to propose to the men of our time the truth of God in its entirety and purity so that they may understand it."[63]

The Council Fathers, however, realized that of themselves they could accomplish nothing and told the world so explicitly: "To be sure, we have neither the riches nor the powers of the earth, but we place our faith in the power of the Holy Spirit."[64] John's vision of the dawn of a new Pentecost in the Church loomed yet more brilliantly before his eyes as he addressed the Council during the closing ceremonies of the first session of the Council, December 8, 1962. He was sick now and spoke as one totally concerned that the "earthly city" be renewed and purified so that it might ready itself as a Bride for the Bridegroom. With the vision typical of a prophetic spirit, he spoke of a Pentecost that will increase the Church's wealth of spiritual strength and extend her material influence and saving power to every sphere of human endeavor: "Then will we see the extension of Christ's Kingdom on earth, and throughout the world will re-echo more clearly, more eloquently, the good news of humanity's redemption; confirming the kingship of Almighty God, strengthening the bonds of fraternal love among men, and establishing that peace which was promised in this world to all persons of good will."[65]

The Documents

After the death of Pope John, the Council continued to meet during the fall of the next three years. Many and dramatic changes in the life and practice of the Roman Catholic community were initiated, and the faithful were challenged to update, "aggiornamento." Relationships between Catholics and other faiths were to be based on openness and on willingness to listen and learn. The duty of Catholics is to scrutinize the signs of the times and hear, distinguish, and interpret the many voices of their age. The Council reoriented a Church of European cultural confinement to the possibility of becoming a world Church. The leap to a world Church can be clearly seen by looking at a few of the sixteen documents promulgated by the Council.[66] First of all, the *Constitution on the Liturgy (Sacrosanctum Concilium)* allows for the use of the vernacular for liturgical services (article 36).[67] This acknowledges that the "individual churches exist with a certain independence in their cultural spheres, inculturated, and no longer a European export."[68]

In the *Declaration on the Relation of the Church to Non-Christian Religions (Nostra Aetate)*, there is a most positive evaluation of the great world religions, which reads: "All human beings form but one community. This is so because all stem from the one stock which God created to people the entire earth (cf. Acts 17:26), and also because all share a common destiny, namely God" (article 1)[69]:

> In Hinduism men explore the divine mystery and express it both in the limitless riches of myth and the accurately defined insights of philosophy (article 2).[70]

> Buddhism in its various forms testifies to the essential inadequacy of this changing world (article 2).[71]

> They (Muslims) worship God, who is one, living and subsistent, merciful and almighty, the Creator of heaven and earth, who has also spoken to men (article 3).[72]

Further, the *Document* states: "The Catholic Church rejects nothing of what is true and holy in these religions. She has a high regard for the manner of life and conduct, the precepts and doctrines . . ." (article 2).[73] Regarding the Jews, the Declaration teaches: "This sacred Council remembers the spiritual ties which link the people of the New Covenant to the stock of Abraham. . . . Nor can she (the church) forget that she draws nourishment from that good olive tree onto which the wild olive branches of the Gentiles have been grafted" (article 4).[74]

The *Decree on Ecumenism (Unitatis Redintegratio)* begins with one of the principal concerns of the Second Vatican Council, viz., "the restoration of unity among all Christians" (article 1).[75] The Decree calls for theological dialogue and pastoral solicitude to break down the confessional barriers and to heal the wounds of both East-West and intraWest divisions (article 11).[76] The focus is not on a return to the traditional Roman Catholic Church, but on its new selfunderstanding: a pilgrim Church moving toward the parousia (article 2).[77] No longer repeating the offensive teaching that the Catholic Church is the only true Church, the Decree asserts that Jesus, in His Spirit, is at work in the Churches and communities beyond the visible borders of the Catholic Church. Repeating one of the chief teachings of the New Testament,[78] the Decree reminds us "that the only-begotten Son of God has been sent by the Father into the world, so that, being made man, he might by his redemption of the entire human race give new life to it and unify it" (article 2).[79] The Council acknowledged that there are many efforts being made throughout the world in prayer, word, and action to attain the "fullness of unity which Jesus Christ desires." All of us are encouraged to take an active and intelligent part in the movement toward unity of all Christians.

Finally, the *Constitution on the Church in the Modern World (Gaudium et Spes)* is evidence that the Church as a totality becomes conscious of its responsibility for the whole of humankind.

A Participant's View

To this day, the very mention of *Gaudium et Spes* makes present again some very special moments in my life. I was privileged to spend three months in Rome — the time of the final session of Vatican II, during the fall of 1965. As a participant in a leadership workshop sponsored by the Movement for a Better World, we were involved in rewriting the retreat exercises in light of the Documents of the Council. Members of the workshop were Christians from every part of the world. We lived, prayed, discussed, wrote, celebrated, and drank Italian wine together. Since it was the first time I had ever traveled anywhere or met persons of color or cultural diversity, it was an unforgettable global experience — an experience that changed my life forever. Some of the "periti" present at the Council came to the center where we lived and worked to share with us what was taking place at the meetings. I met many of the bishops and theologians from all over the world, in Rome at the time, because they were friends of other participants in the workshop. I remember one talk given by Yves Congar in November, 1965, shortly before the close of the Council. He told us that it was the object of Schema 13, as the forthcoming *Constitution on the Church in the Modern World* was then called,

> to develop what hope the church brings to the world — hope of justice, of better economical output, but a planning fully human; for we notice nowadays that the true progress is the progress of the "whole person" and of "all people." We realize better nowadays that everything is interdependent. Peace is total or it is not in the world. If there is war somewhere, there is risk of war for the whole world. Progress is total or it is not progress. It must be of the whole of humankind and for all of humankind.[80]

A few weeks later, on December 8, 1965, we were gathered, along with thousands of others, in St. Peter's Square to celebrate the formal closing of Vatican Council II. Pope Paul VI officially announced the promulgation of the *Pastoral Constitution on the Church in the Modern World* which had been approved by the Council the day before. He then read the opening words of the *Constitution* which still burn in my heart and, I suspect, in the hearts of all present that day and of Christians everywhere:

> The joy and hope, the grief and anguish of the people of our time, especially of those who are poor or afflicted in any way, are the joy and hope, the grief and anguish of the followers of Christ as well.

> Nothing that is genuinely human fails to find an echo in their
> hearts. For theirs is a community composed of persons who, united
> in Christ and guided by the Holy Spirit, press onwards towards the
> kingdom of the Father and are bearers of a message of salvation for
> all humanity. That is why Christians cherish a feeling of deep soli-
> darity with the human race and its history (article 1).[81]

This moment was for me an experience of World Church. This
moment was an experience of global prayer. I thought of Pope
John who had spoken so often of a new Pentecost and of opening
windows and letting in fresh air. This invigorating air is the breath
of the Spirit. The Spirit continues to open our hearts and knock
down barriers between people. Christians today identify more
closely with humankind and its destiny. To achieve this purpose,
the Holy Spirit chose as instruments Pope John XXIII and the
Second Vatican Council. Let us take a look now at the broader
ecumenical movement which began in the Protestant denominations in the early decades of this century.

A GLOBAL EXPERIENCE OF PRAYER:
WORLD COUNCIL OF CHURCHES

Since the first General Assembly of the World Council of
Churches in Amsterdam in 1948, following the devastating
destruction of the Second World War, the WCC has met with the
express purpose of promoting cooperation among the churches
and of helping Christians to see their ministries as a part of the
whole Church in the whole world. The WCC links three hundred
sixteen churches, with a collective membership of four hundred
million. Almost all of the Protestant Churches of the world, as well
as the Orthodox Churches, are members of the World Council.
The Assembly, held every seven years, provides a rich forum for
the participants to share theological insights and experiences of
prayer and renewal. Christians thus learn to speak, act, and pray
together around vital issues and are thereby prepared for that
deeper unity which all of them seek. The venues and themes of
the first seven Assemblies, as well as the one being planned for
1998, are indicators of the global focus of the WCC:

1948   Amsterdam: "Man's Disorder and God's Design"
1954   Evanston, Indiana: "Jesus Christ—The Hope of the World"
1961   New Delhi, India: "Jesus Christ—The Light of the World"
1968   Uppsala, Sweden: "Behold, I Make All Things New"
1975   Nairobi, Kenya: "Jesus Christ—Frees and Unites"
1983   Vancouver, B.C.: "Jesus Christ—The Life of the World"
1991   Canberra, Australia: "Come, Holy Spirit, Renew the
       Whole Creation!"

1998 Harare, Zimbabwe: "Turn to God—Rejoice in Hope" (Meaning of Jubilee).

Come, Holy Spirit, Renew the Whole Creation!

A Participant's View

The Seventh Assembly of Canberra was the first to choose as its theme a prayer, a prayer that focused on the workings of the Holy Spirit: COME, HOLY SPIRIT — RENEW THE WHOLE CREATION! Everything that went on in the Assembly — the plenary sessions, theatrical presentations, small group discussions, biblical reflection sharing, the hymns, liturgy, and prayers, was integrated with this theme. The Assembly also had four sub-themes:

> "Come, Holy Spirit, Giver of Life, Sustain Your Creation!"
> "Come, Holy Spirit, Spirit of Truth, Set Us Free!"
> "Come, Holy Spirit, Spirit of Unity, Reconcile Your People!"
> "Come, Holy Spirit, Transform and Sanctify Us!"

The invocations called all of us who attended to pray for our world and all who dwell therein. With these prayers in our hearts and on our lips, we Christians, more than four thousand of us, eight hundred and fifty-two voting delegates, more than one thousand accredited visitors, delegated representatives and staff from around the world, gathered in February, 1991, in Canberra to participate in the Assembly. Present also were representations of the world religions — Islam, Hinduism, Buddhism, Judaism, as guests. More than any previous Assembly, this one sought to embrace the full diversity of God's people. This south land of the Spirit is a land of stark beauty, where the air is filled with the sharp sounds of exotic birds and the pungent smell of eucalyptus leaves which we, and the Koala bears, found quite appealing. This wonderful background witnessed a new moment in world religious history. It was a pivotal event, occurring during a time of wars and rumors of war, of threats to planet earth and to all the creation it bears, a time of frustration in visions of peace. The presence of people of such diverse cultures, races, and traditions gave rise to multiple expressions of prayers: Christians and the Global Experience of Prayer! The previous Assembly in Vancouver, which I was privileged to attend also, has been called "the praying assembly" because of the outstanding quality of its liturgical life. Canberra continued this excellence with prayers drawn from a variety of cultures and confessions and prepared in four languages. Like Vancouver, worship took place in an enormous tent — symbolizing Christians as a sojourning people. Leaders in liturgy came from Sweden, Taiwan, Brazil, South Africa, Ghana, Indonesia, the former Yugoslavia, and the United States. We participated in morning, midday, and evening prayers, as well as in Bible study, which reflected on the theme, and we held an all night vigil for peace. We celebrated Eucharist using the "Lima Liturgy," based on the widely studied document, *Baptism, Eucharist, Ministry*, and also we participated in special Eucharistic celebrations led by Oriental Orthodox and Eastern Orthodox participants.

The Assembly had two contexts: first, Australia, home to the indigenous, Australian Aboriginal people who figured prominently throughout the events of the Assembly; second, World — and all its concerns. We reflected with the psalmist on "the earth is the Lord's and all that is in it, the world, and those who live in it" (Psalm 24:1). We realized that all of us are called to participate, to respond. I was reminded of this constantly by the reports on the Gulf War and the call to make our voices heard by writing to the Pope, President Bush, and other world leaders, asking them to use their influence to end the war immediately. We were involved in many meetings and activities to coordinate our responses to the Gulf crisis. As we have so often heard, when we pray, meditate, engage in theological reflections, and celebrate liturgies, we must have, in one hand, the Bible, our living traditions, and, in the other hand, the newspaper. In the Bible, we study salvation history; in the newspapers, we realize how much the Good News is still needed today.

Come, Holy Spirit, Giver of Life, Sustain Your Creation!

The first theme: "Come, Holy Spirit, Giver of Life, Sustain Your Creation!," challenged our understanding of, and our relation to, creation. Why are we called to look at the issues of creation? We know the reason is that we, as a human family, have reached a turning point in our history.[82] What we choose now will determine whether we and our earth have a longterm future. We might have hoped that those stunning and wonderful images of the whole earth, beamed back to us from space by the Apollo Missions in 1969, would have taught us once and for all that we are really dealing with a single planetary resource, a common planetary home. That image alone would tell us that we cannot keep living the way we have in recent times because the earth, the water, the air, the atmosphere, this planet we are spinning around on in space, all are limited. What we have now is all we are ever going to have. We cannot go off and get some more some place else. This has been very difficult for us to comprehend. It has been our ignorance and, beyond that, our sin that we have continued to ravage and pollute God's gift of our earth.

The protective ozone shield has been damaged by harmful chemicals, e.g., refrigerating chemicals. Ozone protects the surface of the earth from ultra violet B radiation which is highly damaging to biological molecules like those that make up our bodies. One result is a high incident of skin cancer. In Canberra, Australia, such a dangerous amount of ultra violet radiation was coming through that it was necessary to wear hats, put on layers of sunblock lotion, sun glasses, and walk under umbrellas. Announcements were made on the T.V. and radio to keep the children inside.

Those attending the WCC were painfully aware that the warming of the earth's atmosphere may well be catastrophic. We were reminded that so much carbon dioxide is being produced around the globe that it cannot escape our atmosphere fast enough. The resulting green house effect has accelerated global warming, threatening health and even life. Cutting the forests, which provide us with oxygen, increases carbon dioxide twenty-five percent. Excessive burning of fossil fuels increases the gas seventy-five percent. The United States alone is responsible for one-fourth of the world's generation of carbon dioxide. New York, for example, or Los Angeles, produces more of this concentrated gas than all of China.

A final concern brought to reflection in Canberra is the possibility of biological extinction. As a result of the tremendous population growth all over the world, and as a result of our greedy and unbridled consumption of world resources, we are losing forests and changing habitats all over the world at frightening speed. We are told that in the next thirty years we can expect to see the disappearance of one out of five of all kinds of plants, animals, and microorganisms in the world. As a result of the global system of exploitation, important new and rare drugs, used in treating childhood leukemia and many other forms of cancer, are not, and will not be, available. Sources of the drugs will be extinct.[83] We are obliged to face the extent to which we have wasted and destroyed the richness of creation. At the WCC in Australia, we prayed for the Spirit of Wisdom, of Knowledge, of Counsel, of Fear of the Lord, to guide us in these matters.

Exploring the theme, "Giver of Life, Sustain Your Creation," also exposed particularly Western Christian theological failures of the past which supported such attitudes. "Domination" (Gen. 1:28) was misinterpreted as the right to exploit the earth, and "transcendence," misconstrued as God detached from creation. The more theology stressed only God's absolute transcendence, the more the earth was viewed as a mere secular object, a force to be controlled. As a consequence, nature was not appreciated as a living being interconnected with ourselves as its conscious expression, but as an inexhaustible resource that we could use or misuse at will.

At Canberra, we studied, learned, and prayed from the attitudes and values of indigenous peoples, i.e., the Aboriginal peoples of Australia. Theirs is "one of the oldest continuous habitations of one people in any place on earth."[84] The peoples, laws, traditions, spiritual ceremonies, and prayers go back sixty thousand years beyond the clocks of recorded history, back to the beginning. Anne Pattel-Gray, an Aboriginal Christian, told us that the Aboriginal peoples believe that, in the beginning, the great white spirit came and walked this land. This great white spirit is believed to be God and has given the people laws — laws similar to biblical ones — to love our sisters and brothers, not to steal, and to care for the land. The Aboriginals never believed that they owned the land, but thought, rather, that the land owned them. She writes in her book, *Through Aboriginal Eyes*, "We have always centered our lives in the natural-spiritual world. We are deeply committed to God the Creator and to the earth in consciousness and in instinct. Only through our spiritual connection can we continue in our own identity."[85] The Aboriginals are true lovers of nature. They love the earth and everything about the earth. The love and attachment grow throughout life. They literally love the soil, and that is the reason they want to sit or recline on the ground as it gives them a feeling of being close to a mothering power: "The soil is soothing, strengthening, cleansing and healing. That is why Aboriginals sit on the earth instead of propping themselves up and away from the life-giving forces."[86] This sitting or lying on the ground helps them to think and feel more vibrantly: "We can see more clearly into the mysteries of life and come closer in kinship to other lives around us."[87]

The Maoris are the indigenous peoples of New Zealand. Sir Paul Reeves, an Anglican archbishop, himself a Maori, spoke of the Maoris also as "people of the land" in his sermon during the opening service: "In Maori terms I am *tangata whenua*, a person of the land. A Maori viewpoint is that the land is *Papa-tua-nuku*, our earth, our mother. We love her as a mother is loved."[88] When someone says "land is my mother," it means that, as he/she works the land, he/she is taking part in the sacred act of bringing life to birth: "In Maori, *whenua* is the placenta, the lining of the womb where the unborn child is nourished. No wonder *whenua* is also used to describe the body of the earth mother who nourishes and supports humanity."[89] Maoris also believe that humans are the species through whom the living earth comes to know itself: "The Spirit or liveliness of God affects everything, and our transformation will be a sign of what can happen to the rest of creation. This will happen only when its creatures are reconciled and healed."[90]

Two hundred Aboriginals brought into our midst unforgettable spiritual realities. The mysteries of their spiritual convictions stay with us. They shared with us their values about respect for one another and for mother earth, the identity of humankind with the earth, the sacredness of all of life, the oneness of the secular and the sacred, a sense of belonging each of us one to the other, and a sense of "awe" about all of it. These convictions are common also to the Native American Experience of Prayer, as we will see in the essay of Carol Gallagher. Our futures can be reshaped by these beautiful, talented, spiritual, peoples if we but listen, pray, and repeat with them: we love God's creation because God is our Creator. We respect mother earth in thankfulness to God. Our spirituality begins the day we are born, "continues in how we live, how we care for our brothers and sisters, how we deal with our extended family and how we care for God's creation. It is all balanced and cannot be divided."[91]

In prayers of penance we turn to God to beg forgiveness for the havoc we have wreaked on creation and to thank the Giver of Life for our indigenous brothers and sisters who have helped us Christians to gain a new vision, a new creation theology, and an understanding of ourselves and of our relationship to creation — away from dominance and sovereignty and exploitation to one of mutual respect and cooperation. Let us pray as Christians through the eyes of the Aboriginals in celebration of God's good earth:

> God, Father and Mother of all living things, Creator of the earth and all that is in it, in You we live and move and have our being. You dwell in all You have made. Help us see this world as a cathedral, a church where we can sense Your holy presence. Help us also to treat this world with the reverence that is due to all that is sacred. We offer You our thanks and praise. We ask this through Christ, our Lord. Amen.[92]

Called to One Hope: Prayer in Diverse Cultures

The second issue which emerged strongly at Canberra is the tension which exists between faith and the expression of that faith in prayer and the culture of the times and places we live. Cultural elements have always entered in, but now, in our day of the global community, what a challenge it is. Culture shapes the voice that answers the voice of Christ. We can express our faith only in the culture we know. Only then can we do it authentically. To try to do it from afar, we fail to do it. Karl Rahner reminded us of this when he wrote:

> I suspect that persons in the early church knew what they were supposed to believe when they heard the Apostles' Creed (at least if combined with a brief instruction). I also suspect that, in spite of all the normative significance this creed has and also will have in the future, most persons would understand nothing or almost nothing if I recite this creed to them today, and even if I try to explain it briefly.

What we must do then, Rahner suggests, is to work toward a globalization in theology. We must "let historical events, insofar as they do not condition its actual nature, fall back quietly into a (merely) historical background (only)." What would Christian prayer look like when, "to the world outside the West, elements of its historical conditioning fade away?"[93] While at the Assembly, we had the opportunity to experience the response to Rahner's question. Many Christians from Asian cultures were present. When I realized that Asians are more than half of the world's population, I knew the significance of the Asian context in our search for a global experience of prayer.

It was a young woman, Professor Chung Hyun Kyung of the Presbyterian Church in South Korea, who, in her address on the theme, "Come, Holy Spirit, Renew the Whole Creation," set before us concepts and images of the Holy Spirit drawn from the Buddhist and Shaman cultures of South Korea, thus giving us a glimpse of what Christian prayer, formed by a Buddhist and Shaman cultural background, might look like. The whole of her presentation was a prayer. She began with dance, accompanied by sixteen Korean and two Aboriginal dancers, complete with drums, clap sticks, bells, candles, and gongs, and robed in long white gowns. "I would like to invite all of you," she said, "to get on the holy ground with me by taking off your shoes while we are dancing to prepare the way of the Spirit. With humble heart and body let us listen to the cries of creation and the cries of the Spirit within it."[94] She began prayers of invocation, calling upon the spirits of many persons throughout history who have suffered and died by unjust hands:

> Come. The spirit of Joan of Arc, and of the many other women burned at the "witch trials" throughout the medieval era.
> Come. The spirit of Jewish people killed in gas chambers during the holocaust.
> Come. The spirit of the Amazon rain forest now being murdered every day.

Dr. Chung continued praying, listing the names of those who, throughout history, have been oppressed, exploited, and who have suffered and been killed unjustly. She then slowly rolled the scroll, made of rice paper, into a cone, set it afire, and let the ashes rise like incense into the air.

Explaining a little of the meaning behind her actions, Dr. Chung spoke of Korea as a land of "spirits full of Han." Han refers to the anguished cry of those who have violently died with their misery unappeased: the spirits of the Maryknoll Sisters, the Jesuits, Oscar Romero, Steve Bikko, are in our midst. Spirits are all over the place, seeking the chance to make the wrong right. These spirits open the door to human transcendence: They are icons of the Spirit. It is the living people's responsibility to listen to the voices of the Han-ridden spirits and to participate in the spirits' work of making right whatever is wrong. "These Han-ridden spirits in our people's history have been agents through whom the Holy Spirit has spoken of her compassion and wisdom for life. Without hearing the cries of these spirits," she continued, "we cannot hear the voice of the Holy Spirit. I hope the presence of all our ancestors' spirits here with us shall not make you uncomfortable. For us they are the icons of the Holy Spirit."[95]

When we pray, "Come, Holy Spirit, Renew the Whole Creation," we must guard against an infantile image of God, Dr. Chung warned us, whereby we think there is a magic solution to the ecological catastrophe, or to healing the wounds of war, injustice, poverty, economic injustice, and violence. We can think of God as someone to whom we look when we are in need or have problems beyond our ability to solve. We can think of God as a Macho Warrior who can lead us to victory in any war. Leaving all of it to God, we can become passive, point to prayer as a way out and as an excuse not to get involved in working for peace and justice and not to struggle in solidarity with all forms of life. It is always a temptation. We must be awake, watchful, and alert: "The Spirit of God has been teaching us through the 'survival wisdom' of the poor, the screams of the Han-ridden spirits of our people and the blessings and curses of nature. Only when we can heed this cry for life and can see the signs of liberation are we able to recognize the Holy Spirit's activity in the midst of suffering creation."[96] This is the God on whom we must rely — the compassionate God who weeps with us for life in the midst of the cruel destruction of life. For Dr. Chung, the image of the Holy Spirit as the compassionate God comes from the image of the Kwan In:

> She is venerated as the Goddess of compassion and wisdom by East Asian women's popular religiosity. She is a bodhisattva, an enlightened being. She can go into Nirvana any time she wants to, but refuses to go into Nirvana by herself. Her compassion for all suffering living beings makes her stay in this world enabling other living beings to achieve enlightenment. Her compassionate wisdom

heals all forms of life and empowers them to swim to the shore of Nirvana. She waits and waits until the whole universe, people, trees, birds, mountains, air, water become enlightened. They can then go to Nirvana together where they can live collectively in eternal wisdom and compassion.

Dr. Chung suggests that perhaps this might also be a "feminine image of the Christ who is the first-born among us, one who goes before and brings others with her."[97] She ends her prayer with the challenging plea that, relying on the energy of the Holy Spirit, we "tear apart all walls of division and the 'culture of death' which separates us" and live on this earth "in solidarity with all living beings, building communities of justice and peace." Then, with a vibrant cry she prays: "Wild wind of the Holy Spirit blow to us. Let us welcome her, letting ourselves go in her wild rhythm of life. Come, Holy Spirit, Renew the Whole Creation. Amen."[98]

The young professor's presentation was received and applauded with a standing ovation by most of the Assembly's participants, but, there were some critics also. A small number accused Dr. Chung of heresy, of syncretism, of compromise. Representatives of the Churches of the Orthodox family argued that there can be no new gospel for our time. The only gospel is the one given to the apostles and handed down through the centuries in the traditions of the Church. Controversies regarding the Holy Trinity had been settled once and for all by the Council of Chalcedon in 451. While it is the right of all Christians to understand and preach the gospel in their own context, it is essential to ask, "what are the limits to diversity?" Is there a point at which a particular understanding of the Scripture and Tradition, certain images and expressions in prayer, no longer stand within the Tradition of the one Church? Referring specifically to Professor Chung's presentation, the Orthodox said:

> The Orthodox wish to stress the factor of sin and error which exists in every human action, and separate the Holy Spirit from these. We must guard against a tendency to substitute a "private" spirit, the spirit of the world or other spirits for the Holy Spirit who proceeds from the Father and rests in the Son. Our tradition is rich in respect for local and national cultures, but we find it impossible to evoke the spirits of "earth, air, water and sea creatures." Pneumatology is inseparable from Christology or from the doctrine of the Holy Spirit confessed by the church on the basis of divine revelation.[99]

Dr. Chung responded:

> Who has the right to judge that I am wrong, and on what basis? Why is it wrong for women, Korean women especially, freed from the restrictions imposed by religion, society and culture, to formulate

their experience of and encounter with the Christian gospel in ways different from how it was expounded in patriarchal cultures. Women's experience of the divine has never found voice until our time. For the last sixteen hundred years the doctrines expressed in our prayers have been formulated in western categories, i.e. in Greco-Roman terms, in Platonic dualistic categories. But Asians are not Platonic but ying/yang opposites, needing each other. Theological language can also be the language of mystery, of poetry, not just rational. Only in this way can we listen and hear the pain of others. Western culture has been for centuries the vehicle for transplanting the gospel message into different nations and missionary lands. The conviction held by the colonizers that their own culture and religion was superior led them in many times to reject the culture and religion of the people to whom they brought the gospel. We, in this country, have come to realize the devastating effect this attitude has had on the culture and religion of the indigenous peoples.

Dr. Chung and many Christians question the identification between Western culture and Christianity and are asking for a fuller awareness of the need to formulate Christian belief and prayer anew in their own culture. Could we not use Buddhist terms, Hindu terms, to speak about, and to pray to, the Holy Trinity? No one way says all. God speaks through all cultures and all histories. Give us some time now to try new expressions, new ways, Dr. Chung pleaded. Give us the option to try new modes of speaking, praying, and communicating the Good News. Surely, there can be endless ways to express the mysteries of Christianity and what God has done in Christ.

The debate focuses clearly for us the urgency to continue study, exploration, and dialogue on the question of the relationship between Christianity and culture. What makes Christianity, Christian?: "How can Christians who can and must interpret the gospel in their own culture recognize others in other cultures as belonging to the one family in Christ? Are there real limits to diversity, or is there only a center for the faith, and everything that comes out of and relates to the center is a valid expression of the faith?"[100] And, finally, the authority question must be addressed. Who can say that a particular understanding and response to the faith in prayer, and ritual, puts "a person or community outside the bounds of the church?"[101] Who has the final word? This question of the way the one gospel is related to the many cultures of the world has continued to be the subject of much discussion, the results of which were the substance of the next world mission conference in November of 1996 with the theme, "Called to One Hope: The Gospel in Diverse Cultures." Essential to all cultures in our time must be the Good News of Christianity, addressing effectively the staggering number of world concerns. In prayer, let us focus our attention on women, world peace, and Christian unity.

A GLOBAL AGENDA OF PRAYER

Women

We are now invited to passover and stand among the women of the world. There have been numerous opportunities in the last twenty years for women of different ages, colors, professions, religious traditions, levels of education, political positions, and ideologies to come together at national and international levels. The United Nations declared 1975-1985 as the UN Decade for Women. Three international conferences were held, one in Mexico City in 1975, a middecade conference in Copenhagen, Denmark, in 1980, and the close of the decade conference in Nairobi, Kenya, in 1985. Ten years later, in 1995, the UN again called the women of the world together in Beijing, China. More than 15,000 women came to Nairobi; more than 30,000 journeyed from all parts of the world to Beijing. They came to share their stories of impoverishment, exploitation, abuse, slavery, and political and spiritual oppression. They came to focus on and force change in international law regarding the rights of women and the girl-child. The theme song of the Nairobi conference speaks poignantly to the point: "We are the world, We are the women. We are the ones who do two-thirds of the world's work, get one-tenth of the world's income, and own less than one percent of the world's assets." In Beijing, women again reaffirmed this reality. To what do we attribute this global subordination and oppression of more than one-half of humankind? Without doubt, it is the result of thousands of years of the universal system of patriarchy, validated by Judaism, Christianity, and Islam which we know are patriarchal religious traditions. In the abstract, these religions teach that God is neither male nor female, that God is beyond sexuality, beyond every human characteristic; yet, it is the male face of God that has been visible throughout history. God is the God of Abraham, Isaac, Jacob, and the sons of Jacob. In our Hebrew Scriptures, God is imaged as a patriarchal head of a family, or by other images that bear absolute authority over others: Warrior, Master, Judge, or King. The patriarch exercises complete power over all members of the household. He is the owner of all properties and all possessions, women, too. Relationships within this power structure are in terms of superiority and inferiority, domination and subordination, power and powerlessness.[102] Our history, theologies, social structures have been based on the patriarchal system. It is as strong today as it was 4,000 years ago: "Our society, like all other historical civilizations, is a patriarchy."[103]

Now, women say it is time to change. We must begin with the religious traditions. We must begin with the sacred writings. When women come together to pray, they seek the feminine face of God. We will call upon God in other than exclusively male words. We will use a language, images, symbols that include the life, experiences, reflections, concerns of millions of human beings: women, young people, peoples and nations of other races of skin color. The language we use to pray to God can be a liberating, creative force. It can come from reading the Hebrew Scriptures and being aware of the feminine and motherly traits in God. Can we not only pray to God as a strong father, but also as a loving, tender, nourishing mother who gives birth, is supportive, compassionate and protective (Isaiah 49:15)? In our prayers, can we not speak to God who does all those things a mother would do: teach us to walk, give us food, console and dry our tears when we are grieving, who cannot forget the child of her womb (Isaiah, 66:49)?

Can we not pray?:

> O God of a thousand names and faces
> Mother and Father of all life on earth
> You who live in the cells of all life
> Teach us to know and love you.[104]

Can we not profess?:

> I believe in God
> who created woman and man in God's own image
> who created the world
> and gave both sexes
> the care of the earth. . . .
>
> I believe in the Holy Spirit
> as she moves over the waters
> of creation
> and over the earth . . .
>
> I believe in the Holy Spirit
> the woman spirit of God
> who like a hen
> created us
> and gave us birth
> and covers us
> with her wings.[105]

In the midst of our pain, can we not cry out?:

> O God, you created us in your image, both male and female
> We are female human beings poised on the edge of the new millennium.
> We are the majority of our species, yet we have dwelt in the shadows.
> We are the invisible, the illiterate, the laborers, the refugees, the poor.
> And we vow: NO MORE
>
> We are poised on the edge of the millennium — ruin behind us, no map before us
> the taste of fear sharp on our tongues.
> Yet we will leap.
> The exercise of imagining is an act of creation.
> The act of creation is an exercise of will
> ALL THIS IS POLITICAL. AND POSSIBLE . . .
>
> We WILL make it real, make it our own, make policy, history, peace,
> make it available, make mischief, a difference, love, the
> connections, the miracle, ready.
> BELIEVE IT
> WE ARE THE WOMEN WHO WILL TRANSFORM THE
> WORLD.[106]

In the Christian Scriptures, Luke tells of Jesus who cries over Jerusalem for having killed the prophets and stoned those sent to the city. He says, "How often I have longed to gather your children, as a hen gathers her brood under her wings . . ." (Luke 13:34). These images of God give us a glimpse of the feminine aspects of the mystery of the God who is love, wisdom, compassion. The image of God as Mother persisted throughout Christian history. In the words of Julian of Norwich: "So Jesus Christ, who sets good against evil, is our real Mother. We owe our being to him — and this is the essence of motherhood! with all sweet keeping of love that endlessly follows. As truly as God is our Father, so truly is God our Mother."[107] These images enrich the language we use when we pray, as we see in this African prayer: "O love and hatch us Wondrous hen! We dwell in thy kingdom, Our hen of heaven."[108]

At times, it is helpful to go beyond the cultural legacy of the Hebrew Scriptures and the Christian Scriptures and to include forms of expression, symbols, and images of people with other lifestyles and other cultural heritages. Hear an African woman pray:

God of Fire, God of Light
Are you the God who answers prayers?
Your people are burning and killing each other,
but all they want is land, food, education and the vote.

God of Fire, God of Light
Are you watching over us
Yes! You are holding up the Fire to give us energy,
to fight for what is right and just.[109]

How can we think, speak, and project God beyond sexuality for today and for tomorrow? Can the search to unfold the feminine face of God help us to bring about changes in the way Church and society are organized? Can we break the system of patriarchy? Can we be part of the solution? It is the prayer of women that, by telling their stories, dreaming their dreams, and networking with others, they will be empowered in the struggle for a new world order that is good for all God's creation, a world that is good also for women.

World Peace

O God of the children of Somalia, Sarajevo,
South Africa, and South Carolina,
Of Albania, Alabama, Bosnia, and Boston,
Of Cracow and Cairo, Chicago and Croatia,
Help us to love and respect and protect them all.

O God of children of destiny and despair, of war and of peace
Of disfigured, diseased, and dying children,
Of children without hope and of children with hope to spare and to share,
Help us to love and respect and protect them all.[110]

The institutions of war and the militarism that feeds and supports it have been present throughout human history. For the most part, they are created, controlled, and perpetuated by men. At times, women may support military solutions to conflicts, and, today, in some places, women are in the armed forces. In situations where women lead governments, some promote policies leading to war: "But mostly women and children are the victims of war and militarism."[111] They become refugees, the objects of rape and sexual abuse by occupation forces, and trapped as civilians in the midst of violence. Women are the mothers, sisters, and wives of those killed, those who "disappear," and, with children, are the majority of those deprived of basic necessities needed to live a human life when money is taken from programs that enhance life and given to weapons that destroy life. It is not surprising, then, "that women are often at the heart of movements for peace with

justice and other activities that promote creative nonviolent resolution of conflict."[112] And, women have taken the lead in urging
that adversaries be recognized as full human beings and not as a
projection of the other as enemy. The whole world movement to
cultivate a culture of peace seems doomed to failure when we contemplate the more than thirty armed conflicts in the world, resulting in massive human tragedies. Humankind is embroiled in the
throes of a culture of death. Due to civil war and conflicts, some
twenty million people are on the brink of starvation and death in
African countries alone: Sudan, Ethiopia, Somalia, Angola,
Mozambique, Rwanda, and Liberia. For the most part, the people
of the world are turning a deaf ear. How can we speak of world
peace!

Today, we are called to collaborate with those of other faiths for
peace, justice, and the integrity of creation. The future of the
earth concerns all of us, whatever our religion or ideology. For
centuries, religious differences, prejudices, and mistrust have pre-
cluded any dialogue among religions. All of us lived in deliberate
isolation. Today, Christians are involved in fruitful dialogues with
all the major religious traditions. For Christians, Jesus Christ is the
Light of the world, the Prince of Peace. He is the Way, the Truth,
and the Life. He teaches us nonviolence, peacemaking, forgiveness, and self renunciation. Is Jesus Christ, our Light, compatible
with other lights recognized by millions of others? Do not Christ,
our Light, and Enlightened ones of other faiths, e.g., Gautama
and the Koran, show us clearly the Way to peace? All religions are
messages of salvation, answering basic questions about human life.
All the great religions demand certain standards for living that
guide actions. These are based on an Absolute, valid for millions
of people. All offer ways to live now so as to attain eternal salvation. Five great directives are found in all great religions of
humankind: "You shall not kill! or in positive terms: Have respect
for life! You shall not steal! or in positive terms: Deal honestly and
fairly! You shall not lie! or in positive terms: Speak and act truth-
fully! You shall not commit sexual immorality! or in positive terms:
Respect and love one another."[113]

Religious traditions can be distorted for the motivation, support, and prolongation of war. History shows only too well that
they have often played a disastrous role. Today, in many parts of
the world, religion is used as a force of division and conflict.
Religious language and symbols are being used to exacerbate conflicts. Religious traditions can also produce leaders for avoiding or
shortening conflicts. In this spirit, ten years ago Pope John Paul II
announced the World Day of Prayer for Peace to be held in Assisi,
Italy, on October 29, 1986. All the leaders of the world's religions

were invited to attend. About thirty-three nonChristian representatives and about fifty representatives of Christian churches
attended. Twelve Muslim leaders, ten Buddhists, four Hindus, two
African traditionalists, and representatives of Judaism, Sikhism,
Zoroastrians, and American Indians were present. Each group
prayed as a religious family, and each group offered its prayer in
the public forum. In the words of Pope John Paul II:

> The coming together of so many religious leaders to pray is in itself
> an invitation to the world to become aware that there exists anoth-
> er dimension of peace and another way of promoting it which is not
> a result of negotiations, political compromise or economic bar-
> gaining. It is the result of prayer, which, in the diversity of religions,
> expresses a relationship with a supreme power that surpasses our
> human capacities."[114]

The primary task of religions today is to be a peacemaker, one to
the other. They should address, and clear up, misunderstandings,
heal bitter memories, eliminate stereotypical images of the enemy,
resolve conflicts, diminish hate and destruction. What a blessing it
would be if religious leaders were to speak and act for peace
among the religions and nations. What if, Hans Küng asks, the
years following World War II had been used by the Bishops of the
Catholic Croats and the Serbian Orthodox Bishops to deal with
the crimes committed by both sides? What if, after mourning and
clarifying guilt, they had called the people to penitence (*metanoia*,
a change of heart and mind), asked each other's pardon, and celebrated reconciliations?[115] With our new policies of diplomacy, what
is yet needed is a conversion of our hearts and a forgiveness of one
another. The process of repentance, reconciliation, celebration
may well be a long one. Let us pray:

> How far from you have we strayed, Lord, that this could have
>   happened?
> How long can we be allowed to go on living if we insist on treating
>   fellow human beings in this manner, sometimes even in Your
>   name?
> How can we overcome the sins by which human beings have
>   damaged the moral atmosphere of a world hungry for sanctity?
> Is our earth a fit place for a Messiah?
> Is my own soul such a place?
> Am I praying and working to purify the world from hatred, from
>   bigotry, from the kind of ignorance which can produce yet
>   another Holocaust?
> Dare I pledge, in prayer, a lifelong vow to be alert to evil and to
>   fight it in Your name?[116]

Christian Unity

The nations of the world have heard the urgent call to unity through the recent report on "Global Governance" from the Independent Commission whose mandate was approved by the UN Secretary General in 1991. The UN report, "Our Global Neighborhood," written in the context of celebrating the jubilee of the UN, focuses on issues central also to the ecumenical movement today. The report gives three issues that must be addressed as prerequisites for global unity: the relationship between unity and diversity, the appropriate structures of unity, and methods of cooperation possible on the way to unity. The governments of the world are searching for the ways and means to achieve unity.[117]

The agenda which the nations must address are similar to those being addressed by the Churches as they seek unity together for the sake of humankind. The call for the Churches to seek visible structures of unity is imperative. Throughout most of this century, there have been significant landmarks on the way to Christian unity. Churches have moved from isolation, polarization, confrontation, and from defining themselves in opposition to others, to dialogue, cooperation, respect, sharing of energies, gifts, and ministry. Now, the call is for visible structures of unity. The world of the Faith and Order Commission of the WCC continues to work diligently toward this goal. We note the work undertaken on the "Common Understanding and Vision" in 1995, as well as the publication of *Costly Commitment*,[118] the studies on the "church as the 'koinonia' confessing the faith in each time and place, celebrating the presence of God through worship and commitment to discipleship."[119] Since its unanimous acceptance at the WCC meeting in Vancouver in 1983, the document, *Baptism, Eucharist, and Ministry*, has continued to be discussed and studied at international conferences until today. These dialogues engaged in by the theologians in the Faith and Order Commission and the bilateral conversations have been a great success. The Catholic Church and its theologians are in dialogue about the responses to these statements. Already, responses have been made at the highest levels to the Anglican/Roman Catholic *Final Report* and to the WCC document, *Baptism, Eucharist, and Ministry*. Other dialogues, like the Lutheran/Catholic Dialogue, are resulting in very specific proposals for moving toward visible unity. Dialogues continue today between the Roman Catholic Church and the members of the WCC, all of which are moving us closer to visible unity.[120] As John Paul II reminds us in his letter, "Commitment to Ecumenism":

If Christians, despite their divisions, can grow ever more united in common prayer around Christ, they will grow in the awareness of how little divides them. If they meet more often and more regularly before Christ in prayer, they will be able to gain the courage to face all the painful reality of their divisions, and they will find themselves together once more in that community of the Church which Christ constantly builds up in the Holy Spirit, in spite of all weaknesses and human limitations (22).[121]

The question today is: Shall the dawn of the third millennium rise on our full refound communion? A unity, not only expressed in speeches, documents, theological tomes, but actual unity in reality. Two major ecclesial celebrations to take place in the next few years give reasons to hope the response will be a resounding, "Yes." Two years ago, Pope John Paul II issued an Apostolic Letter to the bishops, clergy, and lay faithful of the Roman Catholic Church, "On Preparation for the Jubilee of the Year 2000."[122] In the second chapter of this letter (9-16), the Holy Father develops the concept of the Jubilee with reference to the two thousandth anniversary of the birth of Christ. The Pope offers a biblical explication of the meaning of Jubilee in the biblical tradition and then outlines an impressive process of spiritual and liturgical preparation for the year 2000. Since the fifteenth century, the Catholic Church has been celebrating every twenty-five years as a "Holy Year," with the main focus on reconciliation. But, in recent years, emphasis has been placed also on spiritual renewal in the love of God, faithfulness to the gospel, reconciliation and commitment to social justice and compassion in human society. Following this tradition, the year 2000 is to be celebrated as a special Holy Year. We read in the Apostolic Letter: "(The Church) invites everyone to rejoice, and she tries to create conditions to ensure that the power of salvation may be shared by all. Hence the year 2000 will be celebrated as the Great Jubilee."[123]

Two years from the end of the millennium, 1998, the Eighth Assembly of the World Council will be held in Harare, Zimbabwe. The Eighth Assembly will be a "Jubilee-Assembly," taking place fifty years after the first Assembly in Amsterdam in 1948. Its focus will be on the motif of an "Ecumenical Jubilee" and what it might mean for the Churches. The theme of the Assembly will be: "Turn to God — Rejoice in Hope." The Eighth Assembly will indeed be a special anniversary and an occasion for much celebration, but the biblical Jubilee motif will call all to seek forgiveness and embrace reconciliation. The parallel focus of these two world bodies gives great significance to the question: An Ecumenical Jubilee — what might it mean for the Churches?

In a recent address to the representatives of the United States Conference of Member Churches of the WCC, Konrad Raiser, the present Secretary General of the World Council of Churches, elucidated numerous motifs of the biblical tradition of Jubilee and their meaning today for the Churches.[124] For instance, it is important to note that the liberty bell in Philadelphia, one of the great symbols of the American Revolution, carries the inscription quoting from Leviticus 25:10: "Proclaim liberty throughout the land to all its inhabitants." To translate for our time, what a prophetic stance it would be if the Churches of the world would raise their united voices to the rich, powerful governments of the world, urging them to cancel the debts, often unjustly calculated, of the poor, developing nations? In the New Testament context, the imperative is forgiveness and reconciliation as the way to reconstitution of community. The forthcoming Jubilees might use this motif as an occasion for the Churches to reflect and to reassess their life. The aim would be to proclaim liberation, to cancel debts, one Church to another, and to practice reconciliation and forgiveness. This is not a turning back, but a reordering and reorientation, a liberation from the bonds of the past and a call to embrace the promise of life. The Secretary General urged the participants to search for new paradigms and for a new vision which will inspire a new generation. The Jubilee motif could serve as a matrix integrating the elements of a new ecumenical vision into the future of the twenty-first century. In the words of Pope John Paul II:

> As everyone recognizes, an enormous effort is needed in this regard. It is essential not only to continue along the path of dialogue on doctrinal matters, but above all to be committed to *prayer for Christian unity.* . . . In these last years of the millennium, the Church should invoke the Holy Spirit with ever greater insistence, imploring . . . the grace of *Christian Unity. Unity, after all is a gift of the Holy Spirit.*[125]

In response to the Holy Father and in the words of the former General Secretary of the World Council of Churches, Emilio Castro, let us invoke the Holy Spirit and pray:

> Come, Holy Spirit — Renew in your people the hunger for unity; renew the sense of guilt for division; renew the awareness of our unity in you, and heighten our imagination and our will to try to express this unity in forms which may be recognizable to the world for which we wish to bear testimony so that it may believe in the Christ who sends us. Come Holy Spirit, Spirit of Unity, Reconcile Your People![126]

CONCLUSION

Planetary prophets from Teilhard de Chardin to Carl Sagan invited us to turn our attention to the things of planet earth and beyond. As planetary pilgrims, we felt the presence of God in the physical universe and in the activating energy of the Risen Christ permeating the entire cosmos.

Listening to the Documents of Vatican II, we realized that the boundaries of our religious tradition need not be barriers, but meeting places where we might learn one from the other as we try to walk together in peace and harmony.

Being present at the Assembly of the World Council of Churches, we grasped the importance of culture as the context and specific content for prayer. Through our experience, we have seen that prayer has taken on a global dimension. A world-wide-web of efforts and prayers for peace, a growing realization and ritualization of the interconnectedness of all creation, the movement by women to elevate the feminine as a worthy and noble image of God, and the urgent struggle for unity among the Christian Churches — all of these speak to the blowing of the wind, the presence of the Spirit in our time. Carl Sagan invites us, "Look again at that pale blue dot — earth photographed by Voyager 1 from beyond the orbit of Neptune. That's here, that's home, that's us. On it everyone you love, everyone you know, every human being who ever was, lived out their lives, the aggregate of our joy and suffering . . . every mother and father, hopeful child, every teacher of morals, every corrupt politician, every saint and sinner in the history of our species lived there — on a mote of dust suspended in a sunbeam."[12] LET US PRAY!

NOTES

[1]Karl Jaspers, *The Origin and Goal of History* (New Haven, CT: Yale University Press, 1953), 1.

[2]Tissa Balasurya, *Planetary Theology* (Maryknoll, NY: Orbis Books, 1984).

[3]Edward Hays, *Prayers for a Planetary Pilgrim* (Easton, KS: Forest of Peace Books, Inc., 1989).

[4]Hans Küng, *Global Responsibility: In Search of a New World Ethic* (New York: Crossroad Publishing Co., 1991).

[5]Alfred T. Hennelly, S. J., *Liberation Theologies: The Global Pursuit of Justice* (Mystic, CT: Twenty-Third Publications, 1996).

[6]Brian Swimme, *The Hidden Heart of the Cosmos* (Maryknoll, NY: Orbis, 1995).

[7]*The Global Brain*, videotape, rec. 1 July 1983, at the Psychosynthesis Conference, Toronto, Canada (London: Peter Russell and Chris Hall Productions, 1985).

[8]Kenneth Kramer, *World Scriptures* (Mahwah, NJ: Paulist Press, 1986), 282.

[9]John Seed, quoted in *Earth Prayers from Around the World*, ed. Elizabeth Roberts and Elias Amidon (San Francisco, CA: Harper, 1991), 35.

[10]Walbert Buhlmann, *God's Chosen Peoples* (Maryknoll, NY: Orbis, 1982), 269.

[11]Wilfred Cantwell Smith, *Toward a World Theology* (Maryknoll, NY: Orbis, 1989), 48.

[12]Diana L. Eck, *Encountering God: A Spiritual Journey from Bozeman to Banaras* (Boston, MA: Beacon Press, 1993), xii.

[13]Ibid., 11.

[14]Anthony de Mello, *Sadhana: A Way to God* (Anand, India: Gujarat Sahitya Prakash, 1984), 13.

[15]A. de Mello, *Wellsprings: A Book of Spiritual Exercises* (Garden City, NY: Image Books, 1986), 314.

[16]Rabindranath Tagore, *Gitanjali* (Song Offering) (New York: Macmillan, 1971), 108.

[17]Eck, 46.

[18]Ewert H. Cousins, "Interreligious Dialogue: The Spiritual Journey of Our Time, *International Religious Foundation Newsletter* II/1 (Jan.-Feb., 1987), 8.

[19]For over two decades, Thomas Berry has been one of only a few voices calling to our attention the religious dimension of environmental issues. See Thomas Berry, *The Dream of the Earth* (San Francisco, CA: Sierra Books, 1988).

[20]P. Teilhard de Chardin, *The Future of Man* (NY: Harper, 1969).

[21]Valentina Tereshkova, "Message from a Cosmonaut," in *Global Survival Conference Report* (NY: Global Forum of Spiritual and Parliamentary Leaders on Human Survival, 1988), 39.

[22]Hays, 12.

[23]Ibid., 184.

[24]Karl Rahner, "The Church in the Future," in Walbert Buhlmann, *The Church of the Future* (Maryknoll, NY: Orbis Books, 1986), 193.

[25]Ibid.

[26]Stephen J. Duffy, "Encountering the Stranger: Christianity in Dialogue with the World Religions," *Yamauchi Lectures in Religion* (New Orleans, LA: Loyola University, 1994), 13-14.

[27]A. Meynell, "Christ in the Universe," in *Selected Poems of Alice Meynell* (London: Burns, Oates, Washbourne, n.d.), 47-48.

[28]Carl Sagan, *Pale Blue Dot: A Vision of the Human Future in Space* (NY: Random, 1994), 397-98.

[29]Hays, 142.

[30]Seder Amram, quoted in Louis Bouyer, *The Eucharist* (Notre Dame, IN: U. of Notre Dame Press, 1968), 126-27.

[31]Karl Rahner, "Toward a Fundamental Theological Interpretation of Vatican II," *Theological Studies* 40 (1979): 721.

[32]Jean Danielou, *The Origins of Latin Christianity: A History of Early Christian Doctrine before the Council of Nicaea*, Volume 3 (Philadelphia, PA: Westminster Press, 1977).

[33]Idem, *Gospel Message and Hellenistic Culture: A History of Early Christian Doctrine*, Volume 2, trans. J. Baker (Philadelphia, PA: Westminster Press, 1973).

[34]Idem, *The Theology of Jewish Christianity: The Development of Christian Doctrine before the Council of Nicaea*, Volume 1, trans. J. Baker (Chicago, IL: The Henry Regnery Company, 1964).

[35]Sebastian Brock, *The Holy Spirit in the Syrian Baptismal Tradition*, The Syrian Churches Series 9 (Poona, IN: Anita Printers, 1979), 11-13.

[36]J. H. Bernard, *The Odes of Solomon*, Texts and Studies 8:3 (Cambridge: Cambridge University Press, 1912), 120-21.

[37]Sebastian Brock, *The Syriac Fathers on Prayer and the Spiritual Life* (Kalamazoo, MI: Cistercian Publications, Inc., 1987), xxvii.

[38]Ibid., 45-53.

[39]*The Ways of the Spirit*. See Theodoret, Letter 145, in NPF 2nd Series, 3:315, and Letter 151, NPF 2nd Series 3:332.

[40]Ephrem of Syria's hymns include numerous references (Hymns on the Nativity 10, 14, 15, 42, Homily on the Faith 21).

[41]Sebastian Brock, *The Harp of the Spirit* (San Bernardino, CA: Borgo Press, 1984), 5-8.

[42]Ibid., 14.

[43]Brock, *The Syriac Fathers on Prayer and the Spiritual Life*, xxxiii.

[44]Brock, *The Holy Spirit in the Syrian Baptismal Tradition*, 12.

[45]"Hymns on the Church," in Brock, *The Syriac Fathers on Prayer and the Spiritual Life*, xxxiii.

[46]Ibid.

[47]Ibid., xxix.

[48]Ibid., xxx.

[49]"Hymns on the Nativity," no. 11 in Brock, *The Syriac Fathers*, 34-35.

[50]Clement of Alexandria, *Stromata* 1.5.

[51]Henry Chadwick, *Early Christian Thought and the Classical Tradition* (New York and Oxford: Oxford University Press, 1966), 1

[52]*De Prescriptione* 7.

[53]Karl Rahner, "Toward a Fundamental . . .," 722.

[54]*Mystici Corporis*, 3rd ed. (New York: America Press, 1957), No. 21.

[55]Antoine Wenger, *Vatican II, Première Session* (Paris: Éditions de Centurion, 1963), 17-18.

[56]Pope John XXIII, "Announcement of Ecumenical Council and Roman Synod," *The Pope Speaks*, 5 (1959), 400.

[57]Idem, "Light on the Ecumenical Council," *The Pope Speaks*, 6 (1959), 236.

[58]Idem, "Sorrows and Joys of the Church," 5 (1959), 403-404.

[59]Idem, "Humanae Salutis," in W. Abbott and J. Gallagher, *The Documents of Vatican II* (New York: Guild Press, 1966), 709.

[60]Idem, "Prayer to the Holy Spirit," in *Journal of a Soul*, trans. Dorothy White (New York: McGraw-Hill Book Company, 1965), 391.

[61]Idem, "The Council — At the Threshold of a New Era," *The Pope Speaks*, 8 (1962), 209.

[62]Ibid., 215.

[63]Idem, "The Council Fathers Speak to the World," *The Pope Speaks*, 8 (1962), 302-303.

64Ibid., 302.
65Idem, "Toward a New Pentecost," *The Pope Speaks*, 8 (1962), 402.
66Karl Rahner, "Towards a Fundamental . . .," 718-19.
67*Sacrosanctum Concilium*, in *Documents of Vatican II*, ed. Austin Flannery.
68Rahner, "Towards a Fundamental . . .," 719.
69*Nostra Aetate*, in *Documents of Vatican II*, Vol. 1, ed. Austin Flannery (Northport, NY: Costello Publishing Co., 1975), 738.
70Ibid., 740.
71Ibid.
72Ibid.
73Ibid., 739.
74Ibid., 740.
75*Unitatis Redintegratio*, in *Documents*, 452.
76Ibid., 457; 462.
77Ibid., 454.
78John 4:9; Col. 1:18-20; Jn. 11:52.
79*Nostra Aetate*, in *Documents*, 453.
80From a mimeographed copy of an unpublished talk given by Rev. Yves Congar, O.P., at Pius XII Center for the Better World Movement, Rome, November, 1965.
81*Gadium et Spes*, in *Documents*, 903. The English translations of the documents of Vatican II still use the term "men" to refer to men and women. While this use of exclusive language was characteristic of earlier times, given the feminist critique of sexist language in most of the English speaking countries of the world, we hope that authors and translators will soon change to inclusive language.
82See Paul F. Knitter, *One Earth, Many Religions: Multifaith Dialogue and Global Responsibility* (Maryknoll, NY: Orbis Books, 1995). In his new book, Knitter shows the way the ecological crisis is central to any serious discussion of the future of humankind and how urgent it is that the world's religions unite in defending the earth.
83I am indebted for information related to ecological issues to a speech given at Saint Louis University by Dr. Peter H. Raven, Director of the Missouri Botanical Garden, "Business Ethics in a Global Environment," April, 1992.
84Muriel Porter, *Land of the Spirit?: The Australian Religious Experience* (Geneva, Switzerland: WCC Publications, 1990), 1.
85Anne Pattel-Gray, *Through Aboriginal Eyes: The Cry from the Wilderness* (Geneva, Switzerland: WCC Publications, 1990), 2-3.
86Ibid.
87Ibid.
88Sir Paul Reeves, Sermon delivered in the opening worship service of the WCC in Canberra, Australia, Feb. 7, 1991. Mimeographed copy of the speech.
89With the understanding of earth as mother and the attitude of respect, love, and reverence we owe to mother, the Maoris, the Aboriginals, and the other indigenous peoples could never do anything to injure the earth, for who can destroy her own mother?
90Ibid.

[91]Anne-Pattel Gray, 5-6.

[92]Ed Eschweiler, *Celebrating God's Good Earth* (Milwaukee, WI: Hi-Time Publishing Corp., 1991).

[93]Rahner, "The Church . . .," 194.

[94]Michael Kinnamon, ed., *Signs of the Spirit: Official Report of the Seventh Assembly of the World Council of Churches* (Geneva, Switzerland: WCC Publications, 1991), 37.

[95]Ibid., 39.

[96]Ibid., 41.

[97]Ibid., 46.

[98]Ibid.

[99]Ibid., 37-46.

[100]S. Wesley Ariarajah, *Gospel and Culture* (Geneva: WCC, 1994), 49-50.

[101]Ibid., 50.

[102]Dolores Greeley, "Patriarchy: A Global Reality," in *Where Can We Find Her?*, ed. Marie Eloise Rosenblatt (New York: Paulist Press, 1991), 80.

[103]Kate Millett, *Sexual Politics* (New York: Doubleday, 1970), 25.

[104]Sharon Owens, *Women's Prayer Services* (Mystic, CT: Twenty-Third Publications, 1988), 25.

[105]Rachel Conrad Wahlbert, *Jesus and the Freed Woman* (Mahwah, NJ: Paulist Press, 1978), 155-57.

[106]Excerpts from *A Woman's Creed*, written by Robin Morgan, in collaboration with Mahnaz Afkhami, Diane Faulkner, Perdita Huston, Corinne Kumar, Paola Melchiori, Sunetra Puri, and Sima Wali, at the Women's Global Strategies Meeting, November 29-December 2, 1994, sponsored by the Women's Environment and Development Organization (WEDO) and attended by 148 women from 50 countries.

[107]Austin Cooper, O.M.I., *Julian of Norwich* (Mystic, CT: Twenty-Third Publications, 1987), 102.

[108]Aylward Shorter, *Prayer in the Religious Traditions of Africa* (Nairobi: Oxford U. Press, 1975), 109.

[109]An African Prayer, in *Through the Eyes of a Woman* (Geneva: WCCP, 1995), 101.

[110]"Prayer to the God of all Children," Marian Wright Edelman, Children's Defense Fund.

[111]"Statement & Appeals on Public Issues," presented by the Seventh Assembly of the World Council of Churches, 1991, in *Signs of the Spirit*, ed. Michael Kinnamon (Grand Rapids, MI: W. B. Eerdmans, 1991), 213.

[112]Ibid.

[113]Hans Küng and Karl-Josef Kuschel, eds., *A Global Ethic*, The Declaration of the Parliament of the World's Religions (NY, NY: Continuum Publishing Company, 1993), 25-32.

[114]Pope John Paul II, "Address in Assisi during the Day of Prayer for Peace," *Origins* 16 (Oct. 29, 1986), 370.

[115]Hans Küng, "Le Christ, la Lumière et les autres lumières. De la problématique des religions mondiales et de l'éthos mondial," *Lumière et Vie* 44:2 (April, 1995): 33-43.

[116]Harry James Cargas, "Help Me to Remember," in *Face to Face*, an Interreligious Bulletin, VII (New York, NY: Anti-Defamation League of B'nai B'rith, 1980), 20.

[117]See Alan D. Falconer, "Faith and Order Report," in *Information* 1996 (Geneva: WCC, 1996), 1.

[118]Ibid., 3.

[119]"The Unity of the Church as Koinonia: Gift and Calling," a document submitted by Faith and Order to the Seventh Assembly of the WCC, Feb., 1991, in Michael Kinnamon, 172. See Faith and Order Study Document, *Church and World — The Unity of the Church and the Renewal of Human Community* (Geneva: WCC Publications, 1990).

[120]Harding Meyer and Lukas Vischer, eds., *Growth in Agreement: Reports and Agreed Statements of Ecumenical Conversations on a World Level* (New York: Paulist, and Geneva: World Council of Churches, 1984); Jeffrey Gros and Joseph Burgess, eds., *Building Unity* (New York: Paulist, and Geneva: World Council of Churches, 1989); Idem, *Growing Consensus*, 1995.

[121]John Paul II, *Ut Unum Sint, On Commitment to Ecumenism.* An Encyclical Letter of John Paul II (Boston, MA: Pauline Books & Media, 1995), 34.

[122]John Paul II, *Tertio Millennio Adveniente* (Quebec, Canada: Mediaspaul, November 10, 1994).

[123]Ibid., 23.

[124]Konrad Raiser, "An Ecumenical Jubilee: What It Might Mean for the Churches." Address at the Annual Meeting of the U.S. Conference of Member Churches of the WCC (Nashville, Tennessee, May, 1995). Mimeographed copy of the speech.

[125]John Paul II, *Tertio Millennio Adveniente*, 44-45.

[126]Emilio Castro, "Report of the General Secretary," in Michael Kinnamon, 166.

[127]Carl Sagan, 8.

Christians and the Hindu Experience of Prayer

William Cenkner

In the early months of 1972, I was initiated into the use of a mantra, along with three other Catholic priests, by a young teacher of Transcendental Meditation. Maharishi Mahesh Yogi had instructed his teachers that ministers, priests, or rabbis were to be initiated only after a series of twenty-seven one hour video lectures by Maharishi on the philosophy of Transcendental Meditation—unlike the noncleric meditators who were given an introductory lecture on one day and initiation on the following day. It was thus several months before I began my mantra practice. For some reason, the Maharishi wanted religious teachers to use the mantra within the context of his contemporary articulation of Vedanta philosophy. Since then, the contextualization of religious practice has been a major concern of mine in coming to understand the Indian spiritual practices. This essay examines Christians and their modes of contextualization in the Hindu paths of devotion, knowledge, and holy action.[1] It is done in two moves: first, five models of contextualization are set forth; second, the experiences of contemporary Christians who have drawn upon Hindu spiritual practices are examined within these five models of understanding.

Models of Contextualization

Although the use of models is not new in theology, Stephen Bevans developed a set of models to bring understanding to intercultural theology within Christianity.[2] The attempt here is to revision his models within intercultural practice between Christianity and Hinduism. Bevans sought expressive models that reflect the interface of intercultural theologies; I seek experiential models that reflect the interface of interreligious practice. The

47

models are neither discrete nor autonomous. Since one can move from one to another and back again, they overlap at significant points. They are not in any sense ontological realities, but contextual models for the sake of understanding the depth and breadth of one's encounter with another culture and with the sacred, and, in this case, one's use of practical methods and spiritual practices. Hopefully, they will reveal the growth resulting from the experience and the value placed on it.

The *translational model* was a common model in theology as Christianity engaged new cultures throughout its history. It assumed that revelation was the communication of truth in verbal form and that truth or meaning can be translated by functional equivalents into other linguistic idioms across time and cultures. It presumes, for our usage here, that prayer or the Hindu spiritual paths can be separated from an Indian cultural context and can function in other cultural and religious contexts. In the process, meaning is translated. For example, ancient Hindu mantras, as repetitive sound to quiet the body and mind, are drawn upon by Christians and are translated as forms of a Jesus prayer. Or, a classical Hindu mantra, as found in Maharishi's form of meditation, is substituted with a nonsense word or syllable with the expectation of similar results and meaning. Another use of this model takes place when a cultural form from Hinduism is used in Christian ritual or prayer with or without its original meaning or usage from the Hindu tradition. Such examples have emerged among Indian Christians who, in liturgical celebration or prayer, may sit in lotus position or use fire in ritual purification and ritual offering.

The *anthropological model* describes well those creative Christian missionaries who view revelation as God's processual self revelation occurring in all cultures. It is not a translation of the old into the new, but a discovery in a new culture of meaning or truth and identifying it as Christian reality and naming it with Western linguistic and Christian theological categories. An anthropological model is prevalent among social scientists and those involved in interreligious dialogue. In revisioning this model, one would find in Hindu prayer or Yoga discipline new meaning and new truth in the Hindu context itself, and only upon reflection would it bring change to the subject in his/her articulation and living of the Christian gospel tradition. This model holds that context affects content and, consequently, does not remove content from its culturally related matrix. For example, in a prayerful reading and reflection upon the Vedic hymns or the *Bhagavad Gita* within a Hindu context of understanding, one then returns to a prayerful reading and reflection of the gospels within a Christian context of understanding, anticipating an enrichment of experience and meaning. In short, the cultural context of the Hindu practice changes, to some degree, the subject in his/her Christian prayer life. This model presumes that a personal encounter with divine presence can take place in more than one religious context. This appears to be the case in conversion experiences, but it is presumed here even when there is no change in religious commitment.

The *praxis model* is a prevalent theological model in Catholic theology today. It is based in the actual experiences of the Christian in which reflection upon life experience results in a new expression of faith and commitment. It images the ageold prophetic tradition and social transformation resulting from gospel reflection in our own history. It brings together word and action, experience and reflection, within the orthopraxis of the subject. In theory, it may well be the most accessible to the Hindu tradition which is fundamentally a tradition of orthopraxis. It is clearly a model of experience underlining a previous theological expression. As a model for understanding Christian use of Hindu prayer, ritual, or meditational forms, it presumes the previous model, that is, sustaining the practice within the cultural context of the other in order to bring about social change in oneself. It articulates well the ancient Hindu axiom, "to know the truth is to do the truth." This model was present in the life of Mahatma Gandhi who drew upon the Western and Jain nonviolent traditions of practice in order to evolve his own reconceptualization of nonviolence. Likewise, Gandhi was enriched with the scriptures and prayer traditions of world religions in his own life and in the religious practices of his communities, all of which moved him and his followers to a commitment in social transformation.

The *synthetic model* in theology combines the best of the anthropological and praxis models because it recognizes the central role of culture in religious expression. Much of contemporary theology utilizes this model under such nomenclature as dialectical, dialogical, conversational, or analogical modalities. It not only tries to develop insight from new intellectual traditions, but also new ways of thinking, perceiving, and judging. The model is both traditional and contemporary, involving both an old intellectual tradition and a new one. It is deeply rooted in one tradition and views it as unique, while accepting a new tradition as significantly complementary. As an experimental model and not merely as an expressive one, it accepts the ritual forms, prayer and meditational methods, and the resulting insights and ways of thinking into one's own practice. In this case, it draws upon aspects of Hindu spiritual practice and brings them into conversation and dialectic with Christian experience. It discovers both similarity and difference, uniqueness and complementarity. This model, I believe, has been successfully followed by John Dunne, with the metaphorical language of "crossing over" to another classical age, another philosophical position, another's personal life, gaining insight, and then returning to one's own tradition with new understanding and spiritual growth.[3] As an experiential model, one would have to enter profoundly into the cultural world and the socioreligious life of Hinduism.

How does the synthetic model differ from the anthropological model? With the anthropological model, one always returns to the primary culture and tradition, but, with the synthetic model, the movement back and forth between two religious traditions and two cultural worlds is an ongoing process. For an anthropologist to do such would be to go native. The early European anthropologists thought that one first enters into the center of the tribal village and gradually moves more and more to the periphery until one is at the village edge, finally outside the village, and never again returns to the center, but functions only as an observer of the village. However, the religious seeker within the synthetic model does not leave the two centers of practice. This does not necessarily mean that he/she has the same commitment to both religious centers. Some Christian seekers who follow such a dual practice remain fully Christian as they carry on their religious practice within the sociocultural context of another tradition. They try to capture the uniqueness of both and the complementarity of one tradition to the other. The differences between the anthropological and synthetic models occur, in my opinion, only on the level of experiential models and not on the level of expressive models, for every effort is made to speak within a Christian context and to articulate as orthodox an understanding as it is possible.

The *transcendental model* reveals similarities between traditional Hindu ways of selftransformation and those found in Western transcendental theology, especially in the epistemology of Bernard Lonergan, in seeking to know the subjective self or, in Hindu thought, to know the true self. The transcendental model seeks a change in horizon, a conversion and radical shift of perspective, an authentic change in subject. In this model, revelation is an event and not merely truth or meaning as content of experience. It takes with utmost seriousness authentic subjectivity rooted in faith. Both Lonergan and Sankara (eighth century C.E.), India's classical thinker, sought understanding through radical and authentic subjectivity. Although they differ in the meaning of such subjectivity, both gave attention to the cognitive and affective operations of the selftranscending subject. Lonergan believed that his theological method — to be attentive, to be intelligent, to be reasonable, to be responsible — was applicable to all cultures and at all times. Such a position would be shared by those scholars, the perennialists, who advance an essentialist view of mystical experience. In Sankara's methodology, which is contextualized in Hindu meditational processes, the focus is also upon the affective and cognitive operations that take place only in meditation in order to bring about a change of normal subjectivity. The subject stands firmly in faith, in the generic sense of trust in the transcendent, as articulated by Wilfred Cantwell Smith.[4] The subject also enters, as fully as it is possible, the cultural and religious context of the other, in this case, Hinduism. This does not mean that one leaves the expressive context of Christianity, but it does imply that one embodies, in a meaningful way, the experiential context of Hinduism. This model can be applied only to those few mystics who become fully intercultural or interreligious, but do not transcend either the particularity of culture or a religion. On the other hand, the perennialist who discovers an essential core in all mystical experience seems to transcend the particularity of both cultures and religion.

Christians and Translational Experience

The Saint Thomas Christians were the first to interface, if not embrace, Indian culture for more than a thousand years before the coming of colonial missionaries.[5] There is evidence that the Saint Thomas Christians were culturally Indian, if not Hindu, in their participation in local customs, festivals, pilgrimages, and social mores. It was only with the colonial missionaries of the sixteenth century that Christian communities became more exclusive in terms of culture and experience. Serious acculturation, however, took place with the coming of Robert de Nobili, S.J., in 1607, followed by John de Britto and Joseph Ascolino in the same century, who took on the role of the Hindu ascetic, the *samnyasi*, in their attempt to inculturate the gospel in Indian life.[6] Nobili was controversial, and Britto was murdered by an enraged local king; both were primarily evangelists who viewed Hindu teachings as misleading and Hindu gods as false. Although they articulated postTridentine Scholasticism, they pioneered new ways of living, studying, and proclaiming the gospel in Christian terms. This may be the first instance of translational theology and lifestyle in which one enters into the culture without a serious entry into the Hindu paths of spirituality. In the present century, the *samnyasi* model was taken up again by the Jesuit Pierre Johanns and G. Dandoy who published a journal, *The Light of the East*, in which Johanns wrote a series of articles, called "To Christ through the Vedanta." This was an instance of translational theology in which Thomistic categories were employed to understand the thought and experience of Vedanta, a classical articulation of Hindu philosophy. These missionaries accommodated themselves to the general cultural life of high caste Hinduism without significant entrance into the prayer life and experience of the Hindu tradition.[7]

One vivid example of significant acculturation, in our own time, of what I call a translational experience is Anthony de Mello, an Indian Jesuit born in Bombay in 1931. Having studied philosophy in Barcelona, psychology in Chicago, and spiritual theology in Rome, he became a worldwide retreat master, teaching meditation in India, Hong Kong, Philippines, Japan, Australia, Europe, and the United States. As the director of an institute for pastoral counseling at De Nobili College, the Jesuit seminary in Pune, India, he trained retreat masters and spiritual guides. He died in 1985, but his legacy is contained in a little book, called *Sadhana: A Way to God*, with a subtitle of *Christian Experiences in Eastern Form*.[8] Appearing in many editions and languages, it is de Mello's testament in meditational experience and in teaching others to pray.

The meditational exercises offered by de Mello fall into three broad categories: awareness meditation, symbolic or image meditation, and devotional meditation. The second and the third are thoroughly Christian in context and content. For example, the Ignatian practice of imaging moments in the narrative of Jesus and symbolically entering into such scenes is common to the second form of meditation, and the Benedictine method of *lectio, reflectio,* and *devotio* is common to the third form of meditation. It is in the first form, awareness meditation or the achievement of silence, that de Mello draws heavily upon the context and content of Indian meditational traditions. He distinguishes prayer from contemplation by indicating that the prior is the use of words, images, and thoughts in one's communication with God, and the latter, contemplation, is the minimum use of words, images, and thoughts in one's relationship with God.[9] Communication with God takes place in awareness exercises of mental prayer, leading eventually to silence. What makes this form of meditation true contemplation is a loving heart or a heartfelt awareness of silence.[10] One of the fundamental principles of his meditational teaching is that prayer is made less with the head than it is with the heart.[11] In detailed fashion, he elaborates meditational exercises that cultivate an awareness of one's own body, breath, physical sensations, and thoughts. In the context of silence, one cultivates an awareness of body parts from head to foot, observing even body sensations and breath as inhaled and exhaled. The awareness of body sensations points to the close link between body and psyche, an insight at the heart of traditional Yoga. Reasoning from the classical definition of Yoga in Patanjali's *Yoga Sutras*, de Mello identifies the silence of the mind as the most significant element in meditational practice. The attempt here is to reduce the mind to one thought, one image, or word, in order to rid oneself of all thought, image, or word. As one reduces mental operations, one then contemplates more with the heart.[12]

Anthony de Mello was a Christian Indian who had a cultural and intellectual grasp of the classical Yoga tradition along with the long history of meditation in the Christian West. He dialogued with Hindu spiritual figures and was well versed and trained in Buddhist meditation, having studied with Theravada Buddhist masters. Some of his meditational exercises are, in fact, taken from texts of Buddhist manuals. On the other hand, he recommended the Hindu mantra, the Jesus prayer, the one thousand names of God, all as repetitive formulas for awareness meditation within a devotional context. In Hindu terminology, he integrated *raja* Yoga and *bhakti* Yoga into a Christian context of meditation.

This is an example of the translational model of interreligious prayer in which core meanings and practices from the Indian tradition are separated from their cultural context and function now in a different cultural context, in this case, Christian.

Significance of Translational Experiences

The form of meditation advanced by de Mello, inner awareness begun by use of mantra, from within the Indian tradition has been popularized by such Western monastics as John Main, Thomas Keating, and Basil Pennington. As a young lawyer in Malaysia, John Main (1926-1982) was initiated into the practice of mantra by a Hindu ascetic, Swami Satyananda, who taught that "mantra is like a harmonic. And as we sound this harmonic within ourselves we begin to build up a resonance. That resonance then leads us forward to our wholeness . . . We begin to experience the deep unity we all possess in our own being."[13] This led Main to Benedictine monasticism and the classical work of John Cassian, along with the medieval text, *The Cloud of the Unknowing*, and, finally, the establishment of a Christian meditation center in Montreal.

In similar fashion, Basil Pennington and Thomas Keating, Trappist monastics, were introduced to the Christian tradition of repetitive prayer through the Hindu method of Transcendental Meditation (TM). Both have become advocates and teachers of repetitive prayer in Christian meditation. Pennington has written that TM leads to pure prayer and corresponds to classical Christian practices. Although the debate on the Christian use of TM continues, Roman Catholic contemplatives seem more open to it than other Christians are.[14] Keating and Pennington, however, view TM as introductory to Christian centering prayer, placing it within Christocentric faith and Western theological culture. In this sense, prayer forms from another tradition fall clearly within the translational model of experience. On the other hand, as a practice leading to apophatic prayer in which a kenosis of the ego and the empirical self occurs, which was the case of Anthony de Mello, the use of a Hindu mantra reflects a deeper translational experience and may even approach a transcendental or anthropological model of experience.

More significant understanding results from contrasting the higher states of awareness in Hindu experience to a Christian counterpart. Such an effort has been made by Kevin Joyce who is knowledgeable in both the literature and practice of Teresa of Avila and Maharishi Mahesh Yogi.[15] In his study, Joyce adopts the method of interiority analysis of Bernard Lonergan in an examination of the higher states of consciousness in both Teresa and Maharishi. This requires, in the analysis, a shift from the content or object of consciousness to the operations of consciousness. According to Lonergan, this shift makes possible an analysis of subjectivity according to the intentional modes of consciousness, that is, the operations of gaining empirical knowledge, understanding, judgment, and responsible action. The mystical and theological language of both Teresa and Maharishi is then transposed to the language of interiority. Joyce's study focuses only on the four higher states that each writer expresses, since the three prior stages are all preparatory to interior prayer. They parallel each other in the following manner:

Teresa	Maharishi
4. Contemplation (prayer of quiet —prayer of Union)	4. Transcendental Consciousness
5. Habitual Union	5. Cosmic Consciousness
6. Spiritual Betrothal	6. God Consciousness
7. Spiritual Marriage	7. Unity Consciousness

Similarities as well as differences will be found in this contrast of two different spiritual masters. Both have in common the same sequential development, but end in distinct experiences.[16] Commonality was found by Joyce in stage four and five where the states of consciousness were clearly similar, but the experiences equally different. The differences were due, not to different doctrinal contexts, but to the different spiritual paths undertaken, that is, devotion to God in Teresa and knowledge of self (atman) in Maharishi. States six and seven were found to be similar only in their sequential development.[17] State six, for example, revealed significant difference regarding extraordinary experience and perception of the external world. Likewise, in state seven there was significant difference in terms of perception and interpretation of relationships among the self, God, and the external world. For example, in Teresa there was in the final stage a union of oneness of two subjects, the divine and the human, while in Maharishi there was complete identification of human and divine consciousness. Joyce argues that the differences in perception and interpretation of similar, but different, experiences are due to the difference in theological and philosophical tradition, namely, contextualization is especially pronounced at the higher states of experience and consciousness. This was not the result in the lower states, four and five, levels of the prayer of union and transcendental consciousness, because both exhibited neither form nor content.[18] This analysis is introduced to stress that greater and greater contextualization takes place at the higher states of prayer experience.

Joyce's study also implies how inconclusive the academic debate is in theology, philosophy or comparative mysticism between the perennialists and the constructionists. The former maintain that all higher religious experiences lead to the same end because they are ultimately all the same, that is, unmediated experiences of God, the One, the universal self, regardless of theological expression. This has been found false in the contrast of Teresa and Maharishi who exhibit different experiences. The constructionists, on the other hand, maintain that all experience is mediated by culture, language, history, and religious tradition. This has been found false in the contrast of Teresa and Maharishi who, in the deeper experiences of the prayer of union and transcendental consciousness, exhibit no mediation through name and form, that is, no cultural contextualization. If the Joyce analysis is correct, following Lonergan's interiority analysis, a more astute examination will have to be made of experience resulting from prayer or mediational practice and the emphasis given to contextualization.

Anthropological Model: Ritual Prayer Contextualized

D.S. Amalorpavadass (1932-1990), an Indian Roman Catholic priest, educator, catechist, and theologian, accomplished more in terms of acculturation in postVatican Council II India than any other individual has. While completing doctoral studies in Paris, he served as an adviser at the early sessions of the Council and returned to India where he established an institute for a new evangelization of Indian priests and laity in renewing the life of Catholicism. Acculturation of Christian life into Indian soil was his

goal as the institute in Bangalore became in time a national biblical center, a national catechetical center, and a national liturgical
center, with research on topics ranging from spirituality to social
development.[19]

Even the art and the architecture of the Bangalore center
reflect the degree of inculturation into Indian life introduced by
Amalorpavadass. As one passes through the entrance gate, the
main focus is the Satchitananda temple dedicated to the Christian
Trinity, a temple, not for liturgical celebration which is done in a
large auditorium, but for prayerful silence and meditation.[20] The
temple is viewed as a microcosm of the macrocosm of the world
within which permeate the divine energy and presence. The tower
of the temple (gopuram) with its sacred vessel (kalasam) on top
draws the eye upwards, symbolizing the human quest for the holy,
built as seven layers signifying successively earth, water, fire, air,
ether, consciousness, and the divine itself. All represent the cosmic mountain where the descending divine energies and graces
flow and ascending earthly efforts meet.[21] The sacred vessel is
shaped as two lotuses, each filled with immortality; the lower lotus
is the earth, humanity, and the human nature of Christ, and the
upper lotus is heaven, eternity, and the divine nature of Christ.

Christ is looked upon as the true teacher, the guru of the center, and the personnel as mere animators, a term Amalorpavadass
used for his own role. He spoke of the center: "As a matter of fact
when one visits the center, one is absorbed by a vision, feels
enveloped into an atmosphere of silence and prayer, and led to an
experience of density in every layer of the air."[22] A focal point in
the temple is the tree of life, a traditional Hindu symbol, in the
middle of which is the tabernacle with the reserved Eucharist. Two
Indian postures are taken by those entering: sitting on one's heels
and touching the ground with the forehead, and a full prostration
on the ground before the tree of life. The above indicates Indian
culture within which Amalorpavadass wished to renew Indian
Christianity.

As examples of the anthropological model of Christian-Hindu
experience with roots in Indian culture, Amalorpavadass, along
with Christian ascetics in the ashram movement, were leaders in
acculturating prayer and ritual in contemporary Indian
Christianity. Catholic liturgical renewal, for example, introduced
new votive masses to parallel Hindu celebrations: Christ as Light
of the World as a Diwali liturgy, Christ as Wisdom of God as a
Saraswati liturgy, as well as various harvest festivals. By 1969,
approval was granted for indigenous customs, such as, postures,
gestures (anjali), prostration, offering of flowers, incense, and fire
(arati). Amalorpavadass introduced into daily worship of the

Bangalore center Indian forms of meditation, mantra, contemplative interiorization, and rhythmic, repetitive singing in which the community repeats what the lead singer chants *(bhajans)*, usually ending in an offering of fire, incense, and flowers.[23] The participants in the weekly seminars, whether in Bible, catechesis, theology, or spirituality, followed a style of community life within a daily prayer setting, similar to the threefold daily prayers *(samdhyas)* of devout Hindus. A morning *samdhyas* consisted of meditation and Eucharistic liturgy; the midday *samdhyas* was community silence or an Indian form of prayer; and the evening *samdhyas* was devotional singing *(bhajan)* and offering *(arati)* to the reserved Eucharist.[24]

Acculturation was a gradual development at the Bangalore center. Amalorpavadass spoke of the first stage as one of creating an Indian atmosphere of worship and prayer; the second moment introduced good translations and Indian *anaphoras* in liturgy according to an Indian idiom; the third stage was a cautious adaptation of world scriptures into Christian liturgy.[25]

Dialogue and the Anthropological Model

The anthropological model of experience is usually evident within a positive situation of interreligious dialogue. Amalorpavadass looked upon dialogue with Hindus as a providential time that had come of age in India among Christian and Hindu communities. He believed that "dialogue becomes a condition and form of service — a new form of missionary action." It includes active participation in social and cultural life of the predominant community, a familiarity with the religious traditions, an openness to the treasures of the other that "a bountiful God has distributed among the nations of the earth."[26] His commitment to dialogue was especially evident when he left the Bangalore center in the 1980s to join a faculty of a state university in order to organize a religious studies program that would engage in dialogue with the religions of the world.

At the heart of acculturation, whether in dialogue or prayer life, was the emergence of an indigenous spirituality. Amalorpavadass believed that an authentic Christian spirituality in India would consist essentially of elements constitutive of Hindu spirituality: an experimental base, awareness and interiority, pilgrimage, renunciation and sacrifice *(yajna)*, liberation *(moksa)*, wholeness *(bhuma)*, discrimination *(viveka)*, a spiritual guide *(guru)*, following a spiritual path *(marga)*, and precise practice *(sadhana)*.[27] These are elements of Hindu anthropology. They imply that Indian Christian experience takes place within a Hindu anthropological world, either with or without Hindu forms of prayer and ritual.

The anthropological model implies a profound dialogue between two cultures as found among anthropologists, Indologists, and comparativists today. Few individuals have entered dialogue more deeply than Raimon Panikkar (b. 1917) who coined the notion of intrareligious dialogue as a mode of experience and understanding.[28] In the preface of a book in Hindu-Christian dialogue, he wrote:

> I have found myself sincerely carrying on the dialogue from both ends of the spectrum. I have played the role of the Hindu, feeling obliged to respond out of a sense of justice and self-respect when Christians misunderstood the Hindu tradition or made a caricature of it. I have also felt called to play the role of the Christian, when Hindus also misunderstood the Christian tradition or made a caricature of it. And each time, I emphasize, without being insincere, syncretistic, or condescending.[29]

For more than thirty years he tried to justify within the academic arena that he is both a Christian and a Hindu. He is not without dual experience in these two traditions, for he affirmed recently:

> I have duly performed Hindu ceremonies (at Guruvayur, one of the most orthodox Hindu temples, for instance) and celebrated the Christian mysteries (in Shillong Cathedral, one of the most "orthodox" Roman Catholic churches, for example). I have been dialoguing in Europe, America, and India: sitting in ashrams, gurukuls, universities, and bishop's houses; living in presbyteries and temples. Karma-bhakti and jnana-yoga are not unknown or foreign to me; the Vedas and the Bible are holy books for me and I have spent long years in practice, study, and meditation of both (sravana, manana, nidhidhyasana).[30]

Panikkar has lived, consequently, within an anthropological model of both experience and expression.

His first popular work in the West was *The Unknown Christ of Hinduism*, first published in 1964 in English.[31] In this book, Christ is the meeting ground for interreligious life, with functional similarities between aspects of Christ's role in Christianity and the role of Isvara in Vedantic Hinduism. A translational model of expression, and possibly experience, could describe this early moment in Panikkar's project, but Christ was an ongoing reality for interpretation and reformulation for the years following.[32] He espoused a fulfillment theology in both Christology and salvation by viewing their fuller emergence in the perfection of other religious traditions.[33] In 1981, after a decade of further reflection and experience, he reformulated and rewrote *The Unknown Christ of Hinduism*, with Christ now functioning as the cosmotheandric principle. This shift in focus reflects a philosophical move from objectivity to subjectivity in which the mediation of Jesus as objective historical reality became a subjective appropriation of the Christ symbol (in cosmotheandric terms) according to the different names and particularity of other religions.[34] The symbol which previously was translationally expressed is now anthropologically expressed as a result of greater experience. Panikkar's shift from objective to subjective analysis was the introduction of a "hermeneutics of otherness" which transcended the dialogic question from "Who am I?" to "Who are you?"[35] From this point onwards, he explicitly thought that, to understand another religious believer, one must participate in that person's tradition. To enter into another's narrative is to take on another anthropological context.

The most practical statement of ritual and meditative prayer is Panikkar's monumental *The Vedic Experience: Mantramanjari*, a ten year effort in preparation, more than nine hundred pages of Vedic text, involving four assistant translators and a greater team of collaborators.[36] It is a book, not to be merely read, but to be used as ritual, prayer, and meditative script. The subtitle reveals its genre: *An Anthology of the Vedas for Modern Man and Contemporary Celebration*. It is designed as a ritual cycle of the spiritual journey: dawn and birth, germination and growth, blossoming and fullness, and twilight. It intends to reflect the personal experiences in one's spiritual quest. The Sanskrit word in the title, *Mantramanjari*, points to the human encounter with the sacred: a mantra is transmitted to another, not merely as sound, but as divine life, as a *manjari*, a cluster of blossoms to humanity.

As an anthropology, Panikkar intends it as an offering of the Hindu universe, with all its richness of objects and subjects, to the world at large. As the canon of Hindu revelation *(sruti)*, it contains the core of the Vedic message. Although the anthology contains introductions to the Vedic hymns, mantras, prayers, and teachings, the volume is intended as ritual prayer. It requires prayer and meditation if it is to be a response to the existential questions of people today; and, when used as such, it allows the hidden dimensions of reality to respond to contemporary questions.[37] Although a text of Vedic revelation, it is neither a study in philosophy nor Indology nor comparative religion. It is intended for the average reader of a modern Western language, culture, and religion, who lives fully in the world with commitment to temporal life and who realizes the global situation in which one encounters other symbols, even essential symbols, with seriousness. Panikkar intends this text for contemporary celebration, and, in this sense, it is not merely a translation of texts arranged according to a classical spiritual quest. The use of the text intends to bring about an existen-

tial reenactment of its revelation. In this sense, it is Hindu orthopraxis, since Indian ritual, prayer, and meditation are forms of sacrifice *(yajna)* for the sake of transformation and reintegration.
Panikkar writes that Vedic revelation engages one in primordial
reenactment: ". . . that he (sic) is called upon to perform the sacrifice that makes the world and even the Gods subsist."[38] A celebration of Vedic revelation may lead to a discovery of new dimensions of life in which, not only the self, but also other human
beings, the universe itself, rediscover their place in the cosmic sacrifice. Prayer and meditation become liturgy as one enters more
fully into life.[39] Panikkar offers a means for drawing one into essentially Hindu experience.

Praxis Model: Social Consciousness and Contextualization

One of the basic teachings of the *Bhagavad Gita* is the centrali-
ty it gives to altruistic action, the holy action of *karma* Yoga as a
means of spiritual liberation. Krishna, the Lord, explains that his
actions sustain the cosmic order by continuing its transformation,
integration, and progressive divinization, just as a devotee's action
done in love and wisdom reenacts and represents the same. Those
who follow the teaching and example of Mahatma Gandhi on the
path of nonviolence are practicing *karma* Yoga as personified by
Lord Krishna. *Karma* Yoga, the path of holy action, exemplifies in
India a praxis model of experience, which requires a heightened
social consciousness grounded in prayer, meditation or contemplative silence, but resulting in greater social commitment.

Charles Freer Andrews (1871-1940), an Anglican priest who
spent almost forty years in India as an intimate friend and col-
laborator of both Mahatma Gandhi and the Nobel poet,
Rabindranath Tagore, pursued the path of holy action and a
praxis model of interfacing Christian and Hindu experience.[40]
Brought up in a British family where his father was an evangelical
minister and his mother a silent devotionalist, he had a transformation experience in his late teens in which he experienced
Christ as Savior and Redeemer. Entering Pembroke College,
Cambridge, he took an immediate interest in social questions and
deep bonding with a tutor, an experience that was to repeat itself
throughout his life. He wrote of this teacher in late life: "He
became almost like a Christ to me, visible and tangible in outward
form, so good and pure was his life."[41] Confirmation in the
Anglican Church and taking a degree in theology soon followed,
but he took a year prior to priestly ordination to work in an industrial city among the poor. He then began teaching theology and
the history of religions at Cambridge.

Yet, his life and interests developed along international lines, not as a result of his theological or literary acumen, but as a result of his capacity, even genius, for friendship.[42] At the end of his life in India, he wrote:

> I have been blessed with wonderful friendships. More than in any other way, my course has been directed by these. They have sprung out of, and have been moulded by, the love which has been ever deepening in my heart for Christ, the Friend of friends. Among the dearest of all friends, in far-off lands, are Muslims and Hindus.[43]

He referred to his entrance into India in 1904 and taking up a teaching position at St. Stephen's College, Delhi, as a rebirth. He established in Delhi his initial friendships with Hindus, Christians, and Muslims. In 1912, he met Tagore in London, who invited him to his experimental school at Santiniketan (Abode of Peace) in Bengal, which became his most stable home. In 1913, he met Gandhi in South Africa where he committed himself to work against race prejudice and colonialism for the rest of his life.

With Tagore in India, Andrews came to understand Christ as the Emancipator from the old social order and, what with his intellectual difficulties with the Anglican Articles of Faith and the Athanasian Creed, withdrew from public Anglican ministry.[44] He was called Deenabandhu, the friend of the poor, by Indians, as he frequently joined Gandhi, but followed through on his own social agenda in India, South Africa, and Fiji. Andrews considered his own support of anticolonialism and Gandhi's noncooperation movement as religious tasks and, in fact, a witness to Christ. He lived and worked, however, more intimately with Tagore in the poet's many literary, educational, social, and international projects. With a prolific literary career of his own, Andrews wrote twenty-two books, edited and collaborated on twelve others, with prevalent themes on Christ, India, social issues, and even on Tagore and Gandhi. He was also a major editor and translator of Tagore to an English speaking audience. He returned to full Anglican communion in 1936, following the unification of the Anglicans of India, Burma, and Ceylon, in which the Articles of Faith were no longer binding and by which time his own creedal problems were resolved.[45] His many biographers speak of the influence individuals had upon him. Andrews wrote of discovering Christ in the suffering poor:

> I have found Christ, and worshipped him, amid the little groups of Indian passive resistors fresh from prison — Hindus most all of them; and among the delicate Hindu ladies with their bright faces marked with suffering, telling me of their joy in prison and among the Tamil coolies who have gone through untold hardship and

played the man, one and all; but I cannot find him in these responsible churches, where a saint like Mr. Gandhi cannot even enter.[46]

Ronald Pachence achieved a perceptive study of Andrews' friendships with Tagore and Gandhi in the context of Andrews' developing Christology. The study concluded that Andrews' theology was a lifelong rearticulation of Christology, trying to thematize the meaning of the personal Christ. Pachence believes that Andrews saw Christ sacramentalized in Hinduism, sacramentalized especially by those in human bondage and sacramentalized in a unique way through interpersonal friendships.[47] Andrews saw the voluntary sacrifice of one's life for others as the highest act of the human spirit, an insight common to Christians, Hindus, and Buddhists, and truly reflective of *karma* Yoga and the teaching of the *Bhagavad Gita.* He wrote: "I must seek and find Christ in human suffering, wherever it is to be found, and must worship and adore him, not in empty words, but in service of the poor in every land."[48] Andrews found in Tagore and Gandhi, Hindus and Muslims, along with Christian friends, images or sacraments of Christ who sacrifice themselves for others. From his life with people of other faiths, in this case primarily Hindus, he practiced *karma* Yoga and, upon reflection, as is true of the praxis model in theology, discovered a renewed personal theology. In India, Christ was revealed to Andrews, not for the first time, but for the first time as universally human and as interpersonal love.[49]

Andrews claimed that he had to go to India to learn the importance of silent contemplation. Tagore favored such meditation in the early morning hours, around daybreak. Andrews was prone to frenetic activity, but, in India, silence and prayer became almost one and the same. In the preface to his book, *Christ in Silence,* he acknowledged this debt to Tagore and Gandhi. Equally significant is the fact that Andrews drew upon Tagore's insight that silence is the source of creativity, whether human or divine. Tagore had defined the human person as a poet, a creator by nature in imitation of the divine poet, the divine creator who creates out of silence.[50] Writing in the 1930s, Andrews focused on prayer, meditations on the gospels, his personal experiences in India, and concluded by defining prayer in devotional terms as a loving response of one person to another.[51]

It is no overstatement, however, that his insight into the role of prayer and renewed Christology came about through friendship. Shortly before his death, he wrote:

> This dynamic quality I found in the two friends who gradually became the formative influence in my thinking — the poet Rabindranath Tagore and Mahatma Gandhi. These two have

brought me quite unconsciously, but very intimately, a fuller interpretation of what the message of Christ actually means in the
modern world.[52]

Andrews looked to Gandhi as a brother, one who became for India
a reconciler, a suffering servant. Tagore was for Andrews the very
best of what Indian literature, thought, culture, and character
could produce, more than a poet and internationalist: a prophet
of a new world. Andrews became known as the hyphen between
Tagore and Gandhi, for he initially brought them into, and kept
them in, loving relationship. He was the link that helped them
overcome their radical differences, in practice and theory, on
most public issues of the day and even in leading a Hindu spiritual
life.

The praxis model of experience, consequently, offers a con-
crete encounter with another religious tradition because it inter-
faces people. Andrews noted that "I have been the receiver rather
than the giver." Upon leaving public Anglican ministry, he was
asked whether he missed Holy Communion and responded by
turning to the children of Santiniketan and said, "These are my
Holy Communion."[53]

Synthetic Model: Christians as Hindu Ascetics

Although not limited to committed ascetics, the path of renun-
ciation (samnyasa) in the Hindu tradition was first pursued by
Jesuit missionaries in the sixteenth century and taken up again in
modern times. Brahmabandhad Upadhyay (1861-1907) was a
nineteenth century Indian Christian who adopted the life of a
Hindu ascetic and, from his own experience, tried to reconcile
Hindu mysticism as articulated in Advaita Vedanta with Roman
Catholic mysticism. Later in this century, two Frenchmen, Jules
Monchanin (1895-1957) and Henri Le Saux (1910-1973),
attempted a synthesis of Hindu asceticism and mysticism with
Christian experience.

Bede Griffiths (1906-1993), however, mirrored most recently a
synthetic model of Christian prayer and contemplation while walking in the footsteps of a Hindu samnyasi. British born Griffiths was
christened and reared in the Church of England and, prior to his
study at Oxford, experienced a dramatic disclosure of the presence of God in nature.[54] This early spiritual awakening exposed
him not only to the sacramental aspect of nature, but also to the
unfathomable mystery that he sought for the rest of his life. C. S.
Lewis was his tutor and friend during the Oxford years as he pursued nineteenth century British Romanticism and continental and
British philosophy, along with the Greek classics and even some

texts from India and China. Due to these influences, he under-
went a conversion to Christian theism and soon after prepared for
ordination in the Church of England. Conversion experiences,
interpreted by Griffiths as a progressive surrendering of oneself,
frequently the surrender of reason, were to continue throughout
his life. Through a reading of Christian mystics and the works of
John Henry Newman, he was attracted to, and was received into,
the Roman Catholic Church and soon after took vows in a
Benedictine monastery. He intensified what was to be a lifetime of
writing on liturgy, contemplative life, and his own practice of
nondiscursive prayer, the Jesus prayer. Continuing his reflection
on the encounter of Christianity and the Asian religions begun at
Oxford, he was challenged by an Indian Benedictine monk,
Benedict Alapatt, who invited him to join an effort to establish a
monastery in India. At the age of forty-nine, Griffiths arrived in
India to enter into an experience of Hindu-Christian monasticism,
asceticism, and ultimately mysticism.

He had already read of Monchanin and Le Saux's attempt at
establishing a Christian ashram in India and now directly observed
their efforts to synthesize Hindu-Christian ascetical life. Along
with Francis Mahieu, a Belgian Catholic priest, and two Indian
priests from Bangalore, he established the Kurisumala Ashram in
Kerala in 1958, which gave him an opportunity for the intrapersonal and interreligious encounter that he sought between
Hinduism and Christianity. During the next ten years at this
ashram, he continued to write, dialogue, and especially enter
more deeply into the prayer and culture of Hindu asceticism.
Vedanta and Christian Faith, one of his early books, began to
explore the implications in what he called "the marriage of East
and West."[55]

Wishing to go further into Hindu ascetical and mystical life,
Griffiths left the ashram in Kerala and went to the Saccidananda
Ashram in Tamil Nadu, established by Monchanin and Le Saux.
The former died, and Le Saux was to begin a more hermetical
stage in the Himalayas. It was at the Saccidananda Ashram or
Santivanam, as it is more commonly known, that Bede Griffiths
became the guru around whom disciples from around the world
would come for spiritual nourishment. It was also here that meditation and prayer became the primary monastic practices, and
communal life and liturgy were the context of such practices.[56]
There was a shift from Benedictine to Hindu asceticism, from
liturgy to meditation, as he began a new affiliation with the
Camaldolese, a more ascetical expression of the Benedictine
Confederation.[57] It is in the final decade of his life that he became
an international figure, lecturing in India and abroad about the

marriage of East and West and seeking a greater synthesis of Hindu and Christian mystical life. Following a stroke in 1990 that did not bring an end to his lecturing, travel, and writing, he tried to extend his synthesis to "Western science, Eastern mysticism and Christian faith," the subtitle of one of his last books, *A New Vision of Reality*.

Throughout his life, Griffiths was in an intrapersonal dialectic with a set of themes in creative tension with one another which gradually advanced his own surrender to the divine mystery.[58] The dialectic could be enunciated as the tension between his own experience and ideas and those of the Catholic Church; between his experience of God in nature and in himself in tension with the revelation in Christ and in the Church; between his attraction to Asian spiritual experience and his ambivalence toward Western reliance upon science. However, the paramount and lifelong tension was between the intuitive, nonrational mind and the rational, logical mind. It was in this pervasive dialectic that Griffiths discovered a fuller meaning of surrender to mystery, of creating a new path, and a new synthesis for modern culture.[59]

In surrendering of the rational self and opening to the intuitive self, Griffiths drew upon an Indian mystical instinct. Always seeking synthesis, however, he nuanced his position in maintaining a complementarity between reason and intuition and a harmonization of reason and intuition not yet found in either the Western or Indian traditions.[60] Likewise, he integrated the Christian notion of surrender with the Hindu notion of renunciation, which is the basis of Indian asceticism. It was especially this factor that helped him achieve self understanding, as he reflected upon his life from his first autobiography in 1954, *The Golden String*, through to his last personal reflection in 1982, *The Marriage of East and West: A Sequel to the Golden String*.[61]

Griffiths sought throughout his life a more direct experience and cognitive understanding of the sacred. He became more aware of the rational and intuitive forces within himself and the need to reconcile these forces for a more profound vision of the unfathomable God. He thus drew upon all his experiences from his youth and university days, from his years as a committed Benedictine monk, and from his most contemplative years in India as a Hindu-Christian ascetic. For example, his experience of an ineffable mystery in nature resulted in a lifelong practice of nature walks and the quieting of the mind during such walks. A commitment to liturgical prayer that was intense during his Benedictine years was never lost, but found lower priority as his meditative life increased. His early use of the Jesus prayer, informed by Yoga once in India, became the *japa* and mantra for situating deeper meditative states. Finally, a need for critical inquiry from his Oxford days continued to his final years, especially in his philosophical study of the Vedanta tradition. Each practice, he believed, brought one to another level of surrender in which God's love and knowledge were more fully experienced.

Although Bede Griffiths encountered the Vedanta as a philosophical study, he did not draw upon the Vedanta as a method of meditation. He used the Jesus prayer as a Hindu would use the *japa*, a silent repetition of the name of God, or as an Orthodox Christian would use the prayer of the heart in order to quiet the discursive mind. Asian methods of meditation, according to Griffiths, were natural means to prepare the meditator for the silencing of the whole person and opening to the action of God.[62] This was interpreted by him as the moment of transition from the natural to the supernatural order. He wrote: "This is the point at which in Christian prayer the action of the Holy Spirit intervenes. All these techniques of yoga, physical, psychological and spiritual, should be seen as a means of preparation for the free action of the Holy Spirit which has to take possession of the soul."[63] Therefore, one could conclude that Griffiths did not fully take up Vedantic meditational practices.

As early as 1930, he reflected again an instinct common to India and British Romanticism: "I still spent all my spare time in long solitary walks in the country among the woods and commons and on the downs . . . But it was no longer the face of nature which seemed to contain the meaning of life for me. I felt now that the real mystery lay within."[64] It is inquiry into the inner self that both Hindu philosophy and asceticism seek through spiritual practice. With this turn to the inner self, Griffiths reconceptualized the Christian notion of *fides quaerens intellectum*, faith looking toward knowledge, to *fides quaerens experientiam*, faith looking toward experience.[65] This was reflected in his move from Roman liturgy to the Syrian liturgy at the Kurisumala Ashram, and again in his move to a Hindu-Christian liturgy at the Shantivanam Ashram. He was approaching the Vedanta nondual experience of ultimacy and the philosophy of Sankara whose vision was based upon intuitive, direct experience of Brahman. In *Return to the Center*, Griffiths spoke of meditation as the means by which one transcends the dualism of oneself, the world and God, to a nondual wholeness of differentiation.[66] Meditation referred to nondiscursive prayer in transcending thoughts and images, in order to experience the ground of consciousness. Contemplation, a broader term, was used for vocal and discursive prayer, liturgy, scripture, labor, and imaginative reflection. One needs to conclude that Griffiths' primary meditation remained the Jesus prayer, but it became, in his final years, a prayer beyond vocality and image, a prayer of the heart in surrender to the mysterious depths of the inner self.[67]

Over the course of three decades, Bede Griffiths was recognized internationally as a synthesizer of Hindu-Christian monasticism and in India as the Christian *samnyasi*. Shantivanam in Tamil Nadu, previously established by Jules Monchanin and Henri Le Saux in 1950, became under Griffiths the testing ground for evolving an interreligious and intercultural spirituality. It attracted some Indians, but a greater number of spiritual seekers came from the West. In a setting that was thoroughly Indian and Hindu in culture, he brought together both Christian and Hindu prayer and meditation forms. Meditation was, however, the center of life and practice at Shantivanam. Griffiths spoke of meditational experience in mystical terms that could be grasped by Christians and Hindus:

> When I turn back beyond my senses and beyond my reason and pass through this door into eternal life, then I discover my true Self, then I begin to see the world as it really is . . . Here all is one, united in a simple vision of being. All the long evolution of matter and life and man, all my own history from the first moment that I became a living cell, all the stages of my consciousness and all human beings, is here recapitulated, brought to a point, and I know myself as the Self of all, the one Word eternally spoken in time.[68]

Griffiths identified mature meditative experience as a nonrational means resulting in an awareness of the nondual nature of reality, which is a typical stance of Advaita Vedanta Hinduism. He, in fact, identified both his philosophical understanding and his personal experiential awakening as one of Christian Advaita. This does not mean that he viewed Christian and Hindu experience as merely two interpretations of the same reality. Griffiths would insist on the fundamental differences between Hindus and Christians, namely, there is a relational aspect to the world and to God that is never lost in Christian nonduality, while in his understanding of Vedantic nonduality all relational experience is transcended. Griffiths drew upon the theology of the Trinity, Incarnation, and Creation to sustain such relational life within nondual experience.

Sustaining an internal dialogue between Christian and Hindu understanding of nonduality over the course of four decades in India, Griffiths' own experience directed his final resolution of the lifelong tension. He saw more clearly the complementarity, not only between East and West, but also between discursive and nondiscursive meditation and between Christian and Hindu nonduality. He exemplified in his own life, as a Hindu-Christian *samnaysi*, the complementarity among cultures, religions, and spiritual traditions. His life reflects a synthetic model of experience.

A synthetic model is based upon significant acculturation and practice in another tradition to the degree that it embraces a "both this and that" way of life. Griffiths was both a Christian and Hindu ascetic; he was discursive in prayer and liturgy and nondiscursive in meditation; he drew upon the rational and nonrational mind in experience. He tried to bring into complementarity Hindu-Christian asceticism and Hindu-Christian experience. The synthetic model of experience may draw upon either dialectical forms or dialogical forms or even analogical forms of discourse. For Bede Griffiths, the internal dialogue of Hindu-Christian experience was projected into an external Hindu-Christian dialogue expressed fully in his writings and lecturing throughout the world. It remained an authentic synthetic model because it retained both the similarities and differences between traditions and experiences. Above all, Griffiths wanted to sustain the fundamental insights and differences in both Christianity and Hinduism. He was not eclectic in terms of forging two distinct traditions into a new universalism. He was a synthetic figure because he embraced to the end of his life both complementarity and uniqueness in contextualized life and cultural experience.

Transcendental Model and Radical Subjectivity

The transcendental mode of intercultural experience evidences a more radical change in subjectivity than the previous models do. The example advanced here is that of Henri Le Saux (1910-1973), better known as Swami Abhishiktananda, whom Bede Griffiths considered as having taken a deeper plunge into Advaita Vedanta than Bede himself did. James Redington observes that "Abhishiktananda might well have passed beyond the stage of dialogue by the end of his life, to a point where he embodied both Hinduism and Christianity."[69] If this did eventuate, then Abhishiktananda attained a radically new horizon and transcended previous subjectivity.

Born in Brittany, Henri Le Saux became a Benedictine monk at Kergonan in 1929 and, after nineteen years as a monastic, at the age of thirty-eight, was drawn to India by Père Monchanin who already was leading the life of an Indian *samnyasi*. Taking the name Abhishiktananda, Joy of the Anointed One, he began a new life at Shantivanam with Monchanin, an asthmatic, along the Kavery River in Tamil Nadu. He visited, within a year upon arriving in India, the renowned South Indian saint, Sri Ramana Maharshi, a silent guru, at Arunachala, a sacred mountain site. It was there as a youth that Sri Ramana achieved realization of the Self *(Atman)* and over the course of years was revered as a saint who lived as a silent guru. Although Sri Ramana died within a year of their initial meeting, it was at their first encounter that Abhishiktananda received his first spiritual awakening to Hindu mysticism. He consistently revisited Arunachala as late as 1958 and, in recalling Sri Ramana's smile, wrote: "A call which pierced through everything, rent it in pieces and opened a mighty abyss . . . New as (these experiences) were, their hold on me was already too strong for it ever to be possible for me to disown them."[70] Along with the Hindu ascetics in the caves of Arunachala, Abhishiktananda gradually assimilated the Advaita asceticism of the Upanishads: renunciation and surrender.

He was introduced to Sri Gnanananda in 1955 whom he considered his guru and from whom he received the transmission of the tradition that takes place between guru and disciple.[71] From this point onward, he sought the Advaita experience of nonduality between the Self *(atman)* and Brahman. Although he was to write in 1966 that "I have tried to make myself transparent to the experience of India," it was the particularity of the Upanishadic tradition of nonduality that centered his spiritual search.[72] The other Christian *samnyasis* broke with Abhishiktananda, for the latter desired more solitude while the former wanted the more liturgical and communal life of Western monasticism. Bede Griffiths took over the leadership of the South Indian ashram while Abhishiktananda entered long periods of solitude in the Himalayas and spent his final years in a hermitage, called Gyansu, in Uttarkashi.

In his earliest years in India, Abhishiktananda sought to find Christ and Christianity at the heart of Hinduism, but, after a decade in India, worked toward a theological integration of Christian faith and Hindu experience. Adapting this goal to a theology of development and fulfillment of Hinduism, he ultimately rejected such a formulation and put aside any theological reconciliation for the sake of existential life. His early writing tried to seek complementarity between the traditions, but he realized that he was "still too much enslaved to Greek concepts."[73] In his final journals, he believed that neither opposition nor incompatibility existed in experience, but occurred only in expression. He did not equate Christian and Hindu experience, but viewed them as two forms of a single faith.[74] Jacques Dupuis speaks about a symbiosis of two traditions that Abhishiktananda achieved.[75]

Although he was not a professional theologian, Abhishiktananda's theology of the Eucharist and the Trinity were truly astute. He welcomed the changes in the liturgy advanced by the Vatican

Council II and tried to inculturate changes within an Indian ethos. Even in the solitude of hermitical life, he offered the Eucharist and recited the breviary. They served as an introduction to his contemplative quest, advanced with the Jesus prayer and quieting of the person, and, finally, resulted in the silence of the inner self. Similar to the Russian mystics and those of the Middle East, the Jesus prayer, begun audibly with the lips and visually with the imagination, matured into the prayer of the heart, without word, image, form, or concept. Meditation was for Abhishiktananda attention to the divine presence: "As we become aware of the divine presence in the secret of our hearts, so too the same divine Presence is all around us."[76] He viewed prayer as both the intellectual reflection on the nature of God and the offering of affective aspirations of surrender, experiencing an absolute dependence upon God. It was still the prayer of silence, bringing the mind to complete quiet and arresting all mental activity, that characterized Abhishiktananda's effort in contemplative practice.[77] He affirmed the classical conception of Yoga as articulated by Patanjali in the *Yoga Sutras*. His profound awakenings came out of such silence, a silence he believed was manifesting the divine spirit, the *shakti* of Hindu experience.

It would appear that the contemplative paths of Abhishiktananda and Bede Griffiths were the same. Yet, Griffiths believed that his companion went further into Advaita experience than Bede himself did. This seems to be the case. Abhishiktananda restricted most of his meditative reflection to the Upanishadic texts and the Advaita method of self realization: ". . . without the Upanishads, I do not know what I should do or become." Again: "For me everything is in the Upanishads."[78] He wrote perceptively of this tradition: "This experience is not prayer, meditation or contemplation in the commonly accepted sense. It is a kind of consciousness, an awareness to which man (sic) finds himself raised beyond the reach of any of his faculties, hearing, seeing, feeling or even thinking . . ."[79] The Upanishadic teaching is imparted, he believed, only in the guru-disciple relationship. His writing on the Upanishads reflected a depth of scholarship and direct experience. He deftly related Upanishadic wisdom to the practical teaching of Sri Ramana Maharshi that he received in his early years in India.

Abhishiktananda's preference for the Upanishads was reflected in his own role as a spiritual teacher: "Thus a sadhu may be expected to give help to others in understanding the deep meaning of the Scriptures . . . the explanation that he gives will not be a learned exegesis, but the overflow of his own silent contemplation of the sacred text. This should be even more true of anything that he may write."[80] The Advaita tradition, closely adhering to the methodology of spiritual liberation in the Upanishads, advocates a threefold process of hearing *(sravana)* the sacred text as extolled by the Vedanta, reflection *(manana)* upon the text in conjunction with one's experience, and finally concentration *(nidhiyasana)* on the meaning resulting in the contemplative silence of meditation.[81] Abhishiktananda, I believe, assimilated into his own practice this Vedantic method within the greater context of his ascetical life as a classical *samnyasi*. He stood within both the Hindu worldview of nondual Vedanta, with its Vedic texts, and the classical method of Self realization as articulated by Sankara, the primary commentator of Advaita Vedanta. This was the singular path of knowledge *(jnana joga)* that he pursued relentlessly from his meeting with Sri Ramana to his final years when he perceived that he had experienced the nonduality of the Self *(atman)* and Brahman.

The attempt to articulate his experience in relation to Christian theological categories was far more difficult for him than it was for Bede Griffiths. Griffiths was more cautious theologically and remained thoroughly within the orthodox parameters of Catholic theology. Abhishiktananda, on the other hand, although theologically trinitarian, attempted an articulation of Vedantic nondual experience in trinitarian terms, possibly through the influence of Raimon Panikkar. In his final year, he said: "The Trinity cannot be understood apart from the experience of Advaita, a nonduality."[82] The mystical intuition of nonduality of Atman-Brahman was interpreted as the mystical union of the Trinity, namely, a discovering of the Spirit indwelling with the Father and the Son. It is similar to the theology of Bonaventure in which a person is a being-with *(co-esse* — the eternally established relationship of Father, Son, Spirit) through discovery of oneself in another.[83] In the mystical moment, one experiences oneself in the Father as Jesus, the Son, did. This goes far beyond an early monograph in which Abhishiktananda dealt with Advaita and the Trinity by identifying the Hindu manifestation of the divine presence of Saccidananda with corresponding trinitarian realities: "Namely, the Father as primordial being *(sat)*, the Son as consciousness of being *(chit)*, and the Spirit as the joy of being *(ananda)*."[84]

He suffered a severe heart attack in 1973 from which he never recovered, but, as a result of which, he had a transformative realization. He declared from the depth of this purificatory experience, in language similar to other mystics, that "what Christ is, I AM." Upon further reflection, he said: "I feel too much, more and more, the blazing fire of this I AM, in which all notions about Christ's personality, ontology, history, etc. have disappeared. And I find his real mystery shining in every awakening man, in every mythos."[85]

Taking up the life of a recluse ascetic, Abhishiktananda has been faulted for not making the linkage with the social world which is the fruition of contemplative experience. Two observations mitigate this criticism. First, his writing projects, resulting in a number of books, monographs, and articles, were a daily practice even during his most isolated moments. His diaries testify, not only to writing, but also to periodic travel in India to speak at conferences, study days, and retreats. He spoke consistently on spirituality, Hinduism, and his own life and self understanding. His extensive writing was directed to a Western Christian and European audience in order to heighten Christian spiritual practice and the Hindu-Christian dialogue. His goals in India were the same.

A second factor also enhanced his concern for the wider social world: accepting a student within the traditional guru-disciple relationship of Hinduism. This included initiation into asceticism and a guru-disciple lineage, Upanishadic and contemplative instruction, and sharing his own experiences. The last twenty months of his life were devoted almost totally to his young French disciple, Marc Chaduc, to the degree that they experienced each other as a single unified self. In a letter to Marc, initiated as Swami Ajatananda, he said: "But that 'Greater One' whom you find lying behind myself and yourself, is not-other-than-you or me. 'The Father is greater than I.' 'I and the Father are one.'"[86] Abhishiktananda believed that it was the disciple who makes the guru, a teacher evolved from a relationship "beyond words . . . frightening, and what a responsibility!"[87] It was Marc Chaduc who was his last link to the greater world, even though he continued his writing and was cared for by Christian sisters in his final illness. It was to the greater society through Marc, who disappeared in 1977, that he summed up his life-quest: "It is under the sign of Jesus Christ that we have awakened the Brahman, God, even if it needed the Veda to make us fully aware of Him."[88]

Abhishiktananda was aware that he wrote from his own experience. In a letter to a European friend, he observed: "It is biography . . . but everything has been rethought by the 'mind' in the aura of a double culture."[89] Reflection upon self experience continued in the year prior to death with the following: "I feel within myself a profound mutation. But this mutation makes me a 'stranger.'"[90] The degree of transformation that took place in Abhishiktananda was not a mere shift in perspective, but a radical change in his person. It is for this reason that he falls within a transcendental model of a Christian and Hindu experience of prayer. A change of horizons, in the sense used by Bernard Lonergan, along with radical shifts in perception, insight, mentality, and ultimately in personality, took place. The transcendental model attains authentic subjectivity through successive changes in horizons. Abhishiktananda, taking up Sri Ramana's sole question — Who am I? — and Sankara's methodological probing of the true Self, discovered and disclosed a new subjectivity. He sought neither a synthesis of two ascetical traditions nor a parallelism between two forms of meditation and prayer. He articulated his experiences to Christians, especially contemplatives, from a consciousness enveloped in the nondual tradition of Hinduism. He models one who does not necessarily express the content of experience as much as the event of experience.

Conclusion

In speaking of the religious fertility of Jerusalem, the prophet Isaiah wrote: "Widen the space of your tent, stretch out your tent clothes unsparingly, lengthen your ropes, make the pegs firm; for you will burst out to left and right."[91] Isaiah's challenge has been grasped by earnest religious seekers throughout the ages. Each person in this study has approached the challenge differently, with different objectives, intensities, and has brought to it different subjectivities. Those Christians who seriously engaged Hindu forms of prayer contextualized within Indian culture sought neither to assimilate an Indian school of philosophy nor another religious tradition. They sought, instead, a form of spirituality which in itself made their lives manageable or even advanced to some degree their present spiritual development. The figures discussed here enjoyed an openness to the greater religious world that is not surprising in global society today.

Raimon Panikkar once observed that, for an individual, there may well be an end to dialogue. So, too, there may be a limit to acculturation in another cultural or religious tradition as well as to the internal dialogue between two spiritual worlds within personal experience. Just as each person is not called to the same level of dialogue due to interests or capacities, so, too, all are not called to acculturation into several religious worlds. We need to ask ourselves, however, what we can learn from those that do. Some have undertaken the task to discover a method that can be assimilated within a Christian context. J. M. Dechanet, writing some thirty years ago, believed that Yoga could be used by Christians as a mere technique.[92] Such motivation is looked upon today as cultural imperialism or a type of neocolonialism. Others, with a more altruistic objective, attempt acculturation in order to understand those who are committed to another religious world in faith and belief. And, still others, with a global consciousness, seek compatibility with, and the reconciliation of, religious pluralism.

More recent are those who speak about a new age of consciousness brought about through the rapid transformations resulting from international life, mobility, and the formation of global culture. Ewert Cousins contends that we live in a second axial age in which a real mutation is taking place.[93] To enter more fully into this new age, he encourages the retrieval of the spiritual heritage of our religious traditions, especially the experiential modes that lie beneath the pluralism of our religious expressions.

As Christians, we have seen a significant development of doctrine, beginning with the renewal of theology in the nineteenth century, and, for Catholics, from Vatican Council I to Vatican Council II, and in the years since those tumultuous events. As prayer and meditation traditions develop, so does theology. Growth in prayer and in one's relationships with the human community, the world, and with God brings about a change in Christology, Ecclesiology, and in the meaning of sacramentality. Contemporary movements, as creation centered and environmental spirituality, are reflective of a transformation taking place in the lives of people. There is no sign that interest in spirituality, prayer, and meditation is on the wane. A second axial age had already begun for the figures considered here as Christians experiencing Hindu forms of prayer. Their journey has come to an end, but opens to a new future in which we share.

NOTES

[1] I interpret prayer throughout this study in a broad sense in order to approach what Hindus do in their context and within their categories. Accordingly, prayer may be expressed as ritual actions, sacrifices and offerings, devotional acts (through music, dance, drama, song, and poetry), meditation, and even as social acts. This implies that Hinduism is primarily an orthopraxis. The earliest moment of Vedic experience was ritual action that in time developed chants and offerings; next evolved meditational traditions whether within or without a philosophical context; and, finally, emerged a parallel development of devotional acts and social acts. All are integral to what could be called a prayer tradition. Instead of creating categories, I will use classical Hindu notions: the path of ritual, the path of meditation, the path of loving devotion, and the path of holy actions.

[2] Stephen B. Bevans, *Models of Contextual Theology* (Maryknoll, NY: Orbis Books, 1992). I am indebted to Bevans for his use of these models. I have also drawn upon these models as used by Peter C. Phan, "Contemporary Theology and Inculturation in the United States," in *The Multicultural Church: A New Landscape in U.S. Theologies*, ed. William Cenkner (Mahwah, NJ: Paulist Press, 1995), 109-30.

[3] Confer John S. Dunne, *The Way of All the Earth: Experiments in Truth and Religions* (Notre Dame, IN: University of Notre Dame Press, 1978).

[4]Wilfred Cantwell Smith, *Faith and Belief* (Princeton: Princeton University Press, 1979).

[5]Confer Stephen Neill, *A History of Christianity in India, The Beginnings to AD 1707* (Cambridge: Cambridge University Press, 1984).

[6]Acculturation throughout this study is used in the sense of socialization into a foreign context. It may be distinguished from enculturation (the process of being socialized into one's own culture through education) and inculturation (a term more common among Christian scholars to refer to the process of Christian culture implanting itself in another culture and renovating it). Acculturation for Western Christian scholars is the process of Christian culture's acquiring elements of a host culture, accommodating itself to some degree, but where a mutual borrowing of cultural elements as myths, symbols, and rituals, may take place. Confer Arij Roest Crollius, "What Is So New about Inculturation?," *Gregorianum* 59 (1978): 721-38; also, Robert Schreiter, *Constructing Local Theologies* (Maryknoll, NY: Orbis Books, 1985), 144-58.

[7]*Samnyasa* is an ascetical state of life, a life of renunciation, the last of the four stages of life in Hinduism, which results in separation from all worldly ties; a *samnyasi* is an individual, a celibate, leading an ascetical life. The term is used here for those Christian missionaries who took on aspects of Hindu ascetical life as a form of evangelization. The *samnyasi* model has been followed by contemporary Christians in the ashram movement, namely, those living in an ascetical community committed to prayer and meditation, but following some forms of Hindu ascetical life. This is much different from what has taken place in the West in this century with the popularization of Yoga, where Yoga as a physical or psychological process is frequently separated from its cultural foundations. Many have come to Yoga out of curiosity, seeking the exotic, or from cultural voyeurism, rather than as observers of its experiential depths. This was true of the early influence of Transcendental Meditation in the 1970s when numbers of significant magnitude began chanting ancient Vedic mantras. It has been estimated that, by 1975, 700,000 Americans were practicing Transcendental Meditation from some 6,000 teachers in 350 TM Centers in the United States alone. (See *Reader's Digest*, Dec. 1975, 114-16; *Time*, Aug. 25, 1975, 39, and Oct. 13, 1975, 114-16.) It is well established that those who persevere in the West in either mantra practice or Yoga are relatively small. Perseverance in Yoga or mantra practice is possible only with significant contextualization within the Indian culture. Those who have maintained such practice for more than a half dozen years are usually those who have acculturated themselves, in some degree, to Indian life. Even to continue in the practice of physical Yoga would require the moral practices that precede and contextualize physical Yoga. Likewise, with the sacred mantras of Transcendental Meditation, unless these are used within an Indian worldview and culture, a totally different significance and meaning result. A lifelong TM meditator is one committed to the teaching of Maharishi Mahesh Yogi and the traditional Indian ideology and culture contextualizing him.

[8]Anthony de Mello, *Sadhana: A Way to God, Christian Exercises in Eastern Form*, 5th edition (St. Louis: The Institute of Jesuit Sources, 1978).

[9]Ibid., 24-25.

[10]Ibid., 26.

[11]Ibid., 3.

[12]Ibid., 28, 31.

[13]John Main, *The Gethsemani Talks* (Montreal: The Benedictine Priory of Montreal, 1977), 4-5.

[14]Confer Basil Pennington, *Centered Living: The Way of Mantra in Christian Meditation* (Garden City, NY: Doubleday, 1986); Thomas Keating, *Open Mind, Open Heart: The Contemplative Dimension of the Gospel* (New York: Amity House, 1986); Thomas Keating, *The Mystery of Christ: The Liturgy as Spiritual Experience* (New York: Amity House, 1987); Basil Pennington, "TM and Christian Prayer," *Contemplative Review* 9 (Spring, 1976): 26-34. Both Pennington and Keating, of course, have become major teachers of the Centering Prayer.

[15]Kevin Patrick Joyce, *A Study of the Higher States of Consciousness and Their Interpretation According to Teresa of Avila and Maharishi Mahesh Yogi*, Unpubl. Ph.D. Diss., The Catholic University of America, Washington, DC, 1991. As a layman, Maharishi was a university student of physics prior to becoming an ascetic in a traditional order under the tutelage of a guru, the Sankaracharya Krishanand Saraswati, the then reigning pontiff of a major Sankara lineage that closely followed the teaching and practice of Advaita (nondual) Vedanta. By 1957, he had become a popular teacher in India with a considerable following and, consequently, began teaching in Western Europe and the United States. TM centers were firmly established throughout the world by 1970, and, by 1980, institutions for the study of Vedic lore were being established in which all learning could be pursued within the context of his understanding of growth in consciousness.

[16]Ibid., 309, 304f.

[17]Ibid.

[18]Ibid., 306.

[19]Confer J. A. G. Gerwin van Leeuwen, *Fully Indian — Authentically Christian, A Study of the First Fifteen Years of the NBCLC 1967-1982) in the Light of the Theology of Its Founder D. S. Amalorpavadass* (Bangalore, India: National Biblical Catechetical and Liturgical Center, 1990).

[20]Satchitananda is a Hindu formulation for God: *sat* as ultimate reality, *chit* as ultimate consciousness, and *ananda* as ultimate joy.

[21]van Leeuwen, 15-16.

[22]Ibid., 16.

[23]Ibid., 103-104.

[24]Ibid., 135-36.

[25]The adaptation of Hindu scripture was foreseen as gradual: first, using these texts for liturgical prayers and hymns; second, the composition of presidential prayers according to Indian ways of praying; third, the composition of Indian anaphoras inspired by the Indian religious heritage; fourth, adapting readings from other religions in the liturgy of the hours. The final moment in acculturation was the preparation of texts that are primarily concerned with the present social context and with the celebration and inspiration for social action, namely, development, peace, and liberation. Ibid., 246-47.

[26]Ibid., 277.

[27]Ibid., 280-85.

[28]Raimundo Panikkar, *The Intra-Religious Dialogue* (New York: Paulist Press, 1978). Born within a Hindu-Christian family in Spain with an academic background and doctorates in philosophy (Madrid, 1946), science (Madrid, 1958), and theology (Rome, 1961), Panikkar matured into a multicultural and multidisciplinary person. The definitive study of his thought was completed recently: Gerard Vincent Hall, *Raimon Panikkar's Hermeneutics of Religious Pluralism*, Unpub. Ph.D. Diss., The Catholic University of America, Washington, DC, 1993.

[29]Harold Coward, editor, *Hindu-Christian Dialogue, Perspectives and Encounters* (Maryknoll, NY: Orbis Books, 1989), x.

[30]Ibid., x-xi.

[31]*The Unknown Christ of Hinduism: Toward an Ecumenical Christophany*, 2nd rev. ed. (Maryknoll, NY: Orbis Books, 1981).

[32]Hall, 122.

[33]Ibid., 129-32.

[34]Ibid., 139-41.

[35]Ibid., 347-48.

[36]Raimundo Panikkar, *The Vedic Experience, Mantramanjari: An Anthology of the Vedas for Modern Man and Contemporary Celebration* (Berkeley & Los Angeles: University of California Press, 1977).

[37]Ibid., 7, 17, 19.

[38]Ibid., 27.

[39]Ibid., 28-29.

[40]Confer Ronald A. Pachence, *Charles Freer Andrews: An Instance of Sacramental Encounter among Religions*, Unpub. Ph.D. Diss., The Catholic University of America, Washington, DC, 1978.

[41]Charles Freer Andrews, *What I Owe to Christ* (London: Hodder and Stoughton, 1932), 111.

[42]Pachence, 144.

[43]Andrews, 19.

[44]Pachence, 164.

[45]Ibid., 177.

[46]Charles Freer Andrews, *Bunch of Letters to Rabindranath Tagore and M. K. Gandhi* (Delhi: Deenabhandhu Andrews Centenary Committee, 1971), 17-18.

[47]Pachence, 183-84, 191, 202f.

[48]Andrews, *What I Owe to Christ*, 208.

[49]Pachence, 240, 249-50.

[50]Ibid., 248. Confer William Cenkner, *The Hindu Personality in Education: Tagore, Gandhi, Aurobindo* (Columbia, MO: South Asia Books, 1976), 29-42.

[51]Pachence, 247-48.

[52]Ibid., 252, from Charles Freer Andrews, "A Pilgrim's Progress," in *Religion in Transition*, ed. Virgilius Ferm (London: George Allen and Unwin, 1937), 81.

[53]Pachence, 317, from Charles Freer Andrews, *Christ and Labour* (London: Student Christian Movement Press, 1924), 182, and *The Good Shepherd* (London: Hodder and Stoughton, 1940), 127.

[54]Throughout this section, I draw upon the most comprehensive study yet of Griffiths: Judson Bemis Trapnell, *Bede Griffiths' Theory of Religious Symbol and Practice of Dialogue: Towards Interreligious Understanding*, Unpub. Ph.D. Diss., The Catholic University of America, 1992, 24f.

[55]Ibid., 44f. In the bibliography to this study, Trapnell has listed ten books and more than two hundred articles by Griffiths.

[56]Bede Griffiths, *The Marriage of East and West: A Sequel to the Golden String* (Springfield, IL: Templegate Publishers, 1982), 23-24.

[57]Trapnell, 49, 53.

[58]Ibid., 60f.

[59]Ibid.

[60]Bede Griffiths, 150-52, 165.

[61]Bede Griffiths, *The Golden String: An Autobiography* (Springfield, IL: Templegate Publishers, 1954 & 1980).

[62]Trapnell, 160.

[63]Bede Griffiths, "Eastern Religious Experience," *Monastic Studies* 9 (Autumn, 1972): 158-59.

[64]Bede Griffiths, *The Golden String*, 56.

[65]Bede Griffiths, "On Poverty and Simplicity: Views of a Post-Industrial Christian Sage," interview by René Weber, *ReVision* 6/2 (Fall, 1983): 29.

[66]Bede Griffiths, *Return to the Center* (Springfield, IL: Templegate Publishers, 1976).

[67]Trapnell, 152, n.8.

[68]Bede Griffiths, *Return to the Center*, 37-38; confer 40-41.

[69]James Redington, S.J., "A Course Called 'The Hindu-Christian Dialogue,'" *Horizons* 12 (1985): 141-42.

[70]Henri Le Saux (Abhishiktananda), *The Secret of Arunachala* (Delhi: ISPCK, 1979), 9.

[71]Ibid.; also, Henri Le Saux (Abhishiktananda), *Guru and Disciple* (London: SPCK, 1974), 201.

[72]James Stuart, *Swami Abhishiktananda, His Life through His Letters* (Delhi: ISPCK, 1989), 201.

[73]Quoted in Jacques Dupuis, S.J., *Jesus Christ at the Encounter of World Religions,* trans. Robert R. Barr (Maryknoll, NY: Orbis Books, 1991), 77. Dupuis, in this book, has a chapter on "Swami Abhishiktananda, or the Spiritual Experience of a Hindu-Christian Monk," confer 75-76.

[74]Ibid., 85.

[75]Ibid., 89.

[76]Henri Le Saux, O.S.B., *Prayer* (London: SPCK, 1972), 21.

[77]Ibid., 35-39.

[78]Stuart, 30, 319.

[79]Swami Abhishiktananda, *The Further Shore* (London: SPCK, 1957), 105.

[80]Ibid., 9.

[81]Confer William Cenkner, *A Tradition of Teachers: Sankara and the Jagadgurus Today* (Delhi & Columbia, MO: Motilal Banarsidass & South Asia Books, 1983, 1995).

[82]Quoted in Odette Baumer-Despeigne, "The Spiritual Journey of Henri Le Saux-Abhishiktananda," *Cistercian Studies* 17/4 (1983): 312.

[83]Wayne Teasdale, "Abhishiktananda's Mystical Intuition of the Trinity," *Cistercian Studies* 18/1 (1983): 59-75.

[84]Confer Swami Abhishiktananda, *Saccidananda: A Christian Approach to Advaita Experience* (Delhi: ISPCK, 1974). This book was first published in French in 1965.

[85]Stuart, 346, 349.

[86]Ibid., 359.

[87]Ibid., 290.

[88]Ibid., 306.

[89]Baumer-Despeigne, 310.

[90]Stuart, 30.

[91]Isaiah: 54:2.

[92]J. M. Dechanet, *Christian Yoga* (New York: Harper & Row, 1960).

[93]Ewert Cousins, *Christ of the 21st Century* (Rockport, MA: Element Books, 1992).

Christians and the Jewish Experience of Prayer

Gerard S. Sloyan

The first thing to be said about the Jewish experience of prayer is that Christians do not know much about it. In an urban area in the Northeastern United States, the Midwest, the West coast, or the contiguous suburbia of such a region, Christians may see a *mezuzah* (Heb., doorpost) affixed to the door frame of a household or apartment, or a cylindrical locket worn as a pendant by a woman or pinned to a man's lapel. Rolled up inside it will be a parchment or paper on which are inscribed Deuteronomy 6:4-9 and 11:13-21, containing respectively the injunction, "Hear, O Israel, the Lord is our God, the Lord alone" (6:4), and the verse, "You shall put these words of mine in your heart and soul, and you shall bind them as a sign on your hand . . . and forehead. . . . Write them on the doorpost of your house and on your gates" (11:18, 20; cf. 6:9).

The *mezuzah* is normally marked *"Shaddai"* (Heb., the Almighty). The earliest reference to the practice of thus encapsulating these texts is found in the *Mishnah* of ca. 200 C.E. in the first tractate, *Berakoth* (Benedictions), 3.3.[1] *Megillah* 1.8 in the same legal corpus requires that the passage be in the square lettering of Hebrew which it calls "Assyrian" (for Aramaic). Five other places in the *Mishnah* (*Mo'ed Katan* 3.4; *Gittin* 4.6; *Menahoth* 3.7; *Kelim* 16.7; and 17.16) speak of times when the texts may not be written, the cleanliness or uncleanliness of their containers, and whether a *mezuzah* may be purchased from a gentile who has acquired one. The text that is placed in a *mezuzah* and its treatment are the same as in phylacteries (Heb., *tefillin*, attachments). Since these leather boxes strapped to wrist and forehead are mentioned in Matthew 23:5, the encasement of the twofold text can be presumed to go back to the late first century C.E. and before, whenever it was that the observant Judaism of the Rabbis took its rise. The reader may not encounter phylacteries very soon, but, if he/she is sharp-eyed, he/she will see a *mezuzah*.

Some contemporary, observant Jews — males only in the case of the Orthodox — can be seen approaching synagogues on Shabbat, or daily if there are a *minyan* (Heb., number), a minimum of ten, for morning prayer. Usually, they will carry a bag of velvet or velour under arm containing their *tallit* (Heb., cover) or prayer shawl with its knotted fringes at each of four corners.

The first of the major public morning prayers is the *Shema* (Heb., "Hear"), namely, the two passages from Deuteronomy cited above, to which was added at some uncertain point Numbers 15:37-41, which begins: "And the Lord said to Moses. . . ."[2] There follows in Numbers upon this introduction a set of instructions for placing blue cords or ribbons at the fringed borders *(tsitsith)* of one's garments to remind the wearer of the Lord's commandments, not to go astray after the desires of heart and eyes, and to be holy to Israel's God. The reference to that five-verse passage, "And the Lord said to Moses," occurs as early as *Berakoth* 2.2 in the *Mishnah.*

The second morning prayer *(tefillah,* prayer) is made up of the *amida* (from *āmad,* because it is said standing) with the so-called eighteen *(shemoneh esre)* benedictions as its core (actually nineteen because the twelfth against slanderers [*minim*] was a later addition); these are subdivided into "praises" (1-3), "petitions" (4-16), and "thanksgivings" (17-19). Of these benedictions, more later. Then follow the *Tahanun* ("Petition") and a selection from the Pentateuch divided into a weekly portion or *Sidra* ("order") for reading on Mondays and Thursdays, market days in ancient Palestine. The concluding parts of the service are composed of Psalms 84:5; 144:15; and 145. Psalm 20 is added when the *Tahanun* is recited, as it is on every day except festival days like those when a wedding or circumcision is celebrated.

The afternoon service *(minha)* begins with Psalm 145 on account of its verse 16, or so say *Berakoth* 4b in the Babylonian Talmud: "You open your hand, satisfying the desire of every living thing." The *Amida* comes next, then a prayer called *Kedusha* (Is. 6:3; Ezek. 3:12; Ps. 146:10, with additions), the short *Tahanun* and the full *Kaddish* — a doxology made up of five paragraphs — and, finally, *Aleynu* ("Laudation") with the *Kaddish* (which also concludes the morning service). The *Aleynu* is a proclamation of God as king over Israel and over the universe. Originally, the latter was a prayer of dismissal recited at the end of a teacher's discourse, the rabbinical *Kaddish,* "with an allusion to the Messianic hope, derived especially from the Prophets and the Psalms."[3] Only in its fifth of five forms, the *Kaddish* of Renewal, is there any men-

tion of the dead. It is used at funerals by the mourners only after
the burial and runs:

> May [God's] great Name be magnified and sanctified in the world
> that is to be created anew, where He will quicken the dead and raise
> them up into the life to come; will rebuild the city of Jerusalem and
> establish a Temple in the midst thereof; and will uproot alien wor-
> ship from the earth and restore the worship of the true God. . . .[4]

This prayer came to be recited over the centuries in times of
personal or people-wide distress. Mention of it as a prayer of intercession for the departed person occurs frequently in the modern
news media, especially when Jews, prominent in public life or
entertainment, who have not been much associated with Judaism
as a religion, announce their intention to sit *shiva* (Heb., seven,
because recited over a period of seven days) and recite *Kaddish* for
a deceased parent, spouse, sibling, or child.

One who is prevented from praying the *Minha* service is told to
recite the *Amida* twice in the evening service, called *Maariv* (from
erev, evening). The two earlier public prayers correspond to the
morning and afternoon sacrifices at the Temple, but the evening
service has no equivalent in Temple liturgy. It consists of two main
sections, the *Shema* and its benedictions and the *Amida*. Many
additions to the variations of all three are catalogued in Idelsohn's
chapter VIII of *Jewish Liturgy and Its Development*, entitled "Daily
Public Prayers."

A very brief chapter on "Daily Home Prayers" follows in that
work. This is paradoxical since the home, rather than the synagogue, is the center of Jewish prayer life. The same relative appor-
tionment of pages occurs in the *Siddur* or Daily Prayer Book,
accounting for Idelsohn's brief treatment. Rabbi Joseph H.
Hertz's *The Authorized Daily Prayer Book*, for example, a first to have
facing pages in English and Hebrew with explanatory notes,
devotes pages 6-959 to public prayers: daily, sabbath, and festival
services. From pages 960 to the end, 1119, roughly one hundred
fifty pages, private prayers and blessings are given. They begin
with the grace over meals and go on to blessings: on various occasions, over various foods, morning and night prayers, the conse-
cration of a house, prayers at a circumcision, in illness, on going
on a long journey, a confession of atonement and praise on one's
deathbed, and a blessing in the house of mourning.

Christians are prone to think of the synagogue (or sometimes,
modernly, the temple) as primarily a place of prayer. They do this
on the analogy of a church building where the baptized gather for
public prayer. But, the synagogue as a structure was a place of
assembly, *Beit ha kneseth*, for every human purpose. So it would

have been called in first century Palestine. The Greek *synagogē* of the Diaspora was the usage that came to prevail, first in the regions outside the land of Israel and then as a loan word among Jews more broadly. There is no evidence that prior to 200 C.E. Jews in either the heartland or the Diaspora had any buildings devoted exclusively to worship. The historian Josephus (d. ca. 100 C.E.) uses *synagogē* regularly to describe both any assembly of Jews and an all purpose building. Once only does he employ *proseuchē*, a prayer term, in speaking of a Jewish meeting house situated in Tiberias. Philo, who died in Alexandria perhaps fifty years earlier, used that term consistently for buildings in which the Jews of his city met.[5] This is not surprising if prayer was one of the many activities they engaged in there, especially if the exposition and absorption of the people's Scriptures are viewed as an act of prayer. Teaching and learning of the Bible and Talmud are prayer, or can be. A recent study of the Hebrew Bible, however, and of other early Jewish literature, of the writings of the above two men, the Second Testament and other Christian sources, the *Mishnah*, and archaeological data, including inscriptions and papyri, has revealed no mention of anything that could be conceived as sabbath liturgy or worship by the Jews (as contrasted to study) before the year 200. The temple priesthood had its cultic duties on the seventh day, but Jewish laity apparently engaged in no worshipful behavior on that day. A sabbath prayer service was a much later development, namely, well after the compiling of the *Mishnah*. That volume describes the sabbath as a day of total inactivity except for the gathering of some in synagogues to hear the reading of the scrolls; readings from the Torah are given priority.[6]

It must be remembered that, although the *Mishnah* describes many things as if they were practices of long standing, the opinions of the Rabbis that are assembled there are a matter only of the preceding one hundred years. The *gerousía* (academy of elders) was founded in Yavneh a decade or so after the sack of Jerusalem. Its first generation members and their successors set about devising substitutes for Temple worship. They did so by prescribing the portions of the Law, the Earlier and the Later Prophets, and the Writings to be read (including Ruth, Koheleth, Esther, Daniel, Ezra, Nehemiah and Chronicles, all of which had more recently been defined as "soiling the hands," i.e., part of the canon). The veneration for some of the Scriptures had begun in the Babylonian exile; these were edited, and others were composed after the return. They became central in the towns and villages of Palestine, although Temple sacrifice daily and especially on the three pilgrimage feasts resumed. All of it came to an end with the destruction of Herod the Great's "Second Temple." When the post-70 Rabbis set themselves to make a fitting substitute for Temple worship spread over the day, they composed a lectionary in which the readings corresponded to the times of Temple sacrifice. But, such attention to the written scrolls in synagogues never became public worship quite as Temple sacrifice had been. It remained prayerful study.

The proposals of the *Mishnah* were prescriptive as much as they were descriptive. The authors wrote up what they would have Jews do everywhere, often as if it were what they had long been doing. It would have taken some centuries for all the legal settlements found in this collection to be adopted. Already in Luke's gospel, however (90 C.E.?), there is testimony to the public reading and exposition of a prophetic book on the sabbath in a local synagogue (4:16-30). Later Christians took this to be a worship service because they were having Sunday liturgies in their homes and, from 250 C.E. onward that we know of at Dura-Europos on the middle Euphrates, in buildings exclusively for this purpose.

Little is said in the *Mishnah* of religious devotion in the home, only a few rules for observing Shabbat in a tractate of that name. These are chiefly prohibited activities and the few that are permitted, such as preparing the body of the dead for burial (23.5). Prescribed is the lighting of the Sabbath lamp, with the grim promise that death in childbirth awaits the woman who is heedless of the laws concerning it (2.6). The front page of each Friday's *New York Times* carries at the bottom a brief advertisement reminding Jewish women and girls to light the Sabbath candles. The *Siddur* provides a meditation to precede the kindling of Sabbath lights:

> Lord of the universe, I am about to perform the sacred duty of kindling the lights in honor of the Sabbath, even as it is written: "And thou shalt call the Sabbath a delight, and the holy day of the Lord honorable". . . . Father of mercy, continue thy lovingkindness to me and my dear ones. . . . Keep thou far from us all manner of shame, grief, and care; and grant that peace, light and joy ever abide in our home. For with thee is the fountain of life; in thy light do we see light (see Ps. 36:9).

After the lamps or candles are lighted, the hands are spread out before them or over the face, while this benediction is spoken: "Blessed art thou, O Lord our God, King of the universe, who hast hallowed us by thy commandments, and commanded us to kindle the Sabbath light." Since the midsixteenth century, a group of mystics of Safed in the Galilee, a city set on a hill, have proposed Psalms 95-99 and 29 and a number of hymns for recitation to welcome "Queen Sabbath." The psalms have rejoicing and song as their theme and stress God's mighty power over nature. Here is a popular hymn from that period, the *Lechoh Dodi* ("Come, my beloved"), the work of Rabbi Solomon Halevy Alkabetz (ca. 1540):

> Come, my beloved, with chorus of praise,
> Welcome Bride Sabbath, the Queen of the Days. . . .
> Sabbath to welcome thee, joyous we haste; . . . .
> Crown of God's handiwork, chiefest of days. . . .
> Rise, O my folk, from the dust of the earth,
> Garb thee in raiment beseeming thy worth. . . .
> Come where the faithful are singing thy praise;
> Come as a bride comes, O Queen of the days.[7]
>   (tr. Solomon Solis-Cohen)

If the reader has the opportunity to welcome the Sabbath by participating in the Friday night meal with a Jewish family, he/she will have experienced the heart of Jewish prayer. At the festive table an ancient chant is sung that welcomes the angels of the Most High in peace and then sends them on their way. After this hymn the father of the family reads from Proverbs 31, beginning at verse 10 in praise of a good wife and mother.[8] The *Havdalah* (Separation) Service is prayed to bid farewell to the Sabbath and mark people's return after sundown on Saturday to the world of household tasks and everyday work. With a cup in the right hand, one says the following:

> Behold, God *(El)* is my salvation *(yeshuati)*: I will trust and will not be afraid: for God the LORD is my strength and song, and he is become my salvation. Therefore with joy shall you draw water out of the wells of salvation. Salvation [which always means rescue or deliverance] belongs to the LORD: thy blessing be upon thy people. The LORD of hosts is with us; the God of Jacob is our refuge. The Jews [of old] had light and joy and gladness and honor. (So be it with us). I will lift the cup of salvation and call on the name of the LORD.
> Blessed art thou, O Lord our God, King of the universe, who created the fruit of the vine.

That last is the only blessing said at the conclusion of festivals, but on other sabbaths a blessing of spices is added — probably aromatic incense, although the custom of burning it at the meal does not continue — and another of "the lights of the fire," nowadays a woven *Havdalah* candle with two wicks. Another blessing is said with cup in hand, thanking God for having made a distinction between holy and profane, between light and darkness, between Israel and the gentiles, and between the seventh day and the six working days. An eleventh century hymn is then sung or said, the *Hamavdil* (the Setter Apart), which asks sins to be blotted out, redemption granted, and sore and wasting sickness delivered from. Finally, the prayer for the coming week is said, which begins *Ribon ha Olamim,* Sovereign of the Universe. It asks God that, as working days approach, the petitioners may be "freed [in them] from all sin and transgression, cleansed from all iniquity, trespass and wickedness." At the same time, God is asked to frustrate the designs of any who might plan for his people Israel anything that is not for its good:

> Open unto us, Father of mercies and LORD of forgiveness, in this week and in the weeks to come, the gates . . . of holiness and peace, of the study of thy Torah and of prayer. In us also let the Scripture be fulfilled: "How beautiful upon the mountains/ are the feet of the messenger who announces peace,/ who brings good news,/ who announces salvation,/ who says to Zion, 'Your God reigns' (Isaiah 52:7)."

To pray the *Havdalah,* one needs to be the guest of a more observant family than one that welcomes the Sabbath only with prayer and song, although some do it with much careful preparation. The second commonest experience of Jewish prayer the nonJew is likely to have after participation in a Passover *seder,* the *Birkat ha Mazon,* is the prayer at the conclusion of a meal that has begun with a blessing of God over food. First, God is reminded that he gave a command [in Oral Torah] to wash the hands, then: "Blessed art thou, O Lord our God, King of the universe who bringest forth bread from the earth." Jews call this prayer *ha Motzey* because it calls God "Source" of all our food and drink.

Psalm 126 is recited or sung before thanks are offered on Shabbat at the end of a meal and before *Birkat ha Mazon* (which is sung if there are three people present), with its reminder of the way the heathen marveled when the LORD restored the fortunes of Zion. Then: "Restore our fortunes, O LORD, like the torrents in the Negev. Those that sow in tears shall reap rejoicing. Those who go out weeping, bearing the seed for sowing,/ shall come home with shouts of joy, carrying their sheaves" (Psalm 126:4-6). A dialogue follows, beginning not unlike the *"Gratias agamus"* that precedes the *Praefatio* of the Roman Eucharistic prayers, with a response that says literally in Hebrew what became in the Latin, *Sit nomen Domini benedictum/ex hoc nunc et usque in saeculum,* "Blessed be the Name of the LORD from this time henceforth and forever." God is then blessed, from whose bounty all have partaken and through whose goodness we live, who gives food to all flesh in which the covenant is sealed:

> Thou gavest to our ancestors a desirable, good, and ample land and brought us forth from the land of Egypt and delivered us from the house of bondage. . . . By thy Torah thou hast taught us and made known to us the life, grace and lovingkindness *(ḥaim, ḥen, ve ḥesed)* thou hast bestowed on us. Thanks to thee for the food with which thou sustaineth us every day, in every season and at every hour.

Two things in particular should be observed about Jewish prayers. Most of the nonbiblical ones were composed in Europe in the Middle Ages, early or late, when Jews were not having an easy life in the midst of the larger Christian body. Consequently, there is a note of sadness at the heart even of prayers of rejoicing, with a cry for deliverance as in the days of Egypt or Babylon. Secondly, the prayers are absolutely God centered. Israel and its needs are correlative, but they are never at the center. God always is. Moreover, all the shorter prayers begin *Baruch atta*, Blessed art thou, meaning may the divine blessedness or state of happiness be acknowledged by all humanity. The Sabbath or the food is not blessed, but always God who is declared the giver of the gift or who is besought to avert some catastrophe like sin. Christians would do well to remember this. How they came to invoke a blessing upon food or anything else primarily is not clear: "*Benedic, Domine, nos et haec tua dona* . . . Bless *us*, O Lord, and these *thy gifts*. . . ." The prayer over the gifts in the renewed Eucharistic rite of the West has it straight: "Blessed are you, LORD, God of all creation. Through your goodness we have this bread to offer," and so on. Our table prayer should similarly read: "Blessed are you, Lord, who have given us these your gifts from your bounty *(largitas)* . . ." All Christian prayer, like Jewish, is God centered. If it is Christ centered or Holy Spirit centered, there is some confusion about it. Christian prayer is made through Christ in the community of the Holy Spirit, the Church, which, for the believer in the mystery of God Triune, does nothing to dilute or deny the oneness or unity of Godhead.

The later written Jewish prayers are either brief blessings or lengthy addresses of praise and petition. The earlier composed *Tefillah* (or *Amida*) is so central to Jewish prayer that it deserves fuller exploration. For purposes of comparison, we might point out concerning the "Our Father" and the Eucharistic anaphora that there is no recorded struggle attending the use of Matthew's version of Jesus' prayer over Luke's, nor do we know what preceded the emergence of the Hippolytan canon in the East and the earliest version of the Roman canon in the West. Both prayers may have been a matter of peaceful popular acceptance, the Eucharistic one in a Greek and a Latin form and the "Our Father" as first found in Matthew's wording in the *Didachē*. Was such the case with the prayer beginning, *"Shema,"* and the *Amida* or Eighteen that begin, *"Birkath"*? It may well have been. But, some contemporary Jewish scholars take their lead from the Talmudic tradition that Gamaliel II of Yavneh was deposed from the patriarchate at the turn of the second century because of a dispute over the regulation of prayers.[9] The argument runs that the *Shema* became the primary rite of the scribal brotherhoods, its Exodus motif functioning as a polemic of scribal triumphalism. The *Tefillah*, by contrast, originated as the main liturgy of the deposed aristocracy represented by the patriarchs, as evidenced by its stress on the kingship motif. With the Temple's destruction, priestly and patriarchal authority was claimed over the community by these client rulers, "implicitly for Rome and explicitly for God." Well after the Bar Kokhba revolt of 135, the years 155-220 it is hypothesized, rabbinic leadership amalgamated its social forces and merged the formerly distinct liturgical rituals into a single service.[10] Very early in the *Mishnah* the tractate *Berakoth* records the opinions of the scribal schools of Hillel and Shammai on fitting bodily postures when reciting the *Shema* (1.3).

Recall that Jesus finds a scribe agreeing with him on the two greatest commandments of Torah in the context of an argument with the aristocratic Sadducees (see Mark 12:29-30). Scribal values are conspicuous in the content of the text of the *Shema*: the uniqueness and oneness of Israel's God who alone is to be loved while false gods are spurned, which is a major Exodus theme; stress on phylacteries and tassels as reminders "to keep all my commandments and be holy to your God . . . who brought you out of the land of Egypt to be your God" (Numbers 15:41). Notice the omission of the Temple, the priests, Jerusalem, and David in the *Shema* — there is nothing sacerdotal or royal about the three Torah texts. The reenacting of the Exodus was placed at the center of the *seder*, a rabbinic ritual. These learned men put a banquet for Torah study in place of the cultic offering and a feast of the paschal lamb in place of a now nonexistent Temple. They retained certain symbolic acts that recalled Temple worship — paschal offering, now understood as "God's having passed over the houses of our ancestors in Egypt," the *matzah* and the bitter herbs. This immensely popular spring festival became an exercise in Exodus recall with scant reference to the cultic activity of the Temple. The priesthood, now no longer able to function as such, must have felt humiliated at being totally dislodged, even in memory.

The eighteen benedictions of *Tefillah*, on the other hand, featured several quite different matters: the fifth, repentance, a cultic theme; the tenth, the gathering of the Jews in exile to their homeland Israel, a national motif; the eleventh, a prayer for the restoration of "our judges and our counselors," perhaps a protest against foreign judges and Roman domination. Benediction fourteen prays for Jerusalem, a priestly theme, and fifteen, for the reinstatement of the royal Davidic dynasty; finally, the seventeenth begs for the restoration of Temple service on Zion, while the nineteenth invokes God's peace through the medium of the priestly blessing.[11]

There has been much recent discussion among New Testament exegetes concerning the twelfth benediction, actually a malediction, against slanderers (informers, apostates). Kaufmann Kohler (see n. 3, p. 399) and W. D. Davies, followed by others, have taken *minim* (sectarians, apostates) to mean the Jewish believers in Jesus. This prayer, says the Talmud, was composed about 100 C.E. after the others, thus making the total nineteen. Actually, the target group was probably Jews who were dividing the community in the wake of the destruction of the Temple, some by apostasy, others by acting the informer to the Romans. Much later, the phrase *ve hannotsrim* was added, "and the Christians," to be eliminated, along with other even later added phrases which the medieval Christians thought alluded to them. After much polemic, lasting down to the eighteenth century, all such phrasing was removed by dint of Christian pressure. But, the ambiguous curse of the *minim* remains in the Orthodox prayer book.

To conclude the contemporary theorizing on the way the *Shema* and the *Amida* and the *Tefillah* came to be joined as the core of daily morning prayer, one supposes that a compromise was struck some time before 220 C.E. between the scribal and priestly factions. The *Shema* recalls the Exodus and the rabbinic practice of wearing a shawl with tassels, but has practically no mention of Temple worship. The eighteen benedictions feature strongly the Temple priesthood and Jewish kingship. The scribes had succeeded in deposing Gamaliel II, as the Talmud says, opening the way to joining the two liturgies in tandem:

> A probable result is that the *Shema* was revised to include the theme of kingship. In this era the priests were relegated to figurehead status in rabbinic communities. The patriarch . . . was excluded from most internal rabbinic affairs. . . . In effect the scribal faction triumphed in the internal rabbinic power struggle, severing rabbinic ritual from meaningful national political structures.[12]

And so it is to this day. The scribes won out over the priests. Judaism is rabbinism. Thus, "rabbinic Judaism" is a tautology.

It may seem strange that the two gatherings for Jewish prayer best known to Christians have been reserved for treatment until now. They are *Rosh ha Shana*, the first day of the year, and *Yom*

Kippur, correctly, *ha Kippurim*, the Day of Atonement, ten days later (Lev. 23:26-32). Popularly called the High Holy Days, the interval between them is referred to by Jews as the Days of Awe. In urban centers like New York and Philadelphia the traffic is notably less on those two days. Synagogues are crowded, but so are major cities' hotel ballrooms, since synagogues could not accommodate the numbers who attend. The first day of the year is not featured in the Bible. The term *rosh ha shana* occurs only in Ezek. 40:1, where it merely means "around the beginning of the year." But, the *Mishnah* has an entire tractate of that name about the day's observance. The Scriptures record conflicting traditions as to which was the first month of the year. The preexilic priestly choice was Abib (its old Canaanite name), Nisan (its Babylonian name), occurring around the time of the spring equinox in March/April (see Exodus 12:2; 13:4; 34:18). Exodus 23:15 identifies this month as the time the Hebrews came out of Egypt. *Pesaḥ* (Passover) was observed on the fourteenth day of the month and the Feast of Unleavened Bread *(matzoth/azymoi)* for eight days beginning on that day. The Feast of Weeks came seven weeks, that is, fifty days, after Passover (*Shabuoth*, Pentecost). The third pilgrimage feast, Booths *(Sukkoth)*, was a seven day observance in the autumn (Deuteronomy 16:1-17; for the agricultural origins of this three-fold observance, see Exodus 23:14-17). Thus, the year began in the spring in the old calendar.

Another calendar which had the year beginning in the autumn month of Tishri had Mesopotamian roots, as did the spring tradition. It cannot be said with certainty that one calendar was in use before the exile and the other after. Passover was kept in spring on the fourteenth day of what Exodus 12:2 calls "the first month of the year." But, the elaborate celebration specified for the first day of the seventh month occurring after spring (that is, Tishri), followed on the tenth day by the Day of Atonement and the fifteenth day the Feast of Booths (see Leviticus 23:43; Numbers 29:1-39), indicates that an autumn new year's observance was winning out. This scheme of first, tenth and fifteenth days provides assurance that the feasts would fall on the same day of the week every year. This calendar, attested to in the pseudepigraphical books of Enoch and Jubilees, was kept by the Qumrân sectaries. If Jesus and his friends also observed it, a hypothesis put forward by the late Annie Jaubert, Wednesday would have been the first day of Azymes. Hence, the Last Supper of Christians would have occurred on Tuesday night, allowing two full days for all the reported incidents leading to his crucifixion. The bulk of Jews, however, were already observing *Rosh ha Shanah* in the autumn month of Tishri, with a clear memory of its once having been observed in Nisan in the spring.

What are the prayers of the High Holy Days? To usher in the new year there is, first, the Service of the Sounding of the Shofar (ram's horn), the "trumpet blasts" of Lev. 23:24. It is a call to repentance and spiritual renewal, sounded in the following sequence: a long, stretched out sound, followed by broken notes, and then staccato notes. Three benedictions follow, one proclaiming the sovereignty of God, a second, divine providence, and a third, the revelation given on Mt. Sinai. Selections from Numbers 28 and 29 about the day itself, the first day of Tishri, are read, next extended prayers that allude to Deuteronomy and the Psalms, and then a reiterated prayer that acknowledges God's reign over the universe. That benediction is called *Malchiyoth*, Kingship. The next has the title *Zichronoth*, Remembrance (of all God's deeds, beginning with the creation, then the flood, the call of the patriarchs, and the giving of Torah). *Shofaroth* (Soundings of the Horn) is the title of the third benediction because it tells of the shofar blasts at Sinai which, in God's good time, will summon all on judgment day. A blessing of the priests is added on this and all festivals that do not fall on a sabbath. Those named Cohen or any derivative of it ascend the steps toward the Ark to receive it: "May our prayer be acceptable unto thee as burnt offering and as sacrifice [they pray]. . . . Restore, we beseech thee, thy divine presence unto Zion, and there will we worship thee in awe, as in the days of old and as in ancient years."

The ten day interval between this holy day and the next is known also as the Ten Days of Repentance. The service for the Day of Atonement is lengthy, as *Rosh ha Shana's* had been. It begins with a reading of Leviticus 16:30 which says: "For on this day shall he [presumably God] make atonement for you; from all your sins shall you be clean before the LORD." The next verse calls this day a "sabbath of sabbaths" on which Jews must deny themselves, that is, by fasting. With a cessation of Temple sacrifice repentance was left as the sole means for the remission of sins, both in act and in expression of sorrow.

The evening service is preceded by the annulment of all vows *(Kol Nidre)*, a practice that may have originated in Palestine, but gained currency in seventh century Visigothic Spain when its Germanic Arian Christians were forcing Jews to apostatize. The renunciation is declared three times by a leader in prayer and sung in a haunting melody in Ashkenazic (but not Sephardic or Yemenite) congregations: "May these our vows . . . our oaths . . . our bonds be no longer considered as binding." Yoma 8.9 of the *Mishnah* had long before made clear that the *Yom Kippur* atonement formula wiped out transgressions between man and God, hence unfulfilled vows made to God, but for transgressions against fellow humans only satisfaction to those sinned against could be adequately atoned for. The *Amida* proper to this day contains these words:

> Thou hast chosen us from all peoples, thou hast loved us and taken pleasure in us, and hast exalted us above all tongues. . . . And thou hast given us in love, O Lord our God, this Day of Atonement for pardon, forgiveness and reconciliation, that we may obtain pardon on this day for all our iniquities, a holy assembly, as a memorial of the departure from Egypt. . . . O God, the God of our ancestors, pardon our iniquities on this Day of Atonement; blot out our transgressions and our sins, and make them pass away from before thine eyes. As it is said: "I have brushed away your offenses like a cloud, your sins like a mist; return to me, for I have redeemed you" (Isaiah 44:22; followed in the text by Leviticus 16:30, *supra*).

Then comes a lengthy confession of sins and crimes:

> We are guilt-laden: we have been faithless, we have robbed, and we have spoken basely; . . .
> We have counseled evil, we have failed in promise, we have scoffed, revolted, and blasphemed; . . .
> We have been rebellious, we have acted perversely, we have transgressed, oppressed, and been stiff-necked;
> We have done wickedly, we have corrupted ourselves and committed abomination; we have gone astray; and we have led astray.

All the wording of this self accusation and repentance is taken from the Bible. The only difference is, these are not the charges of Moses and the prophets laid against the people, but of the people accusing themselves.

I once asked my Temple University colleague, Rabbi Jacob Agus of happy memory — having for many years read newspaper reports of High Holy Days sermons delivered to New York congregations and knowing the character of the *Yom Kippur* observance — "Why is the pulpit rhetoric so little related to the repentance that this liturgical rite is about?" He was a kindly man, and he said with a smile, in defense of his colleagues: "Perhaps they depend on the gentiles to remind the Jews of their many sins and feel no need to scold them once again." I thought of the Christian pulpit which so often rings with the sins of the absent, and of legislators and members of various courts who go unnamed, while seated congregations are the ones who must be told of their need to repent, usually of quite different sins.

There is a lengthier confession of guilt in litanic form that is very specific: sins committed by slander, in business, in meat and drink, by extortion and usury, with lustful looks, with haughty eyes, by talebearing, by causeless hatred. Again: by despising parents and teachers, by violence, by the evil inclination (*yetser ha rah*; base passion), by deliberate lying, by bribery. This is a relentlessly probing examination of conscience. Nineteenth century Christian prayer books and modern Catholic penance services do not nearly approach its honesty. It is no wonder that Jews approach their assemblies on *Yom Kippur* sober of mien and depart from them even more soberly. *Yom Kippur* is followed after four days by *Sukkoth* (Booths), and the week concludes for the pious with the joyous *Simchat Torah* (Rejoicing in the Law), when hasids and others can be seen dancing with the Torah scrolls on certain Jewish populated streets of the Mayfair section of Philadelphia, in Media and Havertown.

The reader may know about one or another minor festival that is an occasion for joyful celebration, *Hanukkah,* for example, the Feast of Dedication or Renewal (in John's Gospel, *egkainía*, at 10:22). It marks the recapture of the Temple from the Seleucid Greeks by the priest Mattathiah and his sons in 168-67 B.C.E. Lights are lighted on successive evenings after sundown in the month of Kislev (early or late December) because "the Temple's glorious ornaments, carried off as spoils" (1 Maccabees 2:9), were put in place after the recapture (2 Maccabees 10:3). This "Feast of Lights" has special currency in our time because Jewish children, living in the midst of Christians, tend to feel deprived in the midst of all the preChristmas gift giving, the Santas, and the crowded stores. The feast has not had that much importance traditionally. The recapture of the Temple, a fact of history, long ago gave way to the myth of a lamp in the Temple that never went out. Secular Zionists, however, resuscitated the narrative of the courageous Maccabees and elaborated Josephus' legend of the suicide of the 960 at Masada (*War* VII, ix). On the first night, a light is lighted, and this prayer is said:

> We kindle these lights on account of the miracles, the deliverances and the wonders which thou didst work for our fathers, by means of thy holy priests. During all the eight days of Hanukkah these lights are sacred, neither is it permitted to us to make any profane use of them; but we are only to look at them, in order that we may give thanks unto the Name for thy miracles, thy deliverances and thy wonders.[13]

Purim is another festival that is likely to come to the attention of Christians who live in proximity to Jews. Whereas *Hanukkah* is primarily a time of grateful rejoicing rather than of merry making with an emphasis on delights for children, having become such only accidentally, *Purim* undoubtedly is a joyous family feast. The story of Esther at its core is both a tale of seduction and grisly

enough, but the cruel end Haman the Agagite and his sons
planned for the Jew Mordecai is submerged by shouts of relief that
the lives of Jews have been spared. *Pur* is an Akkadian word that is
given a Hebrew plural ending and means "lots." The book itself
spells this out as it describes Haman's casting a lot for the time of
the Jews' defeat and destruction (see Esther 9:24-26). The book of
Esther is read on this day in synagogues from a special scroll
(megillah), the last of five read throughout the year. The others in
numbered sequence are (3) *Pesah*, the Song of Songs; (4) *Shabuoth*, Ruth; (5) *Tisha b' Av*, Lamentations; and (1) *Sukkoth*,
Qoheleth; but (2) *Purim*, Esther, came to be known as *the megillah*.
In 9:17 the Jews who lived in the provinces of the Persian empire
are described as feasting and rejoicing on the fourteenth day of
Adar (February/March), the last month of the year in the old
calendar. The reason is that, according to the previous verse, they
had killed 75,000 of their foes without engaging in plunder. The
entire book shares in this exaggerated, almost burlesque, character, hence can be dealt with lightheartedly. In the Middle Ages, the
festival had many aspects of the preLenten carnival which in some
years the Christians were celebrating concurrently. *Hadassah*
means myrtle or ivy and is the Jewish name of the heroine,
whereas Esther, her court name, is probably derived from the
Persian goddess Ishtar, meaning star. Before the reading of the
whole *megillah* in the morning, three blessings are said, two of
which read:

> Blessed art thou, O Lord our God, King of the universe, who
> wrought wonderful deliverance for our fathers in the days of old, at
> this season. Blessed art thou, O Lord our God, King of the universe,
> who hast kept us in life, and hast preserved us, and enabled us to
> reach this season.

After the reading of the scroll, a blessing of God is invoked in
thanks for the just judgment that avenged the wrong done to the
people Israel, resulting in punishment dealt out to its enemies.
But, this is not the basic character the feast has assumed. Rather,
it has been marked over the centuries by one of unbridled joy at
release and freedom. Although Judaism has always discouraged
drunkenness, a Talmudic exchange asks at this season: "How do
you know when you've drunk too much at *Purim*?," and gives the
answer: "When you can't tell Mordecai from Haman." Then it's
time to stop. On this day, children are given a square spinning-top
called a *dreidel*, with a letter of the alphabet on each of the four
sides, *shin, he, ghimel, nun*, the initial letters of "There happened a
great miracle," for a game of chance. When I was retired from
Temple University, a Jewish colleague in political science took me

to lunch and presented me with a chocolate *dreidel.* I trust he assumed I had the heart of a child and not the mind of a child.

The day before *Purim* is a fast for observant Jews because of Esther's proposal of a fast on her behalf in 4:16. Jewish tradition has added four other fast days, two to commemorate attacks on the city of Jerusalem and one the murder of Gedaliah, whom the king of Babylon set over the cities of Judah in 587 B.C.E. (Jeremiah 41:2). The best observed of the four fasts of the Jewish year is *tisha b' Av,* the ninth of Av (July/August). The fast lasts twenty-four hours and remembers the burning of the First Temple in 586 B.C.E. (see 2 Kings 25:8-10). Tradition placed the destruction of the Second Temple on the same day in 70 C.E., likewise the fall of Bethar to Hadrian's troops in the Bar Kokhba revolt of 135. The near destruction of European Jewry in the holocaust continues to be uppermost in the prayers of those who observe the ninth of Av, but a *Yom ha Sho'ah* has begun to be kept in the spring month of Nisan between Passover and Weeks. I was present on the former day in the Conservative Synagogue on Agron Street in Jerusalem in 1976. It was conducted largely in English with a congregation of American Jews. All the prayers and the sermon were Jerusalem centered, bringing home to me forcefully how much the liturgy must mean to the Jews — and to the Christians — who reside there.

Nothing has been said in this essay of the many fine *Piyyutim* (poetic pieces) found in Jewish liturgies: the *Musaf* service (Reform and Reconstructionist Judaism omit this in its entirety because they do not wish the Temple rebuilt) contains the *Avodah* on *Yom Kippur* only, "a lengthy poetic composition recalling sacred history from creation to the establishment of the cult, with Aaron and his descendants as its priests."[14] There is the taking of branches of "majestic trees and palm trees, the leafy trees and willows" of Leviticus 23:40 to yield the *lulav* and the *etrog* of *Sukkot* and the home ceremony of the *seder* at *Pesah* with its accompanying *Haggadah* (legend, tale) liturgy (see Ezra 6:19-22). Any one of these could be the subject of a separate presentation.

If Christians have had a direct experience of Jewish prayer, the most likely observance, after a blessing of God over food, is the Passover *seder* (order). It is above all a family meal — prayerful, joyous (even raucous), and solemn by turns. In it, Jews see themselves completely at one with Moses and the Hebrew children, escaping the Egypt of the Pharaoh across the Red Sea or Sea of Reeds toward the Promised Land. It is a remembrance of divine deliverance that asks God to ensure the future total liberation of the Jewish people from all that threatens them. Those who have taken part in it will surely remember its sequence, known since the eleven century: the opening *Kiddush*, the washing of hands, the partaking of parsley dipped in salt water; then the broken *matzah* with a portion hidden, to be eaten at the end of the meal as the *aphikomon* (Greek, *èpí kōmōn*, "after the merrymaking," see Isaiah 30:2); the *maggid* or story of Israel's deliverance, a further hand-washing and blessing over *matzah*; the eating of the bitter herb, horseradish *(maror)*; then the *matzah, maror,* and *haroseth* (fruit, nuts, cinnamon, and wine) eaten together. The meal follows interspersed with four cups of wine and featuring a shank bone of lamb on a dish (Sephardi Jews have this, the Ashkenazi do not) and a roasted egg to commemorate the festival offering when the Temple still stood. If the reader remembers nothing else, he/she will recall the four questions put by the youngest to the eldest (see Exodus 13 and 14; M. Pesahim 10.4), or the haunting melody *Daiyenu* ("It would have been enough for us. . . ."); or, perhaps, the folk song about "One Kid" bought for two *zuzim*. Like our nursery rhymes, all of which originated in anti royal sentiment in British history, this ditty may at first have been bitter satire over the Temple price of a kid for slaughter. In any case, it has been given all sorts of midrashic and allegorical interpretations unrelated to Second Temple practice. Christians who have been party to a Jewish family *seder* will long remember its warmhearted and cheerful character, but also the sense of identity modern Jews feel with the liberated Hebrew people of three millennia ago. Their use of symbols to bespeak that identity and the unity the symbols accomplish, both among those around the table and between them and all their forebears, is a powerful reminder to the Christian of the meaning of sacrament.

A footnote may be in place here. I think there is nothing good to be said for the recent practice of a "Christian *seder*" on Holy or Maundy Thursday. It arose out of a laudable desire to do as Jesus and his disciples did at the Last Supper. There is no way of knowing, however, whether the details of the observance given in M.Pesah 10, worked out after much argument by the postTemple Rabbis, were the practice of families and other groups of pilgrims while the Temple stood. Needless to say, many of the medieval additions to the rite could not have marked first century practice. More importantly, the Christian practice which may be intended as a friendly reaching out to Jews can be offensive to them. They already know how much of Israel's religion Christians have adopted, sometimes changing its significance in doing so. They may not appreciate this most recent example of the tendency. The disciples of Hillel and Shammai made one adaptation of the Passover meal enjoined in Exodus 12. The Jewish believers in Jesus as the Christ of God made another. Undoubtedly, both adaptations were being observed throughout the second century as the parting of the ways became a reality. The *seder* is the rite of Jews that developed and should not be mimicked. The Eucharistic meal is the rite of Christians on that holy night that likewise developed. It should be celebrated in the full conviction that Christ, the innocent Lamb who achieves our deliverance, is *our* Passover. The ancient biblical rite has taken on two similar, yet dissimilar, meanings, one people centered as in its origins, the other with wider significance than one for Jews only. The developments are distinct and should not be confused.

This brings us to some final considerations of Christians and the Jewish experience of prayer. Modern Jews are delighted when Christians, in fact any gentiles, join them for family or public prayer. This was not always the case. In the Middle Ages especially, but even down to the present century, the presence of nonJews was suspect and that for very good reason. St. John Chrysostom, as a new and over zealous presbyter of Antioch in 386, preached a series of sermons against the many of his flock who were attending Jewish festivals and joining in their fasts. He identified this as "a disease flourishing within the body of the church."[15] All learned Jews are familiar with the overblown and, in places, scurrilous rhetoric against their people found in Chrysostom's sermons. In medieval Europe, Christians would spy on Jews at prayer only to ridicule its "strangeness," by which they meant its unfamiliarity. Only in recent times, specifically in the postShoah period, have Christians shown much interest in Jewish prayer and been welcomed to learn about it or join in it with Jews. Learned interest in Jewish prayer by Christians is another matter. That scholarly inquiry has a long history, just as some modern Jewish scholars have been concerned to identify the Jewish roots of Christian prayer.[16]

The chief and immediate response of Christians to the prayer forms of Jews is their ability to engage in it totally except for the claim to be ethnically of this people, for it is always either biblical or liturgical in the manner of their own liturgical prayer. All of it is directed to God, but without much mention of Messiah or the Spirit of the LORD. The notable difference for the Christian is that there is no intercessor like Jesus, not Moses or any other. Any antiChristian phrases have long since been eliminated, including some that had no such intent, but were mistakenly thought to have had and were excised by Christian political authority. What is there is marked by a depth of feeling and a sublimity of phrasing with which the Christian can resonate totally. Among the characteristics of Jewish prayer that stand out, upon a first Christian discovery of it, is its complete sense of awe in the presence of the divine majesty; its awareness of dependence on God for life itself and every gift of God throughout life; its close familiarity with suffering and a plea to be free of it if it be God's will; its awareness that this is a *people* at prayer, not individuals, and that this people is convinced of its unique relation with the one it calls *ha Shem*, the Name; its taking for granted that this God is a participant in the joys and the sorrows, the peak experiences and the everyday occurrences of a people whose history goes back to Abraham, to the Exodus and Sinai, to David and Solomon, the building and destruction of two Temples, and the emergence of the Rabbis on the shoulders of prophets, priests, and sages.

Spontaneous Jewish prayer utterances are almost identical with Christian: "God forbid!," after mention of a horrible prospect; "May God forgive me," as prelude to a particularly harsh judgment; and "May God strike me dead," in hyperbolic testimony to the truth of a statement. Modern Jews — Conservative, Reform, and Reconstructionist — are more likely to speak of "the days of Messiah" than they are to say, "when Messiah comes," in the manner of the Orthodox.[17] But, the spirit of prayer of all Jews, whichever their tradition, in the measure it derives from, and is patterned on, their formal prayers, can be discovered only by association with a Jew or Jews who pray constantly and not in certain seasons only. To have such associates, we should be so lucky!

A question that Christians are likely to ask is, "What is the personal prayer of Jews like?" By personal they are prone to mean individual, which is a quite different matter. The obvious answer is, "Ask individual Jews." To be sure, they send anguished petitions heavenward in times of distress, or loss, or anxiety, like any believer in a God of power and mercy. Some Jews have favorite psalms committed to memory; many have not. Those who learned a prayer for the opening of the day and one for its close, either in the home or in Hebrew school, have it available for use throughout life, though, like many Christians, they may not be faithful to youthful practice. A crisis of need brings all believers to their knees. Sometimes, but not very often, a Jew who has a Christian as an intimate friend in a culture like ours may say: "You people seem to gather in small groups for prayer. We don't have anything like that"; or, "I hear you speak of going on a weekend retreat with your husband (or wife), with a group of women (or men) you seem close to. That sounds interesting, but it isn't a very Jewish thing to do."

Jewish prayer, like Jewish life, is more communal than it is individual. While the Temple still stood, prayer or the offering of the lips corresponded to the daily offering at the altar. At its destruction, the Rabbis who framed the *Mishnah* placed "Blessings" as the first of its tractates and prescribed times and postures for praying the *Shema*, *Tefillah*, and Summons to Say Grace

Jointly as if the Temple were still in place. Rabbi Lawrence Hoffman is of the opinion that this "fully elaborated system was intended as a disciplinary *regula* for a specific rabbinic social class, and eventually (not until the Middle Ages) was adopted as binding on all Jews."[18] The synagogue service was codified by the *geonim* ("the highly placed") between the conclusion of the Talmud and the eleventh century. They gave attention to specific prayers and their wording and left a record of the considerations that entered into their choices. The tenor of these prayers was cultic, not ethical. That is to say, glory and praise, petition and repentance were directed to the Most High, but ethical uprightness was not made the subject of prayer. How to live justly was argued in treatises on the Law and its precepts — by the same Rabbis who were framing a synagogue liturgy. Tradition was a determining factor in retaining reactions to certain historical events, like the malediction leveled at the *minim* that they "should have no hope" or the citing of Scripture in the Passover *Haggadah*, asking God to "Pour out your wrath on the nations that do not know you" (Ps. 79:6); see the prediction that "God will crush the skulls of the enemy, the hairy heads of those who walk in sin" (68:22). While these prayers remain in some liturgies because of the force of tradition, other Jewish prayerbooks eliminate them. Medieval authorities say they are right to do so when the conditions that led to their inclusion no longer prevail.

A good example of the exercise of this freedom is the *siddur* series of Reconstructionist Judaism, entitled *Kol Haneshamah* ("Total Spirit"). The second volume to appear contains the prayers proper to the Sabbath and feasts.[19] It was preceded by the experimental *Sabbath Evening* and will be followed by a prayerbook for the High Holydays and a daily prayerbook. Featured in the series are transliterations of the Hebrew as well as English translations, extensive commentary by classic and modern authors, and more than one hundred pages of meditations and readings, some of them by gentiles. The first Reconstructionist Sabbath Prayer Book was published in 1945. Because of the conviction of the founding father of the movement, Mordecai Kaplan, that Judaism was the culture of a people rather than a religion, it deleted references to Jewish chosenness, to the Messiah son of David, to the reinstitution of sacrifices, to individual reward and punishment, and to bodily resurrection. For its rationalist tone, it received a public burning as heresy by a group of rabbis, appearing in a photo on the front page of *The New York Times*. Something of that secular spirit remains in the present volumes, but they contain so much biblical material and selections from Jewish piety that they emerge as profoundly religious works. A number of excerpts fol-

low, beginning with a rendering of Psalm 150. Readers of the
Hebrew on the facing page can see what the English does about
modern gender-specific sensitivities:

> Hallelu / Yah!
> Call out to Yah (the Heb. has *El*, "God") in Heaven's holy place!
> Boom out to Yah (Heb., *Hu*, "him"), for all God's (Heb., "his")
>   mighty deeds!
> Cry out for Yah, as loud as God is great!
> Blast out for Yah with piercing shofar note!
> Pluck out for Yah with lute and violin!
> Throb out for Yah with drum and writhing dance!
> Sing out for Yah with strings and husky flute!
> Ring out for Yah with cymbals that resound!
> Cling out for Yah with cymbals that rebound!
> Let every living thing Yah's praises sing, Hallelu / Yah!
> Let every living thing Yah's praises sing, Hallelu / Yah![20]

The repetition of the last line does not appear in the Bible, only
here in the liturgy. "Praise him" is repeated four times in the
Hebrew after "Praise God." The colorful variants in the spirit of
the "Boomlay, boomlay, boomlay, BOOM" of Vachel Lindsay's
"The Congo" may startle the fastidious, but the loud instrumen-
tality of praise in the original is surely conveyed. A more subdued
tissue of Psalms 89:53; 135:21; 72-18-19 follows immediately:

> Blessed is THE ONE (Heb., "YHWH") eternally.
> Amen! Amen!
> Blessed is THE OMNIPRESENT ("YHWH"),
> dwelling in Jerusalem, Halleluyah!
> Blessed is THE MIGHTY ONE ("YHWH") divine,
> The God of Israel who alone works wonders,
> and blessed is the (Heb., "his") glorious name forever,
> and may God's glory fill the earth.
> Amen! Amen![21]

The *Havdalah* service to mark the departure of the Sabbath
opens with a summons to Elijah, the prophet of Tishbe in Gilead,
to come speedily, bringing on the Messiah, son of David. The
prayerbook renders the latter phrase "messianic days" and adds to
the charge of Elijah a composition by a woman rabbi which
declares that Miriam the prophet "will dance with us at the waters
of redemption" (*el mey hayeshu'a*; see Exodus 15:20-21).[22]
    The following is the way the prayer is said in English while the
cup of wine is raised, with its echoes of Is 12:2-3; Pss 3:9; 46:12;
84:13; 20:10; Est 8:16; Ps 116:13:

> Behold, my God of help,
> In whom I trust and tremble not.

Truly my strength and melody is Yah, THE ONE,
who is for me the source of help.
So draw, in joy, the waters
from the Fount of Help.
All help belongs to You.
Upon your people is your blessing. Let it happen!
With us is THE GREAT ONE of the Multitudes *(tsebaoth)* of Heaven,
happy is the human being who trusts in you!
REDEEMING ONE, extend your help.
Our Sovereign, answer us whenever we may call.
The Jews of old had light,
and happiness, and joy, and love—
may it be so for us!
My Cup of Help I raise,
and in the OMNIPRESENT'S name
I call.[23]

The consistent periphrastic rendering of the proper name of
Israel's God and even of the traditional spoken substitute when it
is encountered, Adonai ("my Lord"), will be hailed by most
Reconstructionist Jews and deplored by other Jews, even feminists
who would call their Judaism traditional. The same can be said of
the quality of English poetry and prose in these pages. But, of the
religious quality, the prayerfulness of the prayers, there can be no
doubt.

There are portions of the seven blessings of the festival *Amida*
said standing. They begin traditionally with three short steps forward and bowing left and right, "a reminder of our entry into the
divine presence." First, the introductory words from Psalm 51:17:

Open my lips, BELOVED ONE (Adonai, "my Lord"),
and let my mouth declare your praise.

Then comes a declaration of God's blessedness expressed
through Israel's ancestors. Three matriarchs, the wives of the traditional patriarchal three, are added:

1.   Blessed are you, the ANCIENT ONE ("YHWH"), our God, God
of our ancestors ("our fathers" and "our mothers"),

God of Abraham,	God of Sarah,
God of Isaac,	God of Rebekah,
God of Jacob,	God of Rachel
	and God of Leah

great, heroic awesome God, supreme divinity,
imparting (lit., "doer of") deeds of kindness, begetter of all;
mindful of the loyalty of Israel's ancestors,
bringing, with love, redemption to their children's children
for the sake of the divine name.[24]

Whenever the word *melek*, "King," appears for God, it is rendered "Sovereign" or "Regal One" so as not to attribute masculinity to deity. God is also called, as this blessing proceeds to an end, the shield of Abraham (*magen*, much later David's six-pointed star) and the help of Sarah:

> 2.   You are forever powerful, ALMIGHTY ONE, abundant in your saving acts. . . .
>   In loyalty you sustain the living, nurturing the life of every living thing, upholding those who fall, healing the sick, freeing the captive, and remaining faithful to all life held dormant in the earth. Who can compare to you, almighty God *(ba'al geburot)*, who can resemble you, the source of life and death, who make salvation *(yeshua)* grow?. . . .
> 3.   Holy are you. Your name is holy. And all holy beings hail you each day. Blessed are you, AWESOME ONE, the holy God.
> 4.   You sanctified the seventh day, your signature upon completion of the heavens and the earth. [Gen. 2:1-3 are then quoted in full.]
>   Our God, our ancient God, take pleasure in our rest. Enable us to realize holiness through your *mitzvot* (commandments, deeds of merit), give us our portion in your Torah, let us enjoy the good things of the world, and gladden us with your salvation. . . . Let all Israel, and all who treat your name as holy, rest upon this day. . . .
> 5.   Take pleasure, GRACIOUS ONE, in Israel your people; lovingly accept their fervent prayer. May Israel's worship always be acceptable to you. . . .
> 6.   We give thanks to you . . . our God . . . today and always. A firm, enduring source of life, a shield to us in time of trial, you are ever there, from age to age.
> 7.   Grant abundant peace eternally for Israel, your people. For you are the sovereign source of peace. . . . [B]less your people Israel, and all who dwell on earth. . . . with your peace. . . .

The Mourner's *Kaddish* is, like all similar prayers, a sanctification of God's Name *(Shem)*. It does not refer to the dead, but to the living, expressing the hope that God may "complete the holy realm *(malḥutey)* in your own lifetime, in your days, and in the days of all the house of Israel, quickly and soon." This realm is, of course, God's reign or rule to which a sanctified Israel submits. The lively Pharisee expectation that the dead will live again, which many Jews entertain, does not occur in the rendering of this ancient prayer. The Note attending the *Kaddish* mentions the custom of the mourners and those observing *Yahrzeit* (Yiddish, anniversary) to stand as it is recited and a list of the dead is read or, in more informal settings, added to orally by those in attendance. But, among the proposed readings, most of which feature remembrance of lives lived, one poet concludes his piece about birth and death with,

> But life is a journey,
> A sacred pilgrimage—
> To life everlasting.[25]

And another, addressed to her dead father,

> I will follow after you
> confident as a child
> toward the silent country
> where you went first
> so I would not feel a stranger there.
> And I will not be afraid.[26]

Koheleth provides the tone here, sending "man to his lasting home as mourners go about the streets; /Before the silver cord is snapped and the golden bowl is broken, /And the pitcher is shattered at the spring, and the broken pulley falls into the well, /And the dust returns to the earth as it once was, and the life breath returns to the God who gave it" (12:5), rather than Daniel's confident, "Many of those who sleep in the dust of the earth shall awake; some shall live forever, others shall be an everlasting horror and disgrace" (12:2), or the even greater assurance of the late written Is 26:19. The Reconstructionist prayerbook reminds us forcefully, by its numerous alternative versions to ancient texts, that there is not one Judaism, but many. Its Judaism is unstinting praise of God under every conceivable attribute, each of which became a divine name. God is rich in lifegiving, in mercy, in forgiveness. In turn, it is proper to address God as Just One, Beloved One, Compassionate, Eternal, the Many Named.

It was in August of 1967 that I came down the stairs of an airliner from Washington to Milwaukee, headed for the national Liturgical Week. As I stepped onto the airstrip, I recognized a bearded man from his photographs and greeted him, giving him my name. Abraham Joshua Heschel surprised me completely by saying: "Ah! I hear you're going to Temple." Not many Jewish academics, least of all Orthodox, keep track of the movements of Catholic academics. I was impressed. Days later at the event to which both of us had come, we stood in the wings of an open floor area where a local company of players was celebrating the gospel in a circus motif. He looked at me sadly as he regretted this modern departure from anything like Catholic ritual. I rather deplored it as art, but that was not his point.

That same autumn, I became the departmental colleague of Rabbi Robert Gordis, a spokesman for Conservative Judaism and chairman of the editorial committee that revised its prayerbook. More than once he expressed regret in my hearing at the passing of Latin in the Roman liturgy. He may have had in mind the struggle of American Jews to retain their own ancient tongue in prayer, or else it was simply his commitment to stability in the practice of any religion. Hebrew schools already enjoy better success in preparing their best and brightest to master the modern version of an ancient tongue than Catholic schools ever did with Latinity; possibly the reason for this was they stayed with Cicero and Virgil, seldom taking on the Vulgate or the liturgy. Whatever the case may be with a knowledge of Hebrew for prayer, the current regular gathering of Jews to pray is notably increased over fifty and even twenty-five years ago.

Before World War II in this country, Jews were only too happy to dialogue with Christians over antidefamation, real and perceived, over social issues, over the Zionist hope for a nation state. "Anything but religion," was the chief Jewish ground rule. Its well trained teachers and bureaucratic officers retained bitter memories of medieval public disputations between rabbis and friars that the rabbis were fated to lose. Since that time, interreligious dialogue between Christians and Jews has become a commonplace, although the exchange of serious discussion of prayer practices is still confined to the learned. There is mutual ignorance, but, whereas the Christians show a concern to be quit of theirs, the Jewish eye glazes over at any attempted exposition of a subject like Baptism, the Eucharist, or the nature of the Church. There is still the lively fear of enforced listening.

The one most important thing that has to be said about Jewish prayer is that more and more Jews are engaging in it. Interest in the United Jewish Appeal and concern for the state of Israel continue unabated, but the past few decades have seen a sharp increase in gatherings on the Sabbath, and for some the next day, to learn and to pray. The liturgies have an increasingly traditional character, although experts in Jewish worship admit that they are still drowned with words and only slowly recovering their talent for ritual. The Reform Judaism that Isaac Meyer Wise brought from Germany to Cincinnati and David Einhorn to Baltimore had a peculiarly American cast. Wise was a learned man and an organizer, but his son-in-law, Kaufmann Kohler, later at the Hebrew Union College he founded, was a theologian. So, too, was Einhorn. Both nineteenth century figures were infected by the German romanticism of men like Schiller and Goethe. The Reform movement abandoned the idea of a personal Messiah and put in its place a messianic age of charity and truth. Many congregations after 1885 adopted the forms of liberal Protestant worship — hymns, a soloist, an organ — and some even moved their services to Sunday. Disturbed by this trend, a number of Reform leaders in the east called Solomon Schechter from Cambridge

University in 1902 to be president of its Jewish Theological Seminary in New York. The learned biblical and talmudic scholars he assembled on that faculty formed the Conservativism that Schechter identified as the United Synagogue of America. The movement committed itself to restoring the dietary laws, the Hebrew language in traditional liturgical prayers, and loyalty to Torah and its historical exposition. Also in New York, meanwhile, a Sephardic Orthodox rabbi, named Henry Pereira Mendes, formed a Union of Orthodox Rabbis that founded a seminary to become Yeshiva College, later University. This more recent immigrant group, the Orthodox, had the largest constituency by the mid1930s, concentrated largely in the cities. The suburbanizing trend of U.S. Jewry after the Second World War brought many families to active adherence to the traditional faith their parents and grandparents had abandoned in the new land. With synagogue membership came something like the regular gentile church attendance, but, more importantly, a return to observant practices: circumcision and the *kippah* or headcovering for the men, modified dietary observance in the home, a Jewish education for the young, and notably public prayer in common in the old forms, with such Hebrew mastery as adults could achieve.

Increasingly, Jewish America is a praying community. Even those who gather once on the High Holydays and for Passover in spring, like their Christmas-Ash Wednesday-Palm Sunday-Easter counterparts, take those days very seriously to reinforce their Judaism. What the matching Church attendance means to Christians is anybody's guess.

NOTES

[1] *The Mishnah*, trans. Herbert Danby, D.D. (London: Oxford University Press, 1933), 4; P. Blackman, ed., *Mishnayoth* (7 vols.; London/New York: Judaica Press, 1951-63).

[2] See A. Z. Idelsohn's *Jewish Liturgy and Its Development* (New York: Schocken Books, 1975; first printing, 1932), 88-103.

[3] Kaufmann Kohler in *Hebrew Union College Annual I*, Cincinnati (1923), quoted in Idelsohn, 85.

[4] Ibid.

[5] See Heather A. McKay, *Sabbath and Synagogue. The Question of Sabbath Worship in Ancient Judaism* (Leiden, New York, Köln: E. J. Brill, 1994), 87; see also 42. Reviewed by the present writer in *Worship* 70 (July, 1996): 352-53. Cf. Lee I. Levine, "The Nature and Origin of the Palestinian Synagogue Reconsidered," *Journal of Biblical Literature*, 115/3 (Fall, 1996): 425-48, whose conclusions from an archaeological viewpoint are similar: "From the third century to the seventh a number of customs perpetuating the memory of the Jerusalem Temple were adopted. . . . [T]he destruction of the Temple . . . had a significant influence. . . . [I]t is also

likely that . . . [Christianity's] emphasis on the sanctity of church buildings . . . stimulated Jews . . . to define their place of worship more sharply
in terms of a 'holy' institution, a 'small sanctuary' " (446f.).

[6]McKay, 207f. McKay cites the tractate *Megillah* 4.1-6 and commentary
on it by P. Blackman, *Mishnayoth, II. Order Mo'ed* (New York: Judaica Press,
1963), 453-54. This tractate describes the proper way to read from the
book of Esther, but it gives more general information about the correct
sequence of readings on weekdays and sabbaths.

[7]Rabbi Joseph H. Hertz, *The Authorised Daily Prayer Book* (New York:
Bloch Publishing Company, 1948), 357.

[8]Described by Isidoro Kahn, Chief Rabbi of Livorno, "Jewish Sabbath,"
in *The Jewish Roots of Christian Liturgy*, ed. Eugene Fischer (New York:
Paulist Press, 1990), 128. Text in Hertz, 405. Prov. 31:10-31 is read on
Sunday 33 *in anno*, Year A, in the Roman *Lectionary*.

[9]B. Ber. 27^b - 28^a; Y. Ber. 4.1.

[10]See Tzvee Zahavy, "The Politics of Piety," in *The Making of Jewish and
Christian Worship*, ed. P. O. Bradshaw and L. A. Hoffman (Notre Dame, IN:
University of Notre Dame Press, 1991), 50.

[11]See Zahavy, 56-58; Idelsohn, 92-109.

[12]Zahavy, 62.

[13]Hertz, 949.

[14]Lawrence A. Hoffman, "The History, Structure, and Theology of
Jewish and Home Liturgy: An Overview," in *Liturgical Foundations of Social
Policy in the Catholic and Jewish Traditions*, ed. D. F. Polish and E. J. Fischer
(Notre Dame, IN: University of Notre Dame Press, 1983), 15f.

[15]*Against the Jews*, Homily I.1 (PG 48:844). Robert Wilken has translated
homilies I and 8 in Wayne A. Meeks and Robert L. Wilken, *Jews and
Christians in Antioch in the First Four Centuries of the Common Era*, SBL
Sources for Biblical Study 13 (Missoula, MT: Scholars Press, 1978), 86.

[16]Notably, Eric Werner, *The Sacred Bridge, Liturgical Parallels in Synagogue
and Early Church* (New York: Columbia University Press, 1959); first
Schocken paperback edition, 1970. On the Christian side, see W. Oester-
ley, *The Jewish Background of the Christian Liturgy* (Oxford, 1925); C. W.
Dugmore, *The Influence of the Synagogue on the Divine Office* (London,
1945).

[17]This essay has not, up to this point, featured differences among the
four groups in their prayer forms. Reference should be made to the
recent *Gates of Prayer* of Reform Judaism, with its elimination of certain
harsh locutions and archaic phrasing, and its cognate, the five volume
cycle of Reconstructionism. No mention has been made in these pages of
the many contemporary Passover *haggadoth* that are regularly published
or works like that of Marcia Sachs Littell and Sharon Weissman Gutman,
eds., *Liturgies on the Holocaust. An Interfaith Anthology* (Valley Forge, PA:
Trinity Press International, 1996). The Rabbinical Assembly of America
and the United Synagogue of America acted together as the publisher of
the 1946 *Sabbath and Festival Prayer Book*. Coming out of Conservative
Judaism, it is the book most widely used by congregations affiliated with
that movement. In a brief Foreword, the editors describe their principles
governing the omission and, at times, the expansion of ancient prayer-

book texts. It retains, however, passages like the ancient prayer on the Sabbath of the New Moon, lamenting the laying waste of "our city [and] our Sanctuary" because "we and our ancestors sinned against Thee," and says that "we cannot fulfill our obligations in Thy chosen House, the great and holy temple."

[18]Lawrence A. Hoffman, "Liturgical Basis for Social Policy: A Jewish View," in *Liturgical Foundations of Social Policy in the Catholic and Jewish Traditions,* 157.

[19]*Kol Haneshamah. Shabbath Vehagim* (Wyncote, PA: The Reconstructionist Press, 1994), 882 pages.

[20]Ibid., 230.

[21]Ibid.

[22]Ibid., 521.

[23]Ibid., 522.

[24]Ibid., 596-610.

[25]Ibid., 791.

[26]Ibid., 794.

Getting Real and Becoming No-Thing: Christians and the Buddhist Experience of Prayer

Mary Jo Meadow

My assigned topic, *Christians and the Buddhist Experience of Prayer*, is a bit startling. The Theravadan Buddhist tradition, from which I address you, does not use the concept of prayer. However, the forms of practice in Theravadan Buddhism easily qualify as prayer by Christian definitions of that term.

At the time of this writing, I have "sat" eleven three month retreats of Buddhist meditation, several one and two month ones, and a few shorter ones. Although I am also a scholar of Buddhist thought, most of what I have learned came from these long periods of intensive practice of Buddhist meditation. We call my approach to this essay "speaking from the cushion" instead of merely manipulating concepts. This method mirrors a cardinal Buddhist teaching — that conceptual thought is of little use for understanding spiritual truths. I now spend much of my time teaching insight practice, especially to Christians who want to learn it to enhance their Christian spiritual development.[1]

Basic Background of Buddhist Practice

History. We start with some history. Theravadan Buddhism is sometimes called the "primitive" Buddhism or the Hinayana Buddhism. The latter is a pejorative term that means "the lesser vehicle"; it is not liked by Theravadans. The Theravadan is the sole surviving school of the original Buddhism, based on the early Pali canon of Buddhist Scriptures. Later, Mahayana Buddhism developed additional Sanskrit Scriptures. When I say Buddhist in this essay, I am referring to the Theravadan tradition, unless otherwise stated.

The Buddha lived around 500 BCE. His teachings were given in India and some areas that are now in Nepal. The current stronghold of the Theravadan tradition is southeast Asia — principally Burma, Thailand, Sri Lanka, and Cambodia. By the time of the Christ, the Mahayana (greater vehicle) Buddhist tradition was beginning to develop. This traveled north to China, then through Korea to Japan. It flowered most strongly in China and Japan, taking on some flavor of Taoism and other traditions indigenous to the Far East. When Buddhist practice later traveled into Tibet, it merged with Tibetan folk religion to produce Tibetan Buddhism.

Major practices. Theravadan Buddhism is rather stark to Western tastes. There are virtually no communal rituals outside of chanting the basic moral precepts and taking refuge in the Buddha, the teachings, and the spiritual community. Some monasteries chant loving-kindness blessings at the last sitting of the evening. Sometimes monks chant *suttas* (sermons of the Buddha). Many Buddhist practitioners bow profoundly before the altar on entering a meditation hall and also to their teachers when they go for guidance.

Theravadan meditation is of two principal forms: concentrative and awareness or insight. The latter is the principal practice. The Pali word is *vipassana*, which means wide, clear, broad, "seeing through" — hence the translation as "insight." These two forms of meditation — concentrative and insight — constitute the major practices in Theravadan Buddhism that Christians could call prayer.

In concentrative practice, the meditation method most familiar to Christians, one chooses an object of attention and tries to hold the mind on it. Should thought start or the mind stray, one gently returns to the object of awareness — over and over again.

Buddhist monastics use various objects for concentrative practice. These include the elements, colors, parts of the body, decomposing corpses, virtues, and the Buddha. Teachers choose the most appropriate object for each meditator, based on that person's general development and attitudes. Outside the monasteries, the principal form of concentrative practice is *brahmavi-hara* (divine dwelling places) practice. This practice cultivates caring and compassionate attitudes toward all beings.

In insight meditation, the principal practice, one tries to be aware of as much of one's experience as it is possible. This is not just scattered attention or an unfocused state. There are very disciplined methods for accomplishing this panawareness so that very detailed attention is given to even minute aspects of experience. The Buddha taught that this is the practice that leads people to liberation. It brings both psychological and spiritual insights to the practitioner. Eventually, it develops the wisdom that is spiritual fruition.

We will look at each of these two forms of practice as prayer and discuss what they give us, what they teach us, with the major emphasis on insight practice. The focus with insight practice will be on five of the many major gifts it offers: learning to listen, emptying the unconscious mind, analysis of suffering and the overcoming of suffering, "spiritual realism," and expanding identity from the narrow limits of self to encompass the universe.

Loving-Kindness Practice

We first briefly discuss the *brahmavihara* practices as an example of Buddhist concentrative meditation. *Brahma* literally means noble, and *vihara* means dwelling place or abode. *Brahmavihara* is often translated "abode of the gods." These practices, which develop *agape* love, come the closest to common forms of Christian prayer. They could easily be classified as intercessory prayer, although they are not addressed to any deity.

These practices develop beautiful states of mind and produce deeply absorbed concentration. The taste of the *brahmaviharas* can make one feel as if one is already in heaven on earth. This bliss is far beyond the delights of grosser pleasures. Buddhist monk and meditation master Mahasi Sayadaw said that these states refer to noble living or "living in the exercise of good will."[2] They are called the "illimitables" because one develops them toward all living beings without exception; this gives them a potentially limitless range of influence.

The background of loving-kindness. *Metta* or loving-kindness practice is the first and basic of the four related *brahmavihara* practices. When one day some disciples came running to the Buddha in fear, he taught them the way to live fearlessly among those who frightened them. Here is the story.

The Buddha's monks always spent the three months of each rainy season in a fixed location, doing intensive meditation practice. One year some went together to a distant forest with huge trees under which they could take shelter. The tree demons who lived there were displeased by the monks' presence and tried to scare them away. They harassed them in various ways, often creating very frightening visions and noises at night. Finally, the monks could take it no longer, and they ran back to the Buddha for help. The Buddha taught them loving-kindness practice, telling them to radiate universal love to all sentient beings everywhere.[3] The monks went back to the forest and obeyed the Buddha's instruction. The tree demons were so captivated by the love being sent them that they ceased tormenting the monks and even began to serve them so that the monks could do their meditation practice more easily.

Compassion. The second *brahmavihara* is compassion. This very important attribute is one of the two "wings" of Buddhism, the other being wisdom. *Brahmavihara* practice develops compassion; insight practice, the major practice of Theravadan Buddhism, develops wisdom. However, compassion can also flow from one's willingness to see the suffering in one's own life as it manifests in insight practice.

Compassion *(karuna)* is defined as the quivering of the heart in response to another's suffering. Compassionate beings want to eliminate others' suffering when they encounter it. They cannot bear to remain unengaged when they see suffering. One need not always *do* something; not every instance of suffering calls for active involvement. Sometimes one acts, sometimes just compassionately enters into the suffering.

Compassion is very different from pity or anger over suffering. Pity condescends; it sets itself apart from the suffering and "looks down" on it. Anger dulls awareness of the sheer fact of suffering and makes sharing it compassionately impossible. Attempts to develop compassion have failed if one's efforts produce sorrow, anger, or pity. These states sometimes mask as compassion, but are actually its dangerous "near enemies."

Compassion is aroused by seeing suffering in others. It directly combats cruelty and succeeds when it ends cruelty. Even moderate development of compassion makes behaving cruelly or deliberately inflicting harm on any being impossible. Compassion has its own special and paradoxical quality of joy. It celebrates the delicate savor of human bondedness. In acutely feeling another's suffering, one shares the happiness of human solidarity.

Practitioners can come to feel compassion for those who have wronged them personally because of the great suffering such people have created for themselves. One also can feel compassion for those who create havoc in the world at large. People who prey on others, who murder, steal, cheat, rape, or otherwise abuse others, not only inflict suffering on others, but also on themselves. Often their bad behavior comes out of already existing intense suffering. A measure of one's compassion is how much one can feel it for such people.

Unhappy or anxious people may be uncomfortable to be around, but they are in pain. People with unbridled desires or consuming ambitions also suffer. Being trapped in addictions or other bad habits can be agonizing. Once compassion develops, one easily sees the suffering in others' annoying habits or quirks. When these things draw compassion rather than irritation, the practice has done its work.

In some Buddhist traditions, meditators can take the "*bod-hisattwa* vow*." They vow not to enjoy liberation until they can bring all beings with them. Compassion makes them unable to go to their final reward in isolation, and they are willing to continue in rounds of rebirth until all are saved. Compassionate awareness of the ultimate oneness of all beings makes individual salvation meaningless to them.

Sympathetic joy. The third *brahmavihara* is sympathetic joy, rejoicing in the good someone else has. The characteristic of sympathetic joy is gladness when seeing the success of others. The most important kind of success is spiritual, but sympathetic joy should not be limited to that. One becomes able to be happy for others on the terms in which they define happiness, not judging the source of their happiness. Sympathetic joy is considered the hardest *brahmavihara*; human nature does not easily celebrate someone else's having something we may want for ourselves. Even the smallest taste of sympathetic joy is an extremely beautiful feeling.

Sympathetic joy directly combats envy. When others' good makes one happy, resentment and envy have no place. When sympathetic joy is well developed, one can see others' good without becoming envious; seeing their success causes gladness to arise. Its "near enemy," which looks like it but opposes it, is unfounded merriment, getting caught up in frivolous excitement. Sympathetic joy is successfully developed when it eliminates aversion toward others. When one cherishes others' good as if it were one's own, one feels caring and protective of them. In this way, aversion towards others is first diminished and then vanquished.

The Pali word for sympathetic joy — *mudita* — means rejoicing and getting pleased. It is sometimes translated as gladness. When others' success truly pleases one, one is delighted frequently — whenever one hears of or sees another's happiness. While I was doing intensive *mudita* practice, this reflection came to me: The sun never sets in one place, but it rises in another; when I am happy for those who have sunshine, my own life will never lack it.

Equanimity. The fourth *brahmavihara*, equanimity, is by far the hardest for Westerners to understand. It asks one to remain unmoved by the outcomes, or lack of outcomes, of all one's other *brahmavihara* practice. It asks one to accept, without a negative reaction, whatever happens in one's own and others' lives. It also directly combats what the West calls codependency.

Technically, *brahmavihara* equanimity is one form of what Buddhists call neutrality of mind. The Pali word *(upekkha)* literally means "there is the middleness." This attitude of impartiality and balance prevents bias or preference. When directed toward human beings, it becomes the *brahmavihara* of equanimity. It looks on all beings, and what happens to them, without any prejudices or preference, free of all discrimination.

However, equanimity is not indifference, which is its "near enemy." Were it indifference, one could not feel loving-kindness, compassion, and sympathetic joy. Equanimity also does not mean failing to act when action is called for or accepting all manner of evils without doing anything about them. Equanimity leads one to act out of wholesome motives rather than out of unskillful reaction to events.

Equanimity prevents excesses and keeps loving-kindness, compassion, and sympathetic joy in proper bounds. It also helps one understand that, whatever one might wish for other beings, one cannot control their outcomes. These are determined by their actions, according to the choices they make. Equanimity keeps one's life and relationships in balance. When one is balanced, one does not try forcefully to make the world, other people, or their lives conform to one's own wishes.

Components of Metta Practice

One does *metta*, the loving-kindness practice, by sending blessings to other beings. One sits comfortably and uses a series of phrases to call down these blessings. There are three main parts to the practice: the words or phrases used, the meaning of the words, and some kind of sense or image of the target being to whom the blessings are sent.[4]

Feelings. Feeling emotions of love when doing this practice is not important. Intending the meaning of the phrases is important. Even if one is not sure of really meaning to want the blessings for a particular being, it is enough if one can want to want it. Training the mind to universal love is not always easy, especially for people for whom one has well developed animosities. That is not a problem in the practice. The important point is that one is choosing to train the mind this way and accepting one's limitations. If done faithfully, the practice will have a positive effect on attitudes.

Targets. This practice always begins with oneself. The Buddha said that one can look the wide world over and not find anyone more deserving of one's loving-kindness than oneself; he also said that one who properly loves oneself can never intentionally harm another.[5] When one ponders the great Christian commandment, "Love your neighbor as yourself," one can appreciate this wisdom. If one cannot love oneself properly, what does this say of how one can love others?

After work with oneself, the classical method goes through a series of other personal targets: a benefactor, a friend, a neutral person, and a difficult person. These targets progress from beings easier to love to those who are difficult. Practice then moves to universal groupings that include all sensate beings. Some of these are in pairs, such as all male and all female beings and all saintly and all worldly beings. If approached carefully, the practice can be very helpful in dealing with difficult relationships. One must be careful, though, not to brutalize oneself by trying to force immediate attitudinal change toward very difficult beings — such as with someone who has seriously mistreated oneself. The practice is also not a substitute for dealing with the emotions created by being abused.

Blessings. Since the loving-kindness is to be impartial, one works with the same blessings for all beings. The traditional blessings are very good for that since they are concerned with universal, basic needs of all beings. A common translation of them is: "May you be safe from inner and outer danger; May you be happy and peaceful; May you be strong and healthy; May you tend your life easily." The practice is based on repeating the blessings; repetition is a helpful method for developing concentration and changing mental attitudes. When doing the practice, one repeats the words of the blessings while focusing on their meaning and holding onto some sense of the target being to whom one is sending the blessing. All three components must be present: words, to sustain the focus; the meaning of the words, to change attitudes; and the target being, to direct the loving energy.

A technique note. Keeping the phrases going is very important. When one does concentrative practice, letting go of the tool — be it phrases or a sacred word or any other object — too soon brings problems. Many Christians do not seem to understand this when they practice sacred word prayer; they let go of their word too soon.

If one lets go of the tool before concentration is well developed, thinking starts almost immediately. If concentration is good, one of two things tends to happen. First, one might fall into a deeply concentrated, but somewhat foggy or amorphous, state of bliss. Some even interpret this as the presence of God. This state feels wonderful, and people are reluctant to let go of it, but it is **not** meditation. Meditation requires clear, sharp awareness. Another problem is that contents of the unconscious may erupt when the mind goes empty. This has frightened some people so much that they abandoned meditation. Since sacred word prayer does not provide a method for dealing with such eruptions, one must not leave "space" for them to occur.

Buddhist wisdom says to let go of the tool — phrases or sacred word — only when it becomes impossible to say it. This is echoed in Christian wisdom. Saint Teresa of Avila called it "foolishness" when people try to let their minds go empty; she advised religious superiors to give more work and less prayer time to those who did this, thinking it put them in a high state of prayer. The author of *The Cloud of Unknowing* said that the prayer he described — "empty" prayer — was "by invitation only." The "invitation" seems to be the absolute inability of the mind to repeat the sacred word.[6]

Fruits and Extension of Practice

Loving-kindness practice produces great happiness. As one willingly lets go of animosities to call down blessings universally, one gets happier and happier. As the feeling of loving-kindness grows, so does the bliss.

Love of humanity (agape). *Metta* sounds a lot like *agape* love. They seem to be essentially the same thing. Both are an attitude of universal friendliness and good will toward all beings without exception. The Theravadan tradition offers a solid method for developing *metta/agape* love in one's heart — one that has proved itself for twenty-five hundred years. Buddhist *metta* includes not only human beings, but also animal beings and beings in other realms of existence — like the Christian heaven and hell.

This love esteems others and is concerned for their welfare beyond any personal gain that one can get out of it. The general love of humankind is a sense of responsibility, care, respect, and knowledge that wishes to further the life of any other human being. It is characterized by nonexclusiveness and assumes the basic equality and identity of all persons in spite of incidental differences in status, abilities, and personal development. It combines care and creativity, for, by loving the unworthy, one sometimes stimulates them to become worthy.[7]

Sharing merit. A related practice, which may sound to Christians like praying for the souls in purgatory, is called sharing merit. Merit is said to make one "shine within." Such acts as virtue, piety, goodness, and spiritual practice create merit, which one can share with any other being, living or dead.

To share merit, Buddhists use a simple formula: "May the fruits of my (generosity, virtue, spiritual practice) be for the good of (my daughter, John Doe, all beings everywhere)." They simply name the meritorious action and the person(s) with whom they wish to share. Sometimes they go through a litany, repeating the phrase a number of times, naming a different meritorious action each time, sharing merit with the same or different people.

Understanding Insight *(Vipassana)* Practice

Now insight practice. Since *vipassana* (insight) meditation requires no specific belief commitments, it is compatible with any other religious affiliation or loyalty. This disciplined method of continuing and alert attention uncovers, in orderly sequence, experiences hidden from awareness — including body sensations, emotions, memories, and spiritual insights. Practitioners attain a broadened perspective and, in deeper practice, have experiences that parallel the stages of spiritual unfolding as outlined by many Christian mystics. My major scholarly work with the practice is demonstrating the way it is an excellent method for the spirituality of Carmelite mystic, Saint John of the Cross.[8]

Preparation. To do insight practice, one tries to establish an upright posture that can be held easily without putting excessive strain on any muscle groups. The reason for sitting upright is purely pragmatic. Lying down is conducive to sleep. Leaning back against anything often requires straining muscles to hold the head erect.

Many Buddhists begin their meditation with the invocation, "May I be surrendered to the *Dhamma*." This Pali word *"Dhamma"* (*Dharma* in Sanskrit) is a very rich one. It means eternal law, Truth, the path, Reality, the foundation of all realities, the way, the pattern underlying all that is real, that which supports and upholds us, that which leads us home, the teachings, and so on. Similarities to the Christian *Logos*, or Word of God, as well as the Holy Spirit are obvious. On our *Silence and Awareness* retreats, Christians often begin each sitting with an act of surrender to the Holy Spirit.

Form. Insight meditation is an intense form of practice. It emphasizes interior and exterior silence to facilitate awareness of one's total experiencing. On retreats, one spends all one's waking hours in meditation — sitting practice, walking practice, and the practice method used while involved in necessary self care, such as eating, showering, dressing, and toilet. Meals are taken in silence. Retreatants are told to leave reading material at home and not to plan on journaling, problem solving, or interpersonal interaction. They refrain from speech, reading, music, writing, and voluntary thinking to deepen their silence and awareness.

A *vipassana* retreat is about the opposite of what most Christians expect from prayer or retreat. They often go to fill themselves up with good ideas, beautiful liturgies, and fine reso- lutions. Because of its starkness, insight practice brings one to a greater depth than most retreats can. Experiences are sometimes intense, but the method provides ways of managing this, and indi- viduals "open" to different experiences as their capacity to handle them grows.

The precision of method is certainly an important feature of this practice. Equally important is the discouragement of analysis and speculation — for one must subscribe to no belief items to do the practice, and there are no gods or other metaphysical entities one must be willing to invoke. This makes the practice available to everyone without any conflict with whatever existing religious loy- alties he/she might hold. The method is simply a precise way of paying fine grained, continuous awareness to all one's experiences of mind and body, including many different mental and emotion- al states. The practice is so simple, yet it yields the highest stages of spiritual unfolding as defined by the world's major spiritual traditions — both Eastern and Western.

Vipassana as Prayer of Listening

Saint Teresa of Avila defined prayer as a conversation with one who we know loves us. This understanding of prayer is quite com- mon among spiritually minded Christians.

Understanding Listening Prayer

For many Christians, prayer consists of reciting formally worded prayers or, for those who have a more developed sense of intimacy in prayer, telling God the news or asking God for assis- tance of some kind. Some may wonder how sitting watching breath, body experiences, and mind states (emotions, moods, awareness) can be considered prayerful.

A conversation usually implies two way interaction. If one per- son hogs the floor, one might have a monologue or a diatribe, but one does not have a conversation. To have a conversation, one must be able to listen as well as to speak. When one is faced with one who knows more than one does, who has more to offer than one has, who is one's superior, one profits more by choosing the silence of listening rather than by working at getting one's own words in. How much more true this should be of prayer! Contemplatives have long said that a much higher kind of prayer is listening. How much better off one is, the mystics say, to become still to know God.

Vipassana meditation "empties" one of roles, voluntary experiences, and the other "trappings" of ordinary daily life to make one "available" to God. *Vipassana* practice teaches people the way to become very still. It teaches them the way to listen. It guides practitioners in letting go of the noisy busyness of their mind-chatter, of craving particular experiences in prayer, of wanting to be in charge of their conversation with God. It teaches them the way simply to be there, listening.

Vipassana teaches one the way to be surrendered to the purifying action of the Holy Spirit. It makes one empty of all the things the mystics said must be emptied out to be able to receive God's communication of God Godself.[9] It is an excellent method for being receptive to the purification that many Christian mystics say is necessary for spiritual growth, for the purity of heart that can "see" God. One becomes docile, pliable, before the Spirit.

Fruits of Stillness

Something of what is first communicated to meditators is self knowledge, which many mystics have said is the necessary road to God. One cannot know God if one does not know self. Since one already knows what one is comfortable knowing about oneself, most of this self knowledge is painful. But, it is necessary to see. If one is faithful in listening to this, one is shown even more — getting into the subtle recesses of one's deeply ingrained resistance to purification of one's being.

God then goes on to show even more — to fill one with the gifts of the Holy Spirit, revealing understanding of things earthly and heavenly, even the things of God Godself. Christian mystics have explained that, as one is more and more emptied out, one can be more and more filled with God. *Vipassana* disposes one to this emptiness; it is a way to stay empty before God's action.

When people stay truly empty and let God work on and in them, God more and more purifies them of the discordant tendencies in their minds and the wrongful inclinations of their hearts that keep them from God. The more one is willing, the more will God respond and bring one to the union of wills that transforms one's being. John of the Cross says that very few are those who are willing to be radically surrendered before God, and to stay surrendered when the going gets hard.[10] *Vipassana* is a method for staying in surrender.

What is the goal? To stay receptive enough in the conversation with God that one is pure receptivity — so that nothing is held in the heart that is contrary to God's presence. As one empties out, God "inflows." John of the Cross speaks of this as a transformation that is a union of likeness with God.[11] When there is only God with all else emptied out, all knowing, all loving, and all experience are that of God. In its substance, the soul clings only to God.

Suffering and Overcoming Suffering

The Buddha has often been quoted as saying, "I teach one thing and one thing only: suffering and the overcoming of suffering."[12] He precisely analyzed the causes of suffering, what keeps beings trapped in it, and the way one can free oneself. Buddhist meditation reveals the specific chains of cause and effect that bind beings in suffering. It also clearly shows the places of potential freedom that the Buddha pointed out.

Causes of Suffering

Quite simply, suffering is caused by clinging, by strong attachments. The Buddha listed five major objects to which beings cling, creating suffering for themselves. Buddhist meditation shows the way they bind beings.

Sense desires. First is sense desires. The Buddha said people cling to these out of fear or greed. They think, "I need this," or "I must have this." They feel empty, so they eat or drink too much, or distract themselves with some other momentary pleasure. If one deeply fears doing without these distractions, one may even lie, cheat, or steal to get them. Clinging to such things, the Buddha said, is like clutching a red-hot iron ball. One knows they are hurting oneself; one knows they bring pain rather than real joy, yet one stupidly refuses to let go.

A very effective monkey trap is used in southeast Asian countries. They hollow out a coconut through a small hole just big enough for a monkey to put in its open hand. On the back side, the coconut is firmly attached to a tree or stake. Then, they put a small piece of banana in the hole. A monkey comes along, smells the banana, reaches in, and closes its fist over it. When it tries to pull out its hand, it cannot, because the opening is too small for the closed fist. All the monkey must do to be free is to let go of the banana. But, it does not do that. When the trappers come, there sits the monkey, imprisoned by its own greed. How often people behave like the monkey, tightly holding onto something that has enslaved them but gives no real satisfaction, yet refusing to "let go!" Greed for bits of banana or pieces of tinsel locks beings into bondage; sense pleasure has enslaved them.

Rites and rituals. Another big trap, according to the Buddha, is clinging to rites and rituals. Many people believe that simply going through the motions of certain religious rituals guarantees salvation. The Buddha vigorously attacked this idea, pointing out that magic does not work, that spiritual life involves the hard work of purifying conduct and mind. Jesus also taught that only the pure of heart can see God.

The Buddha would say that those who believe that going to Mass and Communion for nine successive first Fridays of the month guarantees salvation are clinging to rites and rituals. Those who think saying a novena guarantees a certain benefit, or that visiting a particular shrine will make certain things happen, are clinging to rites and rituals. They are expecting from activities something they are not able to deliver. God is not magically commanded by human actions. Even sacraments are not a magician's act; they simply celebrate what already is.

Heavenly rewards. A third clinging the Buddha discussed is wanting the rewards of a blissful afterlife. Buddhist cosmology describes many realms of existence, including delightful heaven realms. The pleasures of some are much like the way some Christians consider heaven, refined sense pleasures with unending delight. To make this the objective is to fall short of the ultimate goal: life in God Godself. It is preferring the gifts of God to God.

Buddhists also define higher heavens, beyond the senses, with extremely blissful states of mind. These match other Christian understandings of heaven, and they, too, can be objects of clinging. They also fall short of the true goal, of final, ultimate joy. Over and again, the Buddha explained that anything other than *nibbana* is a passing satisfaction that will not bring lasting happiness. *Nibbana* is the Buddha's term for the Ultimate Reality, which can be considered one understanding of God as our final end.

Opinions. A fourth mistake is clinging to opinions. Many people have unfortunately been taught that clinging to opinions is virtuous. They consider it a great strength to hold some viewpoints so strongly that nothing will change their minds. They like to consider their opinions invincible.[13] Since some Christians feel that clinging to religious opinions is appropriate, it is a bit jarring when the Buddha says to let go of opinions. Let us look at this more closely.

All people are "victims" of those who had hold of their minds when they were young and vulnerable. Most people were taught the "correct" opinions to have about almost everything. However, just *what* these correct opinions were varies greatly from person to person, depending on who their caretakers were. One's early authorities pass on the training they got, so young children are given various answers about what to believe, about which opinions are true. All human beings are very prone to consider their own opinions the best simply because they are theirs. They usually fail to see the folly of clinging to them.

The misery that other people's clinging to opinions causes can usually easily be seen. Religious fundamentalism, with its insistence that its religious positions are superior to those of others, has made life unsafe for millions of people around the globe across history. Many people can more easily see this in traditions other than their own, such as mideastern Muslim fundamentalism. However, Christians must not forget its presence in both our history and today. Even the medieval Inquisition is still alive today under another name.

One of my all time favorite cartoons shows a Crusader high on a big white horse, holding his spear at the throat of an Arab spread eagled on the ground. The caption reads: "Suddenly I'm very interested in this Christianity of yours. Tell me more."[14] Is it not true that, across human history, more blood has been shed over differing religious understandings than it has been over any other cause? We have only to look at today's world; not only does it occur between faiths — like the Muslims and Hindus in India, but also between different groups within the same faith. Witness the Catholics and Protestants in Northern Ireland, and the Sunni and Shi'ite Muslims in the Mideast.

Theology itself can be the problem. Psychologist Gordon Allport explained the way some religious ideas contain theological invitations to bigotry.[15] Doctrines of revelation claim exclusive possession of the truth and authority for interpreting it. Dissenters are seen as threats to the common good. People thus justify, as a service to their deity, mistreatment of others — aggressive proselytizing, denying others freedom of conscience, even torture and death for the sake of their souls!

Doctrines of election even more clearly divide an ingroup from an outgroup. If the deity has specially chosen some people for salvation or as agents for divine work in the world, surely their opinions should prevail in any disagreement; they are, after all, God's chosen people! If *God* has decided who is important, how can you argue with that?

Allport's final invitation to bigotry is theocracy — having the religious opinions and moral standards of one group be the secular law of the land. This mentality leads to legal persecution of those who differ, to holy wars, to wedding nationalistic and religious interests, and to invoking the name of God to justify exercising unjust power over others.

Self sense. A fifth clinging is clinging to self, to the idea of oneself as a separate entity. We discuss this very difficult Buddhist understanding later in more detail. Here, we will look at it only in terms of self absorption, egoism, self centeredness. Massive narcissistic self absorption governs many lives, with everything referred to ego.

Most people operate much of the time as if they are the center of the universe and everything revolves around them. They often seek their greatest joy in things with a focus on self: their bodies, their health, their appearance, their intelligence, their talents, and so on. They make self actualization the goal of life, usually meaning things that build up ego, that make one feel important or superior.

Even when one turns attention to spiritual life, one gets caught up in fascination with one's own psyche. A major obstacle in *vipassana* practice is becoming so entranced by what one starts learning about oneself that one quits doing the practice as taught. One prefers to gaze in "adoration" at oneself, getting lost in memories, emotions, and self analysis.

This does not mean one should abandon ego strength, the capacity to function with psychological effectiveness. It does not mean one should not have good self esteem. Buddhist teachings emphasize the need for proper self love. However, when one is truly comfortable with oneself, one transcends the excessive concern about personal functioning in which many people are trapped. There is enormous egoism in guilt, self blame, feelings of inferiority or superiority, depression, and scrupulosity; all these keep attention excessively focused on oneself.

Psychology of the Problem

The Buddha clearly detailed the trap in which beings find themselves. Interestingly, his formulation of the problem mirrors the teachings of contemporary behavioral psychology on conditioning. However, the Buddha's teachings differ in one radically important point: he taught that one can break the chain of conditioning, that one can become free of it.

Dependent arising. The Buddha's teaching on dependent arising elaborated the way the law of *karma*, of moral cause and effect, works.[16] The bottom line is that one will continue to be reborn and to suffer until one frees oneself from desires that lead to poor choices. One must stop choosing mind states, speech, and behavior that create suffering for oneself and others. To stop making such choices, one must break the chains of conditioning that bind one. Those who do not accept the notion of rebirth can still see these factors at work in any given present life.

Here are the crucial elements of bondage and becoming free of it. Given an existence created by previous choices made, one has various experiences. These experiences impinge with a feeling-tone — a quality of pleasantness, unpleasantness, or neutrality. Feeling-tone is a karmic consequence that one cannot alter. The quality of one's experiences is created by the mind one has developed in the past.

Beings come conditioned to react to pleasantness with greed; they want to hold onto pleasant experience. They try to get more pleasant experiences for themselves. Behavioral psychology confirms that organisms will work for reinforcement or satisfying conditions. If one can control reinforcements in an organism's environment, one can control its behavior.

Beings also come conditioned to react to unpleasantness with aversion. They want to avoid it or strike out at it; they are sad when experiencing it. They do whatever they can to get rid of unpleasantness. Behavioral psychology similarly explains the way conditioning regarding unpleasantness controls behavior. Organisms will do what is necessary to remove unpleasantness. They can even be conditioned to do what will remove even the threat of unpleasantness before it occurs.

When experience is neutral, one tends to space out, become bored, ignore what is going on. In this way, one puts oneself in voluntary ignorance. Beings attend more easily to the strong meat of pleasantness and unpleasantness; they grip the attention.

The basic problem, then, is that beings are conditioned to grasp the pleasant, react aversively to the unpleasant, and tune out neutral experience. Any time one desires, based on pleasantness or unpleasantness, one is in a very unhelpful attitude. It is a first step toward actual behavioral transgression. The Buddhist viewpoint is not different from a Christian one. Jesus pointed out that the problem is what lurks in the heart, for that manifests as speech and behavior. However, Buddhist meditation practice gives us experiential understanding of the specific points of trappedness and possible liberation.

The points of freedom. The major point of freedom lies in the link between feeling-tone and the reaction to it. The conditioning, the automatic spill over we have just described, is the trappedness that keeps one attached to wrong choices. The liberating task is to be with pleasantness without grasping after it, with unpleasantness without pushing it away or striking out at it, and to stay fully attentive to neutral experience. Buddhist meditation makes one very sensitive to feeling-tone. Being highly aware of, and willing to experience, feeling-tone can eventually break the conditioned reaction to it.

If, however, one has moved from feeling-tone to an unwholesome state of mind, one can still stop oneself before indulging in open, harmful behavior. An intention to act will arise before action itself takes place. If one sees intentions clearly, one can let unskillful urges go by without acting on them; one counters them with other intentions. This prevents transgression, or behavioral impurity. Meditation practice also helps one be able to do this.

Overcoming Suffering

Buddhists have a helpful road map of three different levels at which spiritual practice purifies beings. Each brings a corresponding freedom from suffering and its own unique kind of happiness.

Behavior. First is overt conduct — the things one actually says and does. The five major precepts of Buddhist practice are similar to moral codes in all the world's major religions. They go a bit further regarding some behaviors.

The first precept is not killing — and this includes animals, not only animals people like to touch and pet, but also insects or any life form. Developing such reverence for life prevents many occasions of mental pain. It leads to wanting to foster the well being of all beings.

The second precept is not to take what is not given. It includes refraining from stealing, but seems to go further. One does not borrow anything without its being offered, or would not assume the right to use any goods unless it was clearly meant to be for one's use. In working with this precept, one also becomes increasingly sensitive about owning property that one is not actively using, especially when so many others in the world are in need or want.

The third precept is avoiding sexual misconduct. The teachings do not have many firm statements about what constitutes sexual misconduct beyond ruling out sex by or with someone in a commitment to a third party and sex with those incapable of giving free consent — such as children, the mentally impaired, or prisoners. Sexual misconduct is simply defined as using sexuality in a way that causes hurt or harm to oneself or someone else. Much is implied in this; it certainly rules out all dishonesty, manipulation, force, deceit, trickery, irresponsibility, and so on, in sexual behavior. Keeping this precept would stop unwanted pregnancies and the spread of sexually transmitted disease.

The fourth precept is to avoid wrong speech. The most important wrong speech is lying. Also considered wrong speech is speech that foments discord or disharmony among people, speech that is harsh or unkind unless a very good outcome obviously requires that another person be spoken to harshly, and, finally, idle speech that is simply a waste of time and has no useful purpose. Affectionate talk between intimates to build relationship is not considered idle speech. However, people so often just rattle on for no purpose at all, just filling silence or passing time. Deliberate lying and causing division among people are the main forms of gross immorality in this precept; they are the behaviors that absolutely must be given up immediately.

The fifth precept is to avoid the use of intoxicants, of any substance that alters consciousness or mood, dulls awareness, or causes heedlessness. Medication prescribed by a doctor and necessary for health is permitted, even if it does alter mood. Caffeine is also allowed.

Keeping the precepts of morality takes care of the transgressional level of impurity. Being able to clearly see intentions in the mind before they propel action makes keeping the precepts possible. Such purity brings the great happiness of freedom from guilt, blame, and remorse. Being moral is also prerequisite for deeper spiritual practice. So long as behavior is discordant, one cannot hope for mental cleansing.

Mental contents. Even when conduct is pure, the mind can still harbor much that is unwholesome — coveting, envy, resentment, self pity, impatience, and so on. The second level of purification is from such obsessive impurities. Since all transgressions are first thoughts or states in the mind, those who prevent obsessive impurity do not transgress. Eventually, meditation practice shows one that all mind states themselves are also choices. If one sees feeling-tone clearly enough, one realizes that one chooses reaction to it. When one stops allowing unwholesome mind states, one avoids the obsessive level of impurity, mental impurity. The type of mind created is clearer and purer, less and less inclined to choices that produce suffering. This brings great peace of mind, the second level of happiness.

Latent tendencies. There is still a third level of impurity to deal with — that of more hidden, deeply embedded tendencies — the latent tendencies of mind that draw one toward obsessional or transgressive impurity when there is sufficient provocation. Buddhists say these tendencies are fruits or residues of past choices, latent karmic seeds. Christians might call them the residual effects of original and personal sin.

The Buddha said: "Dig up the root of craving. . . . As a tree with firm, uninjured roots, though cut down, grows up again, so when latent craving is not rooted out suffering again and again arises."[17] One cannot directly attack this level of impurity, but willing work at levels one *can* touch and doing meditation practice eventually bring purity at this level. Only deep, purgative meditative experience removes impurity of this level. While one cannot bring about one's own full healing, one must make oneself available for it, and Buddhist meditation accomplishes that. This purification brings the happiness of touching *nibbana* — or, in Christian terms, knowing God.

Emptying the Unconscious Mind

All beings have some unfinished business lying beneath the surface of life, unfinished business encouraging and sustaining unwholesome states of mind. They torment one and cloud the heart's ability to know God. When not recognized, they can easily lead one into various unskillful actions. More than just understanding the chain of behavior just discussed, one can also become aware of the torments *(kilesas)* in one's own mind. Meditation practices root out even deeply buried mental debris.

Some people are aware of traumas, such as physical or sexual abuse, or of losses and bereavements they have suffered, but have cut off the emotional experience of them. Some have pushed from awareness their own past harmful or discordant behavior. Sometimes one is completely unaware of this unfinished business, and sometimes one knows of it, but is not emotionally connected with it. Many people manage to "keep down" a lot of fear or anger or sadness or boredom, but it still colors perception and behavior.

Uncovering

Insight meditation is designed to draw up such content and has a method that allows the meditator to manage it. Unfinished business lying barely submerged below awareness often surfaces quickly in *vipassana* practice. One may also recall much from the past that was not taken seriously at the time. One ought not be alarmed by this; the practice method handles the impact of such experiences. Also, the meditator must realize that the practice cannot make one feel angry, sad, bored, and so on. It reveals only what is already there, aspects of oneself with which one has not yet fully dealt. All unfinished business, if one does not become fully aware of it and work through it, leaves its mark. This brokenness then tends to make thought, speech, and behavior discordant; it lodges in the hearts as the impurities we have discussed.

This is true of damage inflicted on people by others as well as their own past poor choices. Damage others have done can be considered as each person's own unique burden of original sin. In a very real way, people *do* carry each others' burdens; each child bears his or her parents' mistakes. Some may consider it terribly unfair that one must deal with the way others have warped one's being. But, that is just the way things are. All beings are in this together, and mutual forgiveness is an important part of the path.

All persons have been "bent" by their experiences, and each must deal with the marks they left. When this brokenness — self or other inflicted — surfaces in meditation practice, one accepts it by simply being willing to see it clearly. One works with it by doing the practice according to the method taught. In willingly experiencing one's own brokenness and incompleteness lies the beginning of its healing. This is the task of each unique life.

Unwholesome Contents

The Buddha detailed the common unwholesome states of mind, drawing distinctions that are precise and illuminating. A listing of fourteen major impurities of mind appears in several locations in the Scriptures.[18] We will look at them under the headings of the Christian seven capital sins as they manifest in spiritually minded people. The Buddhist understandings tend to emphasize the elements in each impurity of mind that Christians would call pride. Buddhists, like Christians, recognize the key role it plays in mental defilement.

Vanity. Buddhist understandings of vanity make distinctions that Westerners at first glance may not quite understand. The Pali word *(mana)*, translated as conceit, concerns comparing oneself to others or ascribing certain characteristics to oneself. It does not matter whether the comparison is favorable to oneself or the other person; the comparing itself is conceit.

Conceit also includes ascribing any virtue or holiness to oneself. Seeing oneself as especially holy requires an implied comparison with others. If one focuses overmuch on one's own goodness, one's neighbor looks the worse — and vice versa. Considering oneself the "lowest of the low" requires a tremendous sense of self importance. The Buddha simply said not to compare at all, for comparison always makes one feel special in some way. The comparing mind is a major hazard in spiritual work.

Conceit can progress to arrogance, haughtiness, superiority feeling, scorn of others, holding an exaggerated opinion of oneself that leads to looking down on others *(atimana)*. Here, the comparing attitude moves to frank judging. This judging mind is a common human characteristic. Those who think they do not judge others ought to look more carefully. People also judge themselves — often severely. Buddhists see the bouts of the self centeredness called guilt as negative self judgments that include a component of self hatred. They agree one needs to recognize bad behavior or attitudes, but say that adding self judgment and self dislike to them does not help. Self hatred is unwholesome in itself and conduces one to further bad behavior.

Avarice. Buddhists go beyond simply understanding avarice as wanting more of whatever is appealing. Another kind of greed, strongly tinged with pride, is wanting interpersonal position or reputation. The Buddha described two special attitudes that reflect such greed.

One *(thambha)* is variously translated obstinacy, refusal to show respect, obduracy, impertinence, unwillingness to accept advice and guidance, or lack of respect for objects and persons worthy of respect. Overvaluing one's own good behavior can lead to this attitude. Obstinate people act as if honor or respect were a material object in limited supply, as if any respect shown others takes away something from themselves. This proud avarice would have for oneself all there is of respect or honor.

Proud avarice makes people unteachable, for they cannot acknowledge that another has knowledge or expertise that they lack. This can be very spiritually damaging. The Buddha considered graceful submission to correction or guidance a "great good fortune."[19] He advised people to seek out those who reveal their weaknesses to them.[20]

A related attitude *(sarambha)* goes one step further. It refers to wanting to shine, to showing off and ostentation — being a "superstar" in others' eyes. The ostentatious want an admiring audience, to be the center of attention and hog the limelight. This interpersonal avarice grasps at attention as a commodity in limited supply. It fosters rivalry and presumption. When ostentation is strong, one may even resort to wrongdoing, or put other people in danger, in order to display oneself. For some people, the admiring audience sought may be God.

Lust. The attitude of lust on which the Buddha focused is trying to be especially appealing or attractive to others. Such lust contains a large element of pride. The Buddha described two stances concerned with making ourselves look attractive to others. Most people will find some of these tendencies in themselves if they look carefully.

The first *(maya)* refers to hiding faults and posing as innocent; this can even lead to hypocrisy, deceit, and deception. It is so easy to fall into little self justifications, minimizing mistakes, telling small self protective lies. People may pride themselves on being honest until they start to see such wrong speech that has become part of their verbal habits.

The second attitude of this pair *(satheyya)* goes further by making real pretensions to more attainment than one has. This can be as small as minor exaggerations of one's experiences or small lies that glamorize or dramatize oneself. This fault can be as major as falsely claiming high spiritual status. When one pretends to qualities one does not have, one tries to endear oneself to others or to use these claims for personal advantage. This can create much suffering. Such boastful pretension may lead to fraud or treachery — as we have unfortunately seen in some spiritual leaders.

Buddhists consider this attitude a very serious flaw. People who make untrue pretensions to spiritual advancement can hurt others who look to them for help. Such pretension is one of the major sins a Buddhist renunciate can commit, along with things like murder, splitting the spiritual community apart, and harming a holy person. It is cause for expulsion from the monastic community.

Anger. Anger *(kodha)* also has a large component of proud self importance. Some people become very much annoyed and dejected when the sweetness goes out of their spiritual work. They may become quite irked with themselves and angrily blame themselves. Buddhists see anger as a striking out because of personal dissatisfactions. This comes from putting undue importance on having things be as one wishes them to be. Anger can easily manifest as cruelty to others if one does not learn the way to control it.

When anger starts to seethe, to hang around and stick to one, one holds grudges. Then, anger has progressed to enmity or resentment *(upanaha)*. This poisonous attitude can hold one captive so intensely that it even disturbs sleep. One becomes obsessed with outrage over whatever caused the anger. It makes one want to exact revenge and can spur one to inflict real harm on others. Those who consider themselves spiritual are likely to do it subtly, with their tongue, sulking, carefully timed silences, obstructionist behavior, or the like.

Gluttony. In spiritually inclined people, gluttony manifests mainly as eagerly seeking the delights and satisfactions of spiritual practice. This is a particularly sticky problem, for one easily justifies such desire as wanting spiritual things good for oneself. Buddhists list ten specific experiences to which one is likely to cling; they call them the "corruptions of insight." These include peace, stillness, light, rapture, and intuitive understanding — in themselves, simply beautiful experiences that one has in the course of spiritual practice. Such experiences become corruptions when one seeks them rather than the rugged work of purification of heart.

One Buddhist aspect of spiritual gluttony is the proud desire to enjoy having good qualities within one's own being. One wants to swallow them down, be stuffed with attributes one admires for the sheer pleasure in it. This proud gluttony can manifest as ingratitude *(makkha)*. One depreciates others, the gifts they have given, or the worth of the gifts. One does not want to acknowledge that some good in oneself comes from others. A negative reaction to another's help can even lead to detraction or contempt. Humans have an amazing capacity to turn on those who help them, and wounded vanity that another should "taste" better than one does oneself can be behind it.

A related attitude is pretentiousness *(palasa)*. This desire to consider oneself on a par with those higher than one is intellectually, morally, or spiritually can mislead one seriously. Most spiritual practitioners *do* evaluate themselves and often overrate themselves. This is one reason a spiritual guide can help one progress. Competent guides can recognize subtle pretentiousness and nip it in the bud before one is seriously deluding oneself.

Envy. Envy *(issa)* is sadness over another's good. Spiritual envy sorrows at others' virtues and spiritual good. The Buddha spoke of this sadness at what another has as the exact opposite of sympathetic joy — taking delight in others' good, one of the Buddhist divine or beautiful mind states. Envy is a universal human malady. The human heart easily inclines to envy of another's good. Saint John of the Cross also described this attitude, saying that truly spiritual hearts rejoice when others serve God better than they themselves do. He said truly spiritual persons will do whatever they can to help others progress.[71]

Carrying envy another step further is stinginess *(macchariya)*. One can be miserly about various things, wanting to keep from others not only material goods, but also good qualities or assets that one has — such as beauty, virtue, or intelligence. One can be reluctant to "share" other people in one's life, to be at peace with friends having other friendships. Some spouses and parents want to "own" completely other family members. One can even want to keep spiritual goods from others, to deprive them of what will help them grow spiritually.

Sloth. Spiritual sloth is shrinking from spiritual practices that do not gratify self centered desires. Buddhists hold that it easily springs from self intoxication *(mada)*, based on such givens in life as youth, health, beauty, intelligence, or even virtue. One can get quite "heady" about one's own assets. Such self intoxication lays a basis for sloth.

Overconfidence and negligence lead to heedlessness, careless-ness, indolence, remissness, and lack of proper consideration. In this state *(pamada)*, one never really applies oneself to dealing with faults, developing virtue, and maintaining a meditation practice. Subtle self satisfaction saps motivation to do spiritual work.

Externalizing

Starting to see more clearly the impurities lurking in the heart and the roots from which they came can be very painful. If one recalls misdeeds that one has never acknowledged to another per-son, confession helps the mind settle down. Many Buddhist monastics regularly confess because they know well the effects on the mind of even small unacknowledged faults. Psychiatrist Carl Jung wrote about the negative effects of such secrets.[22] Once one clearly resolves to abandon wrongful actions and attitudes, which confession can help one do, the mind more easily becomes calm.

Buddhists also recommend confession, acknowledgment, of severe trauma or loss that one has not discussed with anyone else. Many people are ashamed of having been victimized. Being badly mistreated often leaves people with the feeling that somehow they must have deserved such ill treatment. Such experiences have affected and continue to affect them. Externalizing them helps people deal with their effect and helps them purge the intense emotions associated with such experiences. It helps the victimized accept themselves and their lives more fully and to forgive those who have "broken" them.

Spiritual Realism and Abandoning Interpretation

A most central idea in Buddhist teaching is the inability of the thinking intellect to grasp truth securely. True understanding can come only in direct, unmediated experience. Apophatic Christian mystics agree with this idea. We have seen that Buddhists are also extremely sensitive to the damage done by insistence on opinions. They consider clinging to views one of the major barriers to spiri-tual growth.

Two important teachings of the Buddha can be very helpful to Christians. The first is on understanding faith.[23] The second is on the problems created by insisting on the factuality of the stories one tells oneself to interpret experiences. Problems with both of these areas stem from clinging to opinions.

Horror of Clinging to Opinions

In 1967, Martin Luther King, Jr., nominated Vietnamese Buddhist monk Thich Nhat Hanh for the Nobel Peace Prize. Nhat

Hanh has developed a code of conduct for lay folks in contemporary times that reflects a solidly Buddhist horror of clinging to opinions. His first three precepts for those who follow him strike at the heart of dogmatic, intolerant ideologies — those which define an ingroup and outgroups, claiming special virtue or rightness for the ingroup.[24]

The first precept reads: "Do not be idolatrous about or bound to any doctrine, theory, or ideology, even Buddhist ones. All systems of thought are guiding means; they are not absolute truth." What an astonishing lesson for those who absolutize the words of their theologies and creeds, who make words the object of idolatry, who have the peculiar belief that faith means holding "right" opinions!

But, Nhat Hanh considers ideas and beliefs too important, too dangerous, not to call for further consideration. The second precept continues: "Do not think the knowledge you presently possess is changeless, absolute truth. Avoid being narrow-minded and bound to present views. Learn and practice non-attachment from views in order to be open to receive others' viewpoints." Clinging to opinions closes off this openness. What a jolting thought for those for whom faith is the comfort of feeling certain, a cozy security blanket to curl up with that has things all sewn up inside a tidy little belief package.

If the first two precepts are horrifying, the third pushes one even further: "Do not force others, including children, by any means whatsoever, to adopt your views, whether by authority, threat, money, propaganda or even education. However, through compassionate dialogue, help others renounce fanaticism and narrowness." One also ought not insist that one's children see oneself as having the absolute, utter, complete, final truth.

Understanding Faith

Most people wrongly understand faith. They think that it is what they believe and that, for faith to be strong, one must feel very certain about these opinions. Some consider assent to creedal or doctrinal positions to be the essence of faith. Distinctions between religions, and even between different sects within a single religion, are typically defined by the different opinions they hold. The ferocity with which creedal positions are held, defended, and promulgated, with inability to give credence to others' experiences, concepts, symbols, or moral conclusions, reveals a spirit difficult to reconcile with a living faith.

Faith and belief. Buddhist philosopher Alan Watts contrasted faith and belief to clarify this. He said that belief sits down in the middle of the road to suck the thumb that points to the truth, instead of following in the direction in which it points. Believers insist that reality be structured as they say it is, while faith is an openness to truth, whatever it may be: "Belief clings, but faith lets go."[25]

Beliefs are an interpretive overlay on personal experience — or, even worse, an interpretive overlay on others' experiences given us as the truth. Beliefs "can" experience by imposing immutability on it and lead to tunnel vision definitions of what really cannot be canned. They obscure what is essential. Watts said that the more beliefs one has — the more one insists on the truth value of particular understandings and interpretations — the less room there is for the openness that faith demands.

Cistercian monk Robert Morhaus said similarly: "Unless you lose your faith in God at least once a day, you are not growing spiritually."[26] That is, unless one is constantly willing to let go of current understandings so more mature ones can appear, one locks oneself into stunted development. This is what Thich Nhat Hanh meant — adding the danger that one may also seriously abuse others with rigid opinions.

The Buddha's teaching on faith. The Buddha said not to believe anything that anyone teaches, no matter on what authority — and that included not to believe what he, the Buddha, said. However, if a spiritual teaching attracts people for any reason, they should try it out. They should see what they get from practicing it, see what fruits it bears in their life. If it makes them less greedy, less angry, less uncaring, less self deceptive, then it is worth continuing. If not, it needs to be discarded.[27]

The Eastern traditions agree that one should never affirm what one has not tested and that agnosticism is the appropriate attitude toward all untried teachings. The saying, "If you meet the Buddha on the road, kill him," means not to accept things on any outer authority — not even that of the Buddha — but one ought to verify in one's own experience what one adopts. Jesus said similarly that the fruits of something reveal its value.

So many people get trapped in dogmas and creeds and other canned opinions. Alan Watts described this imprisonment: "If you try to capture running water in a bucket, it is clear that you do not understand it and that you will always be disappointed, for in the bucket the water does not run. To 'have' running water you must let go of it and let it run. The same is true of life and of God."[28]

These teachings are entirely compatible with that of high mystics in many traditions. From one of them — Christian Saint John of the Cross: "Those are decidedly hindered, then, from attainment of this high state of union with God who are attached to any understanding, feeling, imagining, opinion, desire, or way of their own. . . . Their goal . . . transcends all this, even the loftiest object that can be known or experienced."[29] No human concept or understanding can adequately grasp the ultimate reality. More simply, any idea *about* God is *not* God. Therefore, attachment to any opinion is an obstacle to spiritual fruition.

Religious Interpretation

My very favorite psychologist, William James, had little use for words and concepts in religion. He held that religion is about people's experiences — not theology and philosophy. In 1902, he wrote salty words about theologians:

> What is their deduction of metaphysical attributes [of God] but a shuffling and matching of pedantic dictionary-adjectives . . . something that might be worked out from the mere word "god" by one of those logical machines of wood and brass which recent ingenuity has contrived. The metaphysical monster which they offer to our worship is an absolutely worthless invention of the scholarly mind.[30]

Formulating concepts. This quote from James is a helpful lead into discussing formulating concepts or interpreting experience rather than simply accepting it. James would agree strongly with the Buddha that one adds nothing but obfuscation when one insists on creating networks of concepts — especially about things that are not even the object of personal experience.

Let us look even more closely at concepts. When one forms a concept of something, one "freezes" a particular experience or set of experiences one has had. Thought and language, which is based on thought, make things look permanent and unchanging. When someone forms a concept of an experience, he or she most often considers the experience a "thing." One "catalogs" new experiences, which *will* always differ in some ways, as being the same "thing" as similar experiences that occurred previously. This encourages one to see what is changing and impermanent as lasting.

For example, once one labels as "anxiety" the fluttery feeling in the stomach that comes along with sweaty palms, a sense of foreboding, an accelerated heart rate, shallow breathing, and so forth, anxiety becomes a *thing* from which one suffers. It is no longer only a bunch of simultaneously occurring experiences that one sometimes has and sometimes does not have. It has, in a way, been made "eternal" because the concept does not go out of existence once it has been created, even though the experiences from which it was created have stopped happening.

When one holds onto such a concept, anxiety becomes a "thing" with which one may have to contend at any step in the road. One has created this evil or unwanted thing and then lives in dread of encountering it — never realizing that it is simply a concept and not a thing with a reality of its own. Thus, anxiety becomes a fact of life for one *all* the time, not *only* when one is having experiences one labels as anxiety. This expectation that anxiety may be around any corner colors the mind in such a way that one is even more inclined to experience anxiety. People so often create self fulfilling prophecies with their dread of anxiety or any other particular experience.

Similarly, once one has formed a concept of "crude, insensitive person" to define someone with whom one has had a bad experience, that person has been "cast in stone." One has erected a "graven image" of that other person and can no longer respond freshly to him or her as he or she is experienced in each successive situation. The conceptual labeling, the graven image — which is eternal, immutable — will always get in the way. The reality that each person is constantly changing and never stays the same for very long is lost. One has substituted a creation of thought for it; one has abandoned really real reality for the convention of a concept.

All people, societies, and social institutions have erected their graven images. Different groups develop their own repertoires of these concepts. When confronted with a particular experience in their unique setting, they leap immediately to their concept, their graven image interpretation, thus cutting off openness to explore deeply or even feel genuinely just exactly what is being experienced.

In ordinary life, when dealing with the created or conditioned world, one needs concepts to communicate, but they can hinder spiritual work. They lead one into conclusions that can become opinions to which one tightly clings. One forgets that one's thought *about* God is *not* God; it is just a thought. In the quote from John of the Cross just given, his point is that any thought or image of God — and we can also say of *nibbana* — is *not* its object. Saint John insisted that, if we cling to the thought, we cannot directly experience God.

Interpreting experience. Buddhists also can teach much about interpreting experiences, making stories about what happens. Perhaps the most dangerous story is one claiming experiential knowledge of God for experiences that can be explained more simply.

Someone enters into a vast, delightful sense of "presence" in prayer and immediately concludes that God was present. A

Buddhist would caution that what one has experienced is simply a vast, delightful sense of presence. That is all that need be said. In Buddhist meditation practice, one learns to stay very close to the experienced data without adding anything to them. In one of his shortest sermons, the Buddha responded to someone's request for instruction toward liberation with a few sentences. He said, "In the seen, let there be just what is seen. In the heard, let there be just what is heard. In the sensed, let there be just what is sensed."[31]

An example from my own meditation work will help here. At the center where I practice, one must walk through the dining hall alongside the kitchen to get from the meditation hall to the bedroom areas. One morning, I was going from the hall to continue sitting in my bedroom. As instructed, I was walking with eyes downcast, not looking around, and paying attention to the sensations produced in my legs by walking. When I heard a sound, however, I was not so mindful and did not merely note it as "hearing." I found the question in my mind, "Why should the cooks be frying something at this hour?" This was, of course, adding my own concepts to the simple experience of hearing. I had identified the sound as spattering oil and made assumptions about the way it was being produced. I did all this without mindful awareness of doing it. I was on "automatic" for forming concepts and thinking about and with them. All people are usually this way throughout an entire ordinary day, continually adding their own conceptual creations to basic experiences.

Later, on my way back to the hall, I again heard the sound and again leapt to concepts, saying to myself, "My goodness, they're still frying something." Then, I happened to glance up at the large windows along one side of the dining hall; after this experience of seeing, my mind then said, "Oh, they aren't frying anything; it's rain I'm hearing." And then, in a flash, I saw very clearly all the interpretations I was creating. My experience had simply been hearing a sound with a spattering quality. I had first leapt to the interpretation of spattering grease. When I looked out the window, I added other understandings to the simple experience of seeing; I called all the patterns of shades, colors, and movement I was seeing "rain." Finally, to the raw flow of experience — the simple acts of seeing and hearing — I added the concept of "I," of some observer to whom all this was happening, and concluded that I was hearing rain. This story well illustrates how easy it is to be wrong when we interpret experience.

Although I find this call to realism and Truth most compellingly made in Buddhist literature and in experiencing Buddhist meditation, Christian mystics have also discussed this danger. Both my Carmelite mentors, Teresa of Avila and John of the Cross, frequently cautioned against interpreting experiences. Much of the second book of Saint John's *Ascent of Mount Carmel* catalogs many varieties of experiences and cautions people against making much of them. The very real possibility of error is one reason that John of the Cross urges against interpreting experience.

Believing the story instead of experience. One woman on retreat came in to tell me excitedly that the Holy Trinity had taken up residence in her heart that morning. She was completely unable to tell me anything she experienced; she was so locked into her interpretation of the experience that it had become the only reality for her.

I think a more detailed story will help for understanding this. A born again man told me that Jesus Christ convicted him of sin in his heart. When I asked him just what he experienced, what actually happened to him, he could only repeat, "Jesus Christ convicted me of sin in my heart." I described to him an experience I had while doing *vipassana* meditation on a retreat. I had noticed that the man in front of me seemed to be struggling with a lot of pain, for he kept shifting position and moving around.

An odd sort of delight arose in me, and then the memory came that earlier this man had done something annoying to me. Like a flash, I realized that I was enjoying the discomfort of another person who had previously caused me discomfort. This was followed by hot, searing pain in my chest, disgust with myself, judging myself to be vindictive, deep revulsion to so being, feeling trapped by such a reaction, desire to be freed from this emotional trappedness, burning of my cheeks, a sense of shame, intense remorseful sorrow, and silent tears running down my cheeks. I asked this man if his experience of being convicted of sin in his heart had been anything like my experience. He was genuinely confused and told me that he was talking about a religious experience and that I was talking about feelings I had while doing a pagan practice.

Lest you think this man is especially dense, here is another experience — from a Buddhist-Christian dialogue conference. I had just read my paper comparing the course of spiritual development in Buddhist *vipassana* meditation with what Christian mystic John of the Cross says about it. One man there commented that, although the parallels seemed striking, an unresolvable problem between Buddhism and Christianity is the importance of the concept of grace in Christianity, for which "atheistic" Buddhism has no parallel.

Sighing inside, I told him a story I hoped would help. My Buddhist meditation teacher had, in true Buddhist fashion, emphasized that all have to walk their own road, that nobody will do the work for them, that it is up to individuals to apply themselves to their practice to purify consciousness for enlightenment. At one point, I told him that my experience was different from this teaching. I said, "I have never felt more carried in my entire life." He smiled and said, "Oh, yes, once you start to experience the unfolding of the *Dhamma*, they are both true." I asked my conference questioner, "What difference does it make what we call it — grace or the unfolding of the *Dhamma*? At the level of experience, what happened to me is the same kind of experience most Christians would call grace." The look on his face suggested he did not quite make the connection.

So often people can speak only of their concepts and cannot even recognize the experiences that led to making these concepts. I have often seen this in retreatants. Too often, people seem unable to recognize experience if it does not come described in their own way of conceptually formulating it. It is almost as if an experience does not really exist unless it is described in the "appropriate" words. In both of my stories, does it really matter whether one calls it the prompting of the Holy Spirit or an impulse from *Dhammoja*, the essence of *Dhamma*? What matters is that one recognizes the "grace" in such experiences and cooperates with it.

Becoming Nothing, Becoming Everything

We now see the way Buddhist wisdom helps one understand the way the sense of separate, distinct self starts becoming undermined in spiritual experience. One important realization is radical impermanence, the constant changes occurring. Everything is always changing, is in constant flux. Even the most solid appearing mountain is always eroding in some places and adding bulk in others; its vegetation also continually shifts and changes. Nothing in earthly experience ever stays the same.

Flux and the Nature of Reality

Physicists say that apparently solid material objects are mostly empty space with flecks of stuff floating around in it at a very high velocity. In Buddhist meditation, one can directly experience this. Although the eye is not a sufficiently delicate instrument, the meditative mind can perceive the world that physicists describe.

Change and breakdown of self sense. All this flux is certainly true of what I call "me." Part of what I called "me" this morning went down the drain when I showered and dead skin flaked off. What I called oatmeal yesterday is now becoming what I call "me." Biologists say that no cell in the body lasts beyond seven years. As cells divide, their contents are replaced, using the protein building blocks we have eaten, according to the genetic code in the body's cells. But, mistakes occur; we call them aging. The reproducibility of cells increasingly falters until finally what is reproduced can no longer sustain life. Then, the material process I call "me" ceases.

Not only bodies, but everything else one might call "me" is all in constant flux: emotions, thoughts, images. Even memories change, for people constantly rearrange the way they recall the past. Meditation shows us that beings are each a process, made up of sets of interlocking processes — not a static, permanent "thing." Seeing this insubstantial, process nature of one's being is important for higher levels of awareness to develop. It undercuts long established habits of seeing oneself as a solid, fixed, separate entity.

Meditators must become able to "become" the object of meditation; that is, they have to let go of their sense of personal identity or "I-ness," allowing consciousness to become totally absorbed in its object. Most people find letting go of individual self sense extremely difficult. It is truly a death experience, and, as people feel it coming, they may instinctively shrink back from it. They cannot easily accept the "death" of the mental-psychic self, cannot let go of their "I" or "me." This task also does not get completed once and for all; one must over and over again surrender self.

Interrelatedness. Buddhist meditative wisdom not only explains the process nature of individual beings. This wisdom also teaches one to realize that each being is not an isolated process. The network of processes that is each being interlocks with many other processes. Buddhist meditation gives one direct, immediate experience of this "interbeing." Nothing exists that is not a constantly changing process, constantly affected by the larger cosmic process of which it is part. This includes "I" or "me." In the exchange of solid matter, of fluids, of gasses — the very air one breathes in and expels — constant exchange with the larger environmental process occurs.

Scientists who study chaos, apparently random chance occurrences in the universe, say that everything is interrelated when one looks closely enough. Nothing can really be called an accident. Everything is caused — the Buddha would say conditioned — by all the ongoing processes that affect it. These scientists describe "the butterfly effect," the way a butterfly fluttering its wings in Hong Kong in January affects weather patterns in America the next summer. Truly, as the poet said, no one is an island; all beings are connected. At this level of seeing, beings are not separate selves, but one greater reality. Christians may call it experiential knowledge of the Mystical Body of the Christ. One can see at this level only when one stops clinging to the sense of separate selfhood.

Love and the Cosmic Body

When one talks about expanding understanding of self, one is actually speaking about love. Love is a state of nonseparation, of oneness.

A unitive metaphysics. A unitive metaphysics underlies the love commandments of all the world's great religions. It is described in various symbolic ways — such as, all people being children of the same God, members of the same Mystical Body, possessing the same Buddha-nature, or flowing from the same Source. Buddhist meditation brings the realization that somehow, in one's deepest being, one's fate is inextricably intertwined with that of all, as intertwined as are the fates of a single person's heart and liver. Too much damage to either affects the other adversely.

No sane person would allow one hand to chop off the other because that would hurt the organic unity of the body to which both hands belong. So also a person who truly understands becomes unable to deliberately harm any other being. Harm done to anyone is harm done to oneself, to the larger whole that *is* all beings. Of course, people continue — even against their conscious will — to create suffering for themselves and others, to pass on the pain in their beings to those with whom they deal. Mystic Simone Weil said that suffering is like a bad coin; it keeps getting passed on until finally someone does not pass it on. A strongly developed sense of ego as separate being is behind this.

The body cosmic. So, at this higher level of seeing, beings are not anything separate at all. Each is one small cell in a much larger body. Each one's fate rests upon the fate of the larger whole, as environmentalists urgently remind people. The philosopher Sartre said, "Hell is other people." This understanding says that Sartre, though wrong, is close to right. Hell is *seeing* other people as other. Hell is seeing oneself as some *thing* separate and distinct from everyone and everything else. As one Buddhist teacher put it: "Big self, big problem. No self, no problem."

This higher level of seeing reveals envy, competitiveness, hostility, resentment, vanity — all the ugliness in the heart — for the stupidity it is. Whether I have pleasant or unpleasant experiences, am alone or have good company, am praised or blamed, am prosperous or poor — all this pales to petty insignificance. At this level, the sorrow and suffering of others truly is one's own sorrow and suffering. The joys of others are truly one's joys.

One does not and cannot sustain one's being apart from the larger whole of which each is a part. One does not belong to oneself, but to that which is greater than one, that which upholds one's being and sustains it, that which undergirds all experience.

It is in realization of this that some Buddhists take the *bodhisattwa* vow not to go to their own final reward until they can bring all beings with them. This vow rests on deeply understanding inter-being. Buddhist meditation brings experiential awareness of it.

The signs of our oneness. Seeing all of nature as one body res-onates with long established Eastern views of the cosmic process. Also, Western physicists say that the amount of matter in the uni-verse is constant; it interchangeably manifests as energy and is constantly being recycled. When a single being dies, its matter decays, is processed by nature, and goes to make up the form of other objects or beings.

One can realize directly that each being constantly partakes of the great and beautiful gift of sharing with all beings — whether one wills it or not — in every act of interchange with the environ-ment: in every cup of water one drinks, in every piece of fruit one eats, in every breath one draws. And, all of it is recycled material, made from what other organisms gave back to the larger whole after using it to sustain their own beings.

All not only take from the universe, but also give back to the larger whole what is no longer useful to them. The gasses one breathes out, the waters of one's tears, sweat, and urine. The solid waste that one deposits in the toilet and that one washes off one's body with each shower. And, all this gets processed for reuse by other beings. With each of these "sacraments" of the kitchen and the bathroom, one can acknowledge and celebrate one's connect-edness with all else that is in the cosmos — if not with awareness, then unconsciously. One's relationship with the universe as a whole becomes like that of a child in its mother's uterus — an inti-mate relationship in which one realizes one's utter dependence and lack of separateness, but also utter security.

And Yet More

In a very real way, beings *are* their experiences. If one focuses attention on a solidified understanding of bodily or mental processes as separate self, one *is* that, and one can experience the hell of isolation in it. One can focus attention on the larger cos-mic process in which the processes making up self are embedded. And, one experiences oneness with all. Buddhist meditation can give this experience. One goes beyond living in isolation and fear.

When one stops clinging to the changing processes called self, one can eventually see the only true and enduring Real, what is Ultimate in Reality. One need not quibble about the various ways in which people have described this — God, *Brahman, nibbana.* Many people in different cultures and spiritual traditions have given their testimony that this reality *can* be experienced by those who are willing to let go of narrower self understandings. Buddhist practice leads to this experience.

The Buddhist "touching" of *nibbana* refers to the ground that lies behind *any* image or understanding of God or Ultimate Reality, for such images belong to lower levels of experience. This level brings the highest bliss, but there can be absolutely no sense of separate "I-ness" here. Some Christian mystics — certainly Meister Eckhart and Saint John of the Cross — have experienced God in this way.[32]

This experience involves the complete "dying" of the self into the Ultimate, into that beyond any image into which one has already surrendered self. One cannot bring body and personality — the *things* of one's individual "I-ness" — to this realization. But, when one has become *no* thing, one *will* become everything. Buddhist teachings describe this. Buddhist meditation brings experience of it. May all beings come to this realization.

NOTES

[1]Two books on this work were published by Crossroad Publishers in 1994: Kevin Culligan, Mary Jo Meadow, and Daniel Chowning, *Purifying the Heart: Buddhist Insight Meditation for Christians* (New York: Crossroad Publishers, 1994), and Mary Jo Meadow, *Gentling the Heart: Buddhist Loving-Kindness Practice for Christians* (New York: Crossroad Publishers, 1994).

[2]Mahasi Sayadaw, *Brahmavihara Dhamma* (Rangoon, Burma: Buddha Sasana Nuggaha Organization, 1985), 1.

[3]The text of this teaching is found in the Metta Sutta which is located in the Sutta Nipata of the original Pali canon of Buddhist Scriptures.

[4]For instruction on the way to do this practice, see Mary Jo Meadow, *Gentling the Heart.* For other perspectives from a Buddhist teacher, see Sharon Salzberg, *Loving-Kindness: The Revolutionary Art of Happiness* (Boston: Shambhala, 1995).

[5]Samyutta Nikaya I: 75; Udana 47.

[6]For more complete discussion of this and other problems associated with doing concentrative meditation, see the last unit of Mary Jo Meadow, *Gentling the Heart.*

[7]An interesting discussion of this point is in William James, *The Varieties of Religious Experience,* in the chapter on "Saintliness." This volume was originally published in 1902 by McKay; it has been reissued in paper by Collier Books, 1961.

[8]For some discussion of this, see Kevin Culligan, Mary Jo Meadow, and Daniel Chowning, *Purifying the Heart.* The teachings of Saint John of the Cross can be found in *The Collected Works of St. John of the Cross,* rev. ed., trans. Kieran Kavanaugh and Otilio Rodriguez (Washington DC: Institute of Carmelite Studies, 1991).

[9]For example, see this in the previously cited *Collected Works of St. John of the Cross*: "To arrive at being all, Desire to be nothing. . . . To come to be what you are not, You must go in a way in which you are not" (*Ascent I*, 13:11).

[10]See, for example, the following in his *Collected Works: Ascent of Mount Carmel* II, 22:2, and *Dark Night* I, 7:4.

[11]See, for example, Saint John's *Ascent* II, 7:11.

[12]See Majjhima Nikaya #22, I. 140, Alagddupamasutta.

[13]For a discussion of faith in relation to clinging to opinions, see Mary Jo Meadow, *Through a Glass Darkly: A Spiritual Psychology of Faith* (New York: Crossroad, 1996).

[14]This cartoon appeared in a very early edition of *The National Catholic Reporter* newspaper.

[15]Gordon Allport, "The Religious Context of Prejudice," *Journal for the Scientific Study of Religion* 5 (1966): 447-57.

[16]This teaching is found in Majjhima Nikaya, Mahatanhasankhaya Sutta.

[17]Dhammapada #337, 338. This collection of aphorisms of the Buddha is widely available in many translations and is one of the best introductions to Buddhist wisdom. Having at least two translations helps clarify the places where it may seem obscure to Western minds.

[18]For one such listing, see Majjhima Nikaya, Vatthipama Sutta #7, 3.

[19]Mahamangala Sutta.

[20]Dhammapada #76, 77.

[21]John of the Cross, *Dark Night* I, 2:8.

[22]Carl Jung, *Modern Man in Search of a Soul* (New York: Harcourt, Brace, and World Harvest Book, 1933), 31-34.

[23]My most recent book, *Through a Glass Darkly: A Spiritual Psychology of Faith*, explores many issues about faith from an interfaith perspective. It relies mainly on Christianity, Hindu *ashtanga* Yoga, Theravadan Buddhism, and the Vedanta of Sri Aurobindo.

[24]Thich Nhat Hanh, *Interbeing: Commentaries on the Tiep Hien Precepts* (Berkeley, California: Parallax Press, 1987), 27, 30, 32.

[25]Alan Watts, *The Wisdom of Insecurity* (New York: Pantheon Books, 1951), cited from paper edition (1968), 24.

[26]Robert Morhaus in a talk given at Insight Meditation Society, Barre, MA, in December, 1986.

[27]One of the most important of this often repeated injunction of the Buddha is found in Kesaputtiya Sutta, A., i., 188, sermon to the Kalamas.

[28]Alan Watts, 24.

[29]John of the Cross, *Ascent* II, 4:4.

[30]William James, 349.

[31]Udana 1.10; there is a similar passage at Anguttara Nikaya 4.24.

[32]I refer here to Eckhart's "Godhead behind the image of God" and to the last stanza of Saint John's *Dark Night* poem. In saying, "All things ceased," John describes an experience that directly parallels the Buddhist "touching" of *nibbana*.

Christians and the Islamic Experience of Prayer

Jane I. Smith

Salat is the pillar of religion *(al-din)*; whoever performs it performs religion. It is the connection between the worshipper *(al-'abd)* and his lord. Whoever prays connects himself to God, and whoever cuts off prayer cuts himself off from God. During [prayer] the Qur'an is recited, God is praised and al-Shaytan is reviled. [Prayer] includes physical exercise and spiritual pleasure, and it is the greatest manifestation of all of the manifestations of reverence to God, Lord of all the worlds. The nearest the worshipper can be to God is when he is prostrating himself in worship *(al-sajid)*.[1]

This statement from a recent Islamist publication gives eloquent testimony to the importance of prayer in Islam and to the comprehensiveness of the prayer experience. It is reminiscent of the insistence of the famous twelfth century theologian and mystic, Abu Hamid al-Ghazali, that "Prayer is the pillar of religion, the mainstay of conviction, the chief of good works and the best act of obedience. . . ."[2] All creation, according to the Qur'an, has as its most basic duty and responsibility the worship of God,[3] and the most immediate way of achieving this is through prayer.[4] Worship in its fullest expression is known as *'ibada*, from the same root as *'abd*, the one who responds to the oneness of God in humble submission. As God alone is lord and creator of the universe, so the Muslim acknowledges that oneness by living a life of integratedness, of integrity, and of prayerful response. In this regard, there is a basic distinction between the worship as an activity of God's other creatures, who respond out of their basic nature or instinct, and that of humans, who are given the choice to respond to God or to act in rebellion against him.[5] Worship, then, becomes a vehicle through which the believer can express his or her deep sense of thankfulness and gratitude to God, which Kenneth Cragg calls "the real touchstone of belief."[6]

Worship as an overall response to God, including one's thoughts and one's actions, is a comprehensive experience that encompasses all aspects of human life. One of the most important components of the whole worship experience is the specific act of prayer, which itself is to be found in a variety of forms. In this essay, I will describe the different kinds of prayer that are part of the Islamic understanding of worship, the purpose and function of prayer, the elements that constitute proper preparation for, and execution of, prayer, and some of the characteristics that I see to be most distinctive about prayer in Islam. I will conclude with some reflections about the ways in which Christians may both learn from their Muslim neighbors and share with them in this most significant aspect of the relationship between human and divine.

Muslims understand prayer to be principally for the purpose of attesting to God's glory and giving Him praise and thanks, rather than for supplication. As is the case with many of the responsibilities Muslims accept as part of their worship of God, prayer assumes a regularity and a discipline. Elmer Douglas, a longtime friend of Islam and Muslims, cites an experience in which a young man, having completed his own prayer in a mosque, turned to him and asked, "Do you know how to pray?" Douglas understood this to be a question of some depth, an inquiry as to whether he as a nonMuslim understood the importance of structure and discipline to the Islamic prayer experience.[7] Prayer is not a casual thing for the Muslim. It is specified as a responsibility many times in the Qur'an, as in Sura (henceforward S.) 11:114 {Establish worship at the two ends of the day and in some watches of the night . . .}.[8] Prayer is thus a duty incumbent upon the believer as a direct command of God. Muslim legal scholars have devoted a great deal of attention to the codification of the details of prayer life, including times, places, content, and readiness. The very regularity of the prayer reflects the Islamic intention that one's personal life should reflect the order and coherence of God's creation and God's plan for humankind.

Islam is the only major religion whose very name suggests a bidimensional focus. With a small 'I' *(islam)*, it refers to the individual and personal human response to God. With a capital 'I' (Islam), it means the collectivity of all of those persons who, together in acknowledging and responding to God, form a community of religious faith.[9] Ritual prayer is designed both to bring benefit to, and fulfill the responsibility of, the individual believer and also to set the context for the communal dimension of the Muslim experience. By sharing in the common prayer, the Muslim draws close to his fellow worshipers and participates in the pro-

motion of the life of the entire community. Prayer in this understanding, while entered into freely by the individual, is not really a
matter of individual choice alone. The command to pray comes to
the entire community, and, by participating in communal prayer,
the individual believer automatically shares in a ritual and ceremonial unity.[10] In another dimension of commonality, Muslims
believe that, when in prayer, they are functioning, not so much as
individuals, but as representatives of the human race in its entirety
insofar as a prayerful response to God's being and presence is
basic and natural to all humanity.

There is a good deal of literature by Muslims about the prayer
experience, emphasizing its importance as a kind of protection
against those things that defile and contaminate and as that which
puts under control the animal impulses of the human soul that
urge one to neglect the better impulses of the spirit. It is also
understood to be a strict obligation, the first duty required by God
of the Prophet. From the earliest inception of the Muslim community in Mecca, the Prophet insisted that the faithful persevere
in prayer. Prayer is not only prescribed for the regularized times,
but is enjoined as a constant activity. In its fullest sense, prayer is a
human attitude which permeates all of life. Insofar as one is cog-
nizant of the presence of God, one is in a stance of prayer, and all
of one's activities are said to be reflections of that awareness. Many
of the eschatological writings of Islam emphasize that one of the
rewards of the faithful on the day of resurrection is to be able to
gaze upon the face of God. Muslims understand that the deepest
experience of prayer allows them to be in a meditative state in
which it is possible to experience the joy that comes from such
contemplation of the divine. "The freshness of my eyes is given to
me in prayer," said the Prophet.[11] There is a general belief that, of
all of the rituals and duties incumbent on humans, prayer is the
most important because it most directly allows us to make the connection between this world and the world of the unseen; it gives
us the means to transcend the mundane and to anticipate our ultimate participation in the life of the world to come.[12]

Communal prayers, as we shall see below, have a prescribed
content. In addition, there are a variety of different kinds of
prayers, including invocations, recitations of devotional formulae
and petitions, as well as spontaneous affirmations of praise for the
divine. Connecting all of these kinds of prayer is the common
thread of absolute conviction of God's being, oneness, and relia-
bility. "Allah, we seek of Thee incontrovertible certainty (*yaqin*),"
says a prayer ascribed to the Moroccan 'Ali Abu'l-Hasan al-
Shadhili.[13] This is a reflection, of course, of the conclusive affirmation of the Qur'an concerning the reality of God and of the

events to come to pass at the day of judgment. {Lo! this is certain truth}, says S. 56:95. Whether prayer is public or private, it is seen as the most fundamental activity of the faithful. Some observers have been so struck with the essential nature of prayer to the belief and practice of Islam that they liken it to the importance of the Eucharist as the essential act of the Christian faith.[14]

The *Salat*

> Know that the ritual prayer is the foundation of being a Muslim. It is the master and leader of works. The Presence of Divinity loves no work more than it, for it has been reported that God has made obligatory for His servants nothing more beloved to Him after *tawhid* than the ritual prayer. If He loved something else more, He would make the higher plenum — those who are brought near to His presence — busy themselves with it. But they are all busy with the ritual prayer — some are standing, some are bowing, some are prostrating themselves, and some are sitting in witness. May God place us and you among the people of the ritual prayer, and may He make us worthy of intimate discourse with Him![15]

The image of faithful Muslims bowing their foreheads to the ground in ritual prayer, shoulder to shoulder with their comrades, is one with which most nonMuslims are familiar. It is this formalized or ritualized prayer, identified by the term *salat*, to which the Qur'an most frequently refers. The word *salat* appears ninety-nine times in some ninety verses of the Qur'an, an interesting coincidence in light of the fact that the Muslim "rosary" *(subhah)* usually contains ninety-nine beads (or thirty-three rotated three times) to represent the ninety-nine beautiful "names" or qualities of God,[16] although, according to classical exegesis of the Qur'an, only forty-three of these references are actually to the obligatory form of worship.[17] The word *salat* itself is from the same root as *sila*, relationship or connectedness, which, according to Mahmoud Ayoub, suggests that which forms a bridge between human and divine. "For pious Muslims not only speak to God," says Ayoub, "but, just as Christians do, they speak with God. Thus they add their voices to the Divine voice which from eternity declared 'All praise be to God, Lord of all beings.'"[18] This is often referred to as "talking with the Lord" *(munajat al-rabbi)*.

Ritualized prayer is one of what are often called the five pillars *(arkan al-din)* of Islam. While it is usually listed after the *shahada* or profession of the oneness of God and the apostleship of Muhammad, it always implicitly or explicitly incorporates the *shahada* itself. The other pillars are almsgiving, fasting during the month of Ramadan, and pilgrimage at least once in a lifetime to the holy city of Mecca, of which prayer and worship are an integral part. The *shahada* itself functions as a prayer and, as such, is whispered into the ear of the newborn baby, first in the right and then in the left. Sometimes this recitation is by the child's father, and, at other times, an *Imam* will be invited to do it. It is often the case that the testimony recited in the right ear is an elaboration of the *adhan* or call to prayer that summons the Muslims five times a day.[19] Prayers are recited with great frequency during the month of Ramadan, especially as one participates in the pilgrimage. While *zakat* is not directly connected to particular prayers, it is often associated with the injunction to pray in the Qur'an.[20] Some have interpreted this to mean that there is a direct connection between the efficaciousness of one's prayer and one's willingness to share generously with those who are in need.

Ritual prayer was practiced by the Jews and Christians of Arabia and has been said by some orientalist scholars of Islam to have been borrowed by the Prophet from those communities. Muslims understand a different origin and believe that *salat* is unique among the prescribed duties in Islam because it is the only one to have been imposed through a direct meeting between the Prophet and God when Muhammad took his legendary night journey from Mecca to Jerusalem to the seven heavens. This journey, often called the *mi'raj* or ascent and referred to rather obliquely in S. 17:1, is interpreted by some Muslims as having been a physical trip, by others as a psychological state, and by still others as a mystical experience or an allegory for divine-human communication. In any case, it is highly revered by Muslims and, because of the belief that Muhammad ascended to heaven directly from the holy rock of Jerusalem, is one of the reasons for Muslim veneration of that city. The part of the description relevant for this discussion on prayer is reported by Muhammad's biographer, Ibn Hisham, this way:

> When Gabriel took him up to each of the heavens and asked permission to enter he had to say whom he had brought and whether he had received a mission and they would say "God grant him life, brother and friend!" until they reached the seventh heaven and his Lord. There the duty of fifty prayers a day was laid upon him. The apostle said: "On my return I passed by Moses and what a fine friend of yours he was! He asked me about how many prayers had been laid upon me and when I told him fifty he said, 'Prayer is a weighty matter and your people are weak, so go back to your Lord and ask him to reduce the number for you and your community.' I did so and He took off ten. Again I passed by Moses and he said the same again; and so it went on until only five prayers for the whole day and night were left. Moses again gave me the same advice. I replied that I had been back to my Lord and asked him to reduce

the number until I was ashamed, and I would not do it again. He or
you who performs them in faith and trust will have the reward of
fifty prayers."[21]

The Qur'an itself does not specify that prayer must be done five
times daily, although it does indicate, as in S. 90:103, that it should
be done at particular times {. . . Worship at fixed hours hath been
enjoined on the believers}. It is generally understood by scholars
of Islam that, in the earliest days of the Prophet, community
prayers were not enforced five times a day, but, rather, two or perhaps three. There is evidence, for example, that, while he was still
in Mecca, before the *hijra* or emigration with his followers to
Medina, the Prophet recommended that prayer be performed in
the morning and in the evening only (see S. 20:130 and 17:78). It
then appears that, after the *hijra*, a third prayer was added, namely, one to be done at the middle of the day (see S. 30:17f.).[22] Some
have argued that Muhammad himself was most dedicated to the
evening prayer, perhaps in imitation of the Jacobite and Nestorian
monks.[23] In any case, it is probable that the insistence on five *salats*
did not come into being until the end of the seventh century.

The tradition cited above provides a rationale for that insistence, at the same time that it underscores God's mercy, one
might even say reasonableness, in not requiring that His devotees
pray fifty times each day. Qur'an commentators have devoted
some energy to a consideration of whether, in fact, the apparent
negotiation that took place between Muhammad and God, egged
on by Moses, really constituted a kind of bargaining session. The
general conclusion has been that, in the end, God must be seen,
not as a negotiator, but as the one Who imposes His divine will on
humankind. In any case, the traditions do avoid suggesting that
there was actually direct conversation, to say nothing of arguing,
between the Prophet and God.[24] In another often quoted tradition
of the Prophet, it is said that the angel Gabriel (Jibril) actually
descended from heaven five times in one day and, in the presence
of the Prophet, performed the *salat*. The Prophet then emulated
his angelic mentor who, incidentally, was also his guide on the
mi'raj and himself prayed five times and, therefore, set the example for the rest of the believers. Some traditions reflect the Islamic
understanding that the *salat* of the individual believer is a kind of
parallel to, or emulation of, the *mi'raj* of the Prophet and that, as
he ascended to the realm of the divine, the faithful, too, through
prayer, can come into communion with God.[25] "Prayer is *mi'raj*
(ascent) for the *mu'min* (faithful)," the Prophet is reported to
have said.[26]

When one performs *salat* alone, there is obviously no need for
a designated prayer leader. If at least two people are praying, how-

ever, one must serve as leader of the prayer or *imam*, from the Arabic word meaning to lead (as in prayer). Technically, any Muslim who is morally upright and who knows the routine of the *salat* can serve this function. According to the classical understanding, one assumes the title of *imam* only for the time during which he is actually leading the prayer. Today, the role of *imam* is being expanded considerably. As mosques in many places, particularly in the United States and Canada, come to take on more functions paralleling those of churches, it is increasingly the case that the roles and responsibilities of the *imam* have enlarged considerably. The *imam* generally is expected to have some degree of training in Islamic theology and science. An *imam* now often serves in a capacity similar to that of a Christian pastor, with this title designating his full role as leader of the activities of the mosque congregation as well as of the prayer.[27]

Despite the fact that Islamic scholars have been in agreement as to the requirement of five times daily for prayer, commentaries on the Qur'an make it evident that they have had difficulty identifying those times as associated with specific verses in the Qur'an. The exact times of day for performing the *salat* are, however, clearly established in the *hadith* or traditions and have been codified in the *fiqh* or law. Specifically, they are the *salat al-fajr* (also called the *salat al-subh*) at dawn before the rise of the sun, the *salat al-zuhr* after the sun passes its highest point, the *salat al-'asr* in the late part of the afternoon, the *salat al-maghrib* just after the setting of the sun, and the *salat al-'isha* sometime between sunset and midnight. If one is ill or is on a journey, combining the noon and afternoon prayers, or the sunset and evening prayers, is acceptable.

Salat five times a day, then, for most of the history of Islam, has been understood to be obligatory for all Muslim adults who are sound of mind and body. The mosque is considered to be the best place for performing the *salat*, but it is permissible to pray anywhere with the appropriate ritual purification. The Prophet is reported to have said: "The whole earth has been made a mosque for me."[28] In the same way, prayer alone is acceptable, although it is much preferable to pray with others. Children often begin to learn the way to participate in the formal prayer around the age of seven and are expected by ten to be fully involved.

It is clear from the Qur'an that women, along with men, are subject to all of the requirements of the faith and also are privy to the rewards promised to the faithful at the day of resurrection. However, some restrictions exist on women praying under certain conditions, such as, while they are menstruating (up to ten days) or during childbirth and nursing (up to forty days). Women did participate in communal prayer at the time of the Prophet, and, while in the mosque compound, they were not cut off from men even by a screen or curtain, although they did form a line behind the men. Succeeding centuries, however, saw women generally secluded and excluded from public life and thus constrained to pray, if at all, in the solitude of their homes or rooms. There is a great deal of discussion in the contemporary Muslim world about the appropriate modes of women's participation in public prayer. It is increasingly being recognized that participation in some way is true to the understanding promulgated by the Prophet Muhammad and that, with some kind of separate placement of men and women necessitated by the performance of the prostrations, women should be full participants in the prayer life of the community. Many mosques have a separate entrance for women who then participate in the prayer in a place apart from the men from which they can see and hear the *imam*. Often, they will have their younger children with them throughout the prayer service.

Visitors to the Muslim world over the centuries have seldom failed to be struck, sometimes enchanted, by the call to prayer (*adhan*, literally proclamation or announcement) through which the faithful are reminded of the necessity of interrupting the daily routines and taking time to acknowledge the presence of God in their lives. The first *mu'adhdhin* (person to give the call to prayer), appointed by the Prophet Muhammad, was a freed Ethiopian slave by the name of Bilal.[29] Traditionally throughout the centuries of Islam, the call to prayer has been sung from atop a minaret or tower of the mosque. (As Muslims have established communities throughout the world, and often worship where there is no formal mosque, other venues have been used for the *adhan*.) While the call to prayer in some senses parallels such reminders in other traditions, as, for example, the *shofar* (ram's horn) in Judaism or the tolling of bells in Christianity, it is unique in its reliance on the human voice.[30] The *mu'adhdhin* receives careful training as to proper intonation and vocalization, and his craft has been seen as one of the great arts of Islam.

So important is the ritual prayer in Islam that the *mu'adhdhin* has been said to be worthy of special merit in many of the traditions of the Prophet: "All that hear the Muezzin's cry, be they jinn, human, or whatever, will testify for him on the Day of Resurrection." Or: "The hand of the All-merciful is on the Muezzin's head until he completes his Call to Prayer." Or: "If a person performs Prayer in a wilderness, an angel prays on his right and an angel prays on his left. If he also gives the Call to Prayer and the signal to begin, angels perform Prayer behind him in rows like mountain ranges."[31] If one is alone and is not privy to the call to prayer from the *mu'adhdhin*, one is praised for giving the call to prayer himself: "Your Lord delights as a shepherd who, on the peak of a mountain crag, gives the call to prayer and prays. Then Allah (glorified and exalted be He), says: 'Look at this servant of Mine, he gives the call to prayer and performs the prayers; he is in awe of Me. I have forgiven My servant [his sins] and have admitted him to Paradise.'"[32]

There has been some discussion as to whether this call can be considered "music," although most Muslims would reject this because of the association of music with secular texts.[33] There is, nonetheless, a very lilting, at the same time haunting, quality to the intonation of the *mu'adhdhin* as he allows his voice to trail, one syllable after another, over a range of notes. He, and it is always a man who carries out this responsibility, ascends to his place of call just before the time that the prayer is scheduled, turns toward Mecca, and begins his recitation. In recent times, particularly in the major Islamic cities, the noises of traffic and industry have forced the replacing of the live human voice with a recording played over a loud speaker. Sadly, the compelling nature of the call is sometimes compromised when *adhans* from different mosques are slightly out of synchronization and almost seem to be competing with each other.

The elements of the call to prayer are as follows: "God is greater" (four times), then two times each, "I testify that there is no other god than God," "I testify that Muhammad is the Messenger of God," "come to the prayer," "come to the *falah* (thriving, success, salvation),"[34] "God is greater," and, finally, said once by Sunnis and twice by Shi'is, "There is no other god than God." Shi'ite Muslims add after the saying, "come to the *falah*," the phrase, "come to prosperity."[35] It is part of the tradition of Islam that the individual worshipper repeats, either orally or in his or her heart, the words of the *mu'adhdhin*, signifying one's participation, not only in the prayer itself, but in the acknowledgment of its advent.

In Islam, one does not simply begin to pray without very careful preparation. Essential to entry into the state of prayerful contemplation in Islam is the attaining of a state of ritual purity or *tahara*. This involves the outward elements, such as, cleansing of the body {O ye who believe! When ye rise up for prayer, wash your faces, and your hands up to the elbows, and lightly rub your heads and (wash) your feet up to the ankles . . .} (S. 5:6) and making sure that one is wearing modest and clean clothing {Thy Lord magnify, Thy raiment purify, Pollution shun!) (S. 74:3-5),[36] as well as the purification and readying of the mind and the heart. A man's body should be covered at least from his waist to his knees, and, by most interpretations, a woman should have only her face and hands uncovered. Essential to the initiation of the prayer is the declaration on the part of the believer that he or she is ready to enter into a state of worship. This is called the *niyya*, or intention, and serves to help one make the transition from ordinary daily activity to the special state of prayerful attention. Intention, in fact, is essential for the performance of all of the religious responsibilities of the Muslim. That which is done without the proper intention lacks efficacy: "Intention is the root of the matter. If there be no words, let there be no words: words are the branch."[37] There is a specificity in each *niyya* such that one is clear exactly what the details of the act will be. Thus, the *niyya* before prayer indicates how many prostrations will be done, et cetera.

The minor ritual washing or oblation, *wudu'*, is taken very seriously by the believer. The details of the washing are outlined in the Qur'an, and the traditions supply enormous detail. Mosques generally have separate facilities in which the wouldbe supplicant can meet these requirements. The following steps are carried out three times: hands are washed up to the wrists, and the arms up to the elbow; the mouth is rinsed, and sometimes a brush is used; water is sniffed into the nostrils and expelled; the face is washed from the forehead to the chin and from ear to ear. The head and ears are wiped with one's wet fingers and thumb; the neck is cleaned, and the feet are washed up to the ankles, beginning with the right. Washing of the neck is sometimes said to refer to the Qur'anic reference to the day of judgment when sinners will be chained by their necks. Symbolically, washing casts off these chains and affirms that the believer will not suffer this fate.[38] The order outlined above is that generally followed, although variation is allowed. If water is not available for washing, it is acceptable to use sand, earth, or even snow. This is called *tayammum* or substitution and is subject to similar, but less stringent, specifications. Once one is in a state of ritual purification, he or she must not be subject to any emission of bodily fluids or substances, or it will be necessary to perform the *wudu'* over again. If there has been a major bodily impurity, performing what is called the major purification *(ghusl)*, rather than the minor *wudu'*, is obligatory. According to some Muslims, the *ghusl* is also required for the Friday prayer and that done on the major *'eids* or holidays, 'Eid al-Fitr and 'Eid al-Adha.[39]

Thus, the act of *wudu'* awakens the believer both physically and intellectually. *Salat* in Islam must be carried out with a clarity of mind that parallels the purity of the physical. The ritual washings both symbolize and actualize the intention of the Muslim to be pure, to make the transition from the mundane to the holy, and to appropriately prepare him or herself for communion with God. As cleansing prepares one for prayer, so prayer itself serves to cleanse the heart and soul of the worshipper. The very process of cleansing not only moves one toward prayer, but also becomes a kind of prayer in itself that God will cleanse the worshipper of his or her sins and wrongdoings. Purification of the limbs is accompanied by purification of the inner heart and soul and becomes a way of praying for forgiveness and for God's guidance. Purity in this understanding is an expression of integrity, of the human ethical and moral response to the oneness of the divine. "After ablution and inward declaration of intention to perform the prayers," says Bill Musk, "the Muslim proceeds through a series of verbal and kinetic announcements of his yieldedness before his Lord."[40] This brief statement, in fact, encompasses the essentials of the act of prayer in Islam: the intention, the preparation, the readiness and the "yieldedness" by which one expresses his or her submission, *islam*, to God.

As the times for the ritualized prayer or *salat* are of particular importance in Islam, so is the physical or spatial orientation involved in the act of prayer. Prayer should be directed toward Mecca, the holiest city of Islam and the home of the *Ka'ba* or sacred house, believed to have been built originally by Adam and later remade by Abraham and his son Isma'il, in pilgrimage to which all Muslims must go once in a lifetime. Historically, prayer was not always directed to Mecca. In the earliest days of the Muslim community, it is clear that the Prophet Muhammad directed his followers to turn toward Jerusalem in prayer. This obvious acknowledgment of the sanctity of that city (called *al-quds*, the holy, in Arabic) marks another reason for the deep regard in which Jerusalem is held by Muslims. Sometime after the *hijra*, however, and probably in connection with the Prophet's rather unsuccessful negotiations with members of the Jewish community living in Medina, he apparently told the faithful that they should now turn toward Mecca for prayer.[41] This prayer direction or orientation is called *qibla*.[42] The very fact of turning in prayer in the same direction or, rather, toward the same centering point that is faced by all of one's coreligionists, enhances the Muslim's sense of community and corporate identity. While the actual times of prayer differ from place to place because of the different positions of the sun, the spatial orientation remains constant, reinforcing a geographical unity that transcends the variations of national and cultural identities. It is not only in prayer that the *qibla* is acknowledged; during the ritual surrounding the death of a Muslim believer, for example, the body is laid so that the face is directed toward Mecca, the final act of God-directedness performed by one's family and community on his or her behalf.

The physical orientation toward Mecca has been interpreted by many spiritually minded Muslims as only symbolic of the true prayer direction, which is toward God Himself. As the Prophet is reported to have said, "[God] is in truth present in the *qibla* of every one of you."[43] Or, in the words of Abu Hamid al-Ghazali:

> As for facing the Qibla, in doing so, you turn your external face away from all other directions and toward the House of God, Exalted is He. Do you then suppose you are not also required to turn your heart away from everything else, directing it towards God, Great and Glorious is He? What an absurd notion, since this is the whole object of the exercise! . . . The Prophet, on him be peace, said: 'When a man stands up to pray, directing his desire, his face and his heart towards God, Great and Glorious is He, he will come out of that Prayer as on the day his mother gave him birth.'[44]

Mosques are oriented in the direction of Mecca, and the worshipper in the mosque is aided in knowing the precise direction in which to pray by an indentation or niche in the front of the prayer hall, called the *mihrab*. It is generally a recession of a number of inches or even a few feet, often decorated or inlaid with stone or tiles, sometimes done in calligraphic style. This has provided an opportunity for Muslim artists to apply their creativity, within carefully set boundaries of what is appropriate, to what is essentially the most important place in the mosque. In a few of the very old mosques, for example in Cairo, one can find today small signs indicating that the geography of early Muslim scientists sometimes lacked precision and that the accurate direction is slightly to the left or right of that signified by the *mihrab*. Worshippers travelling today can make use of small mechanical devices to help orient them toward Mecca, and many hotels in Islamic cities provide indicators of the prayer direction in the rooms.

Also, a part of the physical directedness of the worshipper, but, again, the physical as it points to and enables the one intending to pray to become psychologically and spiritually oriented in the proper direction, is the prayer mat upon which the actual prayer is carried out. The word *sajada* in Arabic means to bow down in worship, to prostrate oneself. The place in which community prayer is performed is thus called the *masjid*, generally translated as mosque, and the rug or mat on which one prays is the *sajjada*. By locating oneself on such a mat, not only does one practically avoid the discomfort of having the forehead touch bare or possibly unclean ground or floor, but also one psychologically and symbolically designates a space apart from the world of the mundane, a special enclosure in and on which communication between human and divine can be facilitated. Often, one may be in a place at the time for prayer when it is not possible to produce a special mat or rug on which to perform the prostrations. Any piece of fabric, or even newspaper, can be "sanctified," as it were, and designated to provide this kind of private space for the worshipper. On the streets of crowded metropolitan cities, one can see the faithful kneeling for prayer on any materials readily available.

For the Muslim, prayer is not simply a mental or spiritual attitude, a chance to sit and converse with God or to lift petitions in the hope of response or solace. Nor is it even simply a matter of thanksgiving of the mind and heart. It involves a total physical, bodily response, a putting of oneself in a series of positions in which one's every bone and muscle attest to the intensity of the prayer experience, to the absolute submission of the individual in relation to God. {Thou (O Muhammad) seest them bowing and falling prostrate (in worship), seeking bounty from Allah and (His) acceptance. The mark of them is on their foreheads from the traces of prostration. . . .}, says the Qur'an (S. 48:29). And, indeed, those Muslims who have dedicated themselves to a lifetime of prayer often do have smoky marks on their foreheads "from the traces of prostration . . ." It has been said that to place one's forehead on the ground, thus exposing the back of the neck, is to assume a position of complete vulnerability in an ultimate act of submission and trust. And, in fact, the history of Islam has recorded more than one incident of a man who has fallen to the sword of his enemies when in just such a position.

Each of the five daily prayers consists of a series of ritual *ruku'* (sing. *raka'*), which means ritual bowing or bending of the body and dropping to one's knees. Each of these movements, including standing, bowing, prostrating oneself completely and then sitting, is accompanied by the appropriate prayers and invocations. The exact nature of these differs slightly from one legal school to another, as do the specific requirements of the prayers at different times of the day, but the basic pattern is the same. Some Muslims in the contemporary world have tried to suggest alternatives to the traditional execution of the prayer, such as sitting on chairs rather than on the floor, or bowing the head rather than prostrating themselves. Such efforts have been strongly discouraged, however, on the basis of both destroying the intention of the full physical efforts as part of the prayer and of impugning the uniformity of all Muslims participating in the exact forms of the prayer ritual.[45]

Raka' is also the term used to designate one complete prayer cycle. In the initial position of the prayer, that of standing *(qiyam)*, the believers extend their arms in a gesture that for some is reminiscent of ancient oriental and occidental liturgies preserved from antiquity.[46] In this position, the worshipper faces Mecca, puts his (or her) hands to his ears, and declares his intention to pray. One must not turn away from the *qibla*, which represents God Himself, at any point during the prayer. Then, he lowers his arms and puts the right one on top of the left and says a prayer of praise to God. At this point, the Fatiha is recited. The Fatiha is the opening Sura or chapter of the Qur'an, consisting of seven verses beginning with the invocation, "In the name of God, the merciful, the compassionate." Some have likened this Sura to the Lord's Prayer in Christianity, a comparison that applies, not to structure or content, perhaps, but certainly to its importance in the minds and hearts of Muslim believers. The Fatiha, which is recited in every *raka'*, is understood by most Muslims to be the essence of prayer itself. A *hadith qudsi*, or saying attributed to God although not part of the Qur'an, attests that "a prayer performed by someone who has not recited the Essence of the Qur'an [i.e. the Fatiha] during it is deficient . . ."[47] Mahmoud Ayoub notes that the quality of mercy attributed to God when he is called *al-rahman* in the Fatiha (and also in all but one of the one hundred fourteen chapters of the Qur'an) is a quality that is God's alone. "This Divine attribute of universal and infinite mercy is symbolized by God's holy and everlasting countenance or face which is turned towards creation and which sustains it and gives it life," says Ayoub. The second divine aspect invoked here, however, *al-rahim*, he says, can also be applied to humans when they show mercy towards others: "This attribute of Divine mercy can and must be shared by human beings."[48] As God is one, humans respond by living lives of integrity. As God is just, we are called upon to express justice in our lives. And, as God is merciful, we are enjoined to express the quality of mercy in all of our human interactions. Thus, the very act of worship becomes the occasion in which the worshipper not only acknowledges and praises God, but, in the process of doing so, assumes the obligation to reflect the divine qualities in her or his own living. The rest of the Fatiha is considered to be divided between God and humanity, so to speak, with the first half describing the divine and the second applicable to humans. Ayoub quotes a *hadith qudsi* in which the rationale for this division is clarified:

> I [God] have divided the prayer *(salat)* between me and my servant, and my servant shall have what he prays for. For when the servant says, 'All praise be to God, the Lord of all beings,' God says, 'My servant has praised me.' When the servant says, 'The All-Merciful, the Compassionate,' God says, 'My servant has magnified me.' When the servant says, 'Master of the day of judgment,' God says, 'My servant has glorified me . . . this is my portion and to him belongs what remains.'[49]

After the Fatiha is recited, another passage of the Qur'an is then recited, with the understanding that the words from the last verse of the Fatiha, "guide us on the straight path," in fact elicit the response from God that is represented in the words of the succeeding verses. This is based on the assurance of S. 42:51 that God will not speak to any mortal unless it be by revelation. Thus, it is through the Qur'anic verses that follow the recitation of the Fatiha that God indeed does speak to the worshipper. The prayer becomes the vehicle for humans to express their praise of God at the same time that it opens the heart of the believers to receive continuing guidance from God. This is the direct way that the believer learns how to conduct himself in his daily living.[50] The worshipper then says the *takbir*, God is greater, and moves through the rest of the *raka'* which includes the sitting *(jalsa, qa'da)* and prostration *(sujud)* positions. The full *raka'* is repeated several times, depending on which prayer is being performed. At the end of the prayer, the worshippers say the *taslim* or salutation, invoking peace by which one both greets those who are worshipping around him or her and again signals one's absolute submission to God.

Some have invested the different postures with particular symbolic significance, often connecting them with letters of the Arabic alphabet. Goolam Karim, for example, says that the first or standing position, *qiyam*, symbolizes the first letter of the alphabet, *alif*, which is a (more or less) straight vertical line. This draws the immediate connection between the human at the lower pole and God at the upper pole. It also illustrates the strong Muslim conviction that there are no intermediaries between human and divine. When one bows at the waist, it represents the letter *lam*; when one rises from bowing, it symbolizes God's listening and responding to the one who is in praise of him. The prostration represents the letter *heh* and finds its parallels in both the Hebrew Bible and the New Testament (Joshua falling on his face in 5:14, Elijah casting himself upon the earth in I Kings 18:42, Abraham in Genesis 17:3, and Jesus prostrating himself in prayer in Matthew 26:39). Karim goes on to say that the two prostrations essential to every *raka'* or prayer segment represent, first, Iblis' disobedience when he refused to prostrate himself before Adam and was ejected by God from the Garden (S. 2:34) and, second, the obedience of the angels who obeyed God's command.[51] "If a human being prostrates himself at an appropriate point in his recitation of the Qur'an," says a tradition from the Prophet Muhammad, "the devil withdraws, weeping as he says: 'Alas! This man was bidden to prostrate himself and he has obeyed, so Paradise is his. I was also commanded to make prostration, but I disobeyed and so Hell is my lot.'"[52]

Throughout all of the ritual of the prayer, the believer concentrates with heart and mind on the realization of God. The ability to be aware of God's presence through contemplation naturally depends on one's spiritual readiness *(isti'dad)*. While the prayer is structured and stylized and one has the experience of participating in the community of all those who worship together, there is, nonetheless, an inevitable and important sense of individuality in the way each worshipper both presents and responds to the elements of the prayer. Each believer's experience of God, in other words, is *uniquely* his or her own, again expressing both the vertical and horizontal dimensions of the very word *islam/*Islam.

Friday Prayer

This bidimensionality is illustrated most specifically in the Friday prayer, the congregational time when the believers are called to come together to worship in unison. {O ye who believe! When the call is heard for the prayer of the day of congregation, haste unto remembrance of Allah and leave your trading. That is better for you if ye did but know}, says S. 62:9. This day of the week is called in Arabic *al-jum'a*, from the Arabic root *jama'a*, meaning to gather together or unite. Friday has been called "the best day on which the sun shines," its excellences applying not only to the noon worship, but to all times of the day. Friday is the auspicious day for works of piety, for personal supplications in addition to the congregational prayer, for reciting the Qur'an, for performing works of piety and almsgiving, and so on.[53] The most powerful experience of the unity and solidarity of all Muslims is perhaps experienced on the *hajj* or pilgrimage, when many hundreds of thousands of worshippers join together in prayer and circumambulation of the *ka'ba.* This experience of the oneness of the community of Islam in its acknowledgment of the oneness *(tawhid)* of God is shared on a smaller scale every Friday at the time of congregational prayer.

The mosque is generally the locale for the Friday prayer. In some areas of the world, there are so many people responding to the call to the Friday prayer that the mosque itself is filled to overflowing. In that case, one can see the courtyard or even the sidewalk outside the mosque occupied by men, and, in that case, it is only men, going through their prayer prostrations. The experience of praying physically in close proximity to one's fellow believers is one in which I have, on occasion, joined both in this country and in the Middle East. Because of these experiences, in which I have been warmly welcomed by Muslim women friends, I can understand the reason converts to Islam in America cite the power and beauty of congregational prayers ("standing feet to feet, shoulder to shoulder") as one of the most compelling aspects of their new faith. While traditionally women have not joined in the congregational Friday prayers,[54] this is changing in many parts of the world as Muslims are seriously rethinking roles that women can, and should, play in the public worship life of the community.

The beauties of the Friday congregational prayer have been extolled through the ages. Al-Ghazali, for example, cites the Prophet as saying that "the merit of congregational prayer surpasses that of individual prayer by twenty-seven degrees," and that "to perform the prayer in congregation is to fill one's throat with worship." Since much of the faith of Islam is expressed in relation to the day of resurrection, al-Ghazali cites a tradition about the importance of the congregational prayer in that context:

> It is said that on the Day of Resurrection a group of people will be assembled, their faces like shining stars. The angels will ask them: "How did you conduct yourselves in life?" To this they will reply: "On hearing the Call to Prayer, we used to set about our ablutions, letting nothing else distract us." Another group will then be assembled, their faces like radiant moons. In answer to the same question, they will say: "We used to make our ablutions ahead of time." The next group to be assembled will have faces like the sun. They will say: "We used to hear the Call to Prayer inside the Mosque."[55]

One of the important ingredients of the Friday prayer which distinguish it from the other times of congregational worship is the delivery of the *khutba* or sermon. In fact, the Friday prayer service is considered "valid" only if there is a sermon delivered by a *khatib* or preacher, who, like the worshipper, must be ritually pure. The *khutba* actually consists of two parts, between which the preacher sits down to rest. The sermon itself follows a certain set pattern, including the appropriate times for standing and sitting, phrases of respect for God and the Prophet Muhammad, prayers for the faithful gathered, and the like. Normally, the sermon is delivered from an elevated position *(minbar)* so that the preacher can be seen by all of those worshipping in the mosque, said to have been the practice of Muhammad toward the end of his life. The tradition of having a *khutba* is not Qur'anic, but probably dates from the time of the Prophet.[56] The actual topics of the sermons can range widely, being sometimes very political in nature and sometimes directed toward the spiritual edification of the listeners. Any topic considered to enhance the welfare of the community is appropriate for the *khutba*, which is designed to instruct and educate the masses, to awaken in them a sense of duty, and to exhort them to appropriate action.[57]

Du'a' (Private Prayer)

{Praise be to God Who hath given me, in my old age, Ishmael and Isaac! Lo! My Lord is indeed the Hearer of Prayer [du'a']. My Lord! Make me to establish proper worship, and some of my posterity (also); our Lord! And accept the prayer} (S. 14:39-40). These verses, from the famous prayer of Abraham in the Qur'an, testify to the importance of the kind of prayer in Islam that is not formal and ritualized. This is du'a', the spontaneous prayer of the heart that can be uttered at any time and for any occasion. Often referred to as "inner prayer," it is one of the ways in which the believer is in constant remembrance of the presence of God in his or her life. It comes from the Arabic verb da'a, to call or summon, or to invite, and expresses the opportunity of the individual believer to call upon God and to know that his call will be answered. (This is also the verb that is used for the missionary effort in Islam, that movement (da'wa) through which Muslims call upon those who are not Muslim to hear and understand the truth of the revelation to the Prophet Muhammad.) The invocatory nature of this kind of prayer finds its justification again in the Qur'an, as in S. 7:180: {The most beautiful names belong to God: so call on Him by them . . .}.[58]

The salat or ritual prayer in Islam has been so venerated in traditional Islam that there have been those of a more purist orientation who have eschewed the legitimacy of this kind of personalized prayer. (In fact, a rare few have questioned whether prayer of any kind is possible because predestination is already determined, or no prayer is worthy of God, or patience in the face of affliction is the best response.[59]) Extraritual prayer, however, occupies an inextricable place in Muslim worship life. The many prayers recorded throughout the Qur'an as having been uttered by the great Muslim prophets and messengers of God are considered du'a', as are the private prayers offered by the Prophet himself throughout his life and ministry.[60] These prayers, overheard by his associates and preserved in the traditions, offer the believer an opportunity to know more intimately what was in the mind and heart of the Prophet as he went through the experiences of establishing his new community. They relate the content of Muhammad's conversations with God and, in turn, become the basis for instruction of his followers in the essentials of prayer life.

Du'a' is actually one of the meanings of the term salat as it is found in the Qur'an. The exegete, al-Tabari, specified four places in the Qur'an where this is the case, interpreting it to mean that calling on God in this way in the context of the ritualized prayer has the effect of promoting a calmness and confidence in the worshipper.[61] "In the best hands *Du'a'* stays very closely with the temper and the themes of *Salat* and with the *Fatihah*," says Kenneth Cragg, "which, it can be claimed, is central to both."[62] And, indeed, the Fatiha is often called the *surat al-du'a'*, the chapter of the private prayer.[63] Despite the relationship of the formal and informal kinds of prayer, however, the appeal of *du'a'* is that it is freer, more personal, and, generally, based on the particular concerns that one is having in his or her own immediate situation. It is, in a word, a personalized prayer in which the believer is able to tailor his or her appeal to God to meet life's daily exigencies. The link between the two forms of prayer is also underscored in that a *du'a'* or private prayer can be said at specified times during the ritual prayer, at the time of the call to prayer, in the standing position, during the prostration, or even in the time of sitting. While the *salat* must be performed by recitation in Arabic, *du'a'* can be made in any language.

Du'a' prayer is offered in a regularized way during the performance of the *hajj* or pilgrimage. This includes a prayer of supplication and praise during the *ihram* or initial state of sacred prohibitions; prayers in Mecca on entering the mosque, beholding the *Ka'ba*, and passing under the arch before the sacred enclosure; a prayer while circumambulating the *Ka'ba*; prayers read atop the mountains of al-Safa and al-Marwah; prayers on entering the Valley of Arafat, read at the mosque of the Sacred Grove, and read on approaching Mina; and a prayer read by the pilgrim departing Mecca for the trip home. When one visits Medina, the second of the holiest cities of Islam, *du'a'* prayers are read on entering the mosque, at the tomb of the Prophet, at the tomb of the first caliph, Abu Bakr, and at the tomb of the second caliph, 'Umar.[64]

These personalized prayers technically are considered to be beyond that which is required, i.e., the ritual prayer, and in the realm of supererogatory performance (*nafila*, pl. *nawafil*) or work of supererogation. Doctors of the law recommend that, before offering the private prayer, one should be in the same state of ritual purity, achieved by doing ablutions, that is required before performing the *salat*, and that *du'a'* should be prefaced with the *niyya* or intention.[65] In fact, spontaneous prayer is just that and often leaps to the mind and heart of the worshipper without the strict formalities required of the ritual prayer. Many traditions support the Qur'anic promise that God will indeed be present to the one who calls on him, as in S. 2:186, {I answer the prayer of the suppliant when he crieth unto Me}. In one famous *hadith qudsi* or holy hadith, God is believed to have said: "My servant continues drawing nearer to Me through supererogatory acts until I love him; when I love, I become his ear with which he hears, his eye with which he sees, his hand with which he grasps, and his foot with which he walks. And if he asks Me [for something], I give it to him. If indeed he seeks My help, I help him."[66] Another often-quoted holy saying assures the believer that God will not only respond, but will, in fact, outdo the believer in eagerness to draw closer:

> I am as My servant thinks I am. I am with him when he makes men-tion of me. If he makes mention of Me to himself, I make mention of him to Myself; and if he makes mention of Me in an assembly, I make mention of him in an assembly better than it. And if he draws near to Me in a hand's span, I draw near to him an arm's length; and if he draws near to Me an arm's length, I draw near to him a fathom's length. And if he comes to Me walking, I go to him at speed (sometimes translated "If he walks toward Me, I will run toward him").[67]

Such assurances of the nearness of God and the willingness of God to respond to the one who calls on Him in prayer provide great comfort in the lives of those who are facing trials and calamities and offer an opportunity for the spontaneous word of praise of God that may come at any time from the believer.

The supplicatory nature of the private prayer is often one of its most distinguishing characteristics. The believer prays in petition, asking something of God (although generally this does not mean a request for material goods) in a way that is not true of the ritual prayer which is generally declaratory. It is sometimes said that a prayer for others is one that will always be answered and that one is obligated to pray for one's family and loved ones, as well as for those who have been part of one's life journey. Annemarie Schimmel notes that many Persian, Turkish, and Urdu epic poems invite the reader, at the end, to pray for the author and the scribe.[68]

An important dimension of the petitionary aspect of private prayer is the seeking of forgiveness, *istighfar*. There are a number of traditions which make it clear that asking forgiveness was a reg-ular practice of the Prophet, so much so that he has been called *sayyid al-istighfar*, the master of forgiveness: "Thy glory I extol, O God! And Thy praise I hymn. I testify that there is no god save Thee. I seek Thy forgiveness, and unto Thee I turn penitent."[69] The Qur'an itself indicates that God called upon Muhammad to ask forgiveness for living believers, as in S. 47:19 {Know, therefore, that there is no god but God, and ask forgiveness for thy fault, and for the men and women who believe}. According to the Hanifi school of law, asking forgiveness of God is an essential part of the valid prayer-rite, and, even for those who do not make it condi-tional, some form of *istighfar* is considered Sunna, or according to the tradition of the Prophet, during the prayer.[70]

The question of intercession often comes up when the matter of prayer in Islam is discussed. The Qur'an refers to intercession *(shafa'a)* and intercessor twenty-nine times. For the most part, it is clear that intercession is unacceptable and that no one can intercede with God, although there seems to be some flexibility in terms of the possibility that angels, true witnesses, and those who have made a covenant with God might be able to perform this function. Among the true witnesses, of course, is the Prophet Muhammad, although he is not mentioned in any of the twenty-nine references. Qur'an 47:19 (cited above) indicates that God did expect him to intercede in asking forgiveness for the members of his community. Constance Padwick, perhaps the best known of the Western chroniclers of Muslim prayer practices and manuals, notes that the greatest of all opportunities for intercession is actually on the pilgrimage, citing the petition of the Prophet, "O God, forgive the (Mecca) pilgrims and forgive those for whom the pilgrims ask forgiveness."[71] The best of the *du'a'* prayers are those that are made out of deep love of, and trust in, God and with no attention to human wishes and interests. For the mystic, this becomes the prayer of pure selfless love, beyond human fear and hope, which carries one beyond even the desire for eternal existence in the Garden of Paradise. This was most beautifully expressed by the early woman mystic and saint, Rabi'a al-'Adawiyya (d. 801) of Basra, who proclaimed: "O my Lord, whatever share of this world Thou dost bestow on me, bestow it on Thine enemies, and whatever share of the next world Thou dost give me, give it to Thy friends — Thou art enough for me."[72]

Dhikr

Basic to the understanding of prayer in Islam is the importance of remembering God, referred to in the Qur'an as *dhikr*. It means calling forth in one's deepest imagination the reality of God's presence both by thought and by the process of specific mention. Among the many Qur'anic references to *dhikr* are S. 33:41-42 {O ye who believe! Remember Allah with much remembrance, and glorify Him early and late}, S. 78:3 {So remember the name of thy Lord and devote thyself with a complete devotion}, and S. 13:28 {Verily in the remembrance of Allah do hearts find rest!}. More specifically, *dhikr* implies thinking about God with the necessary preparation and focus: "Doctrinally speaking, the *dhikr* is the becoming aware by the creature of the connection that unites him for all eternity to the Creator. Seen in this way, the *dhikr* constitutes the very essence of religion. . . ."[73] In its more generalized sense, *dhirk* can be used to describe the process of remembering God by all believers as they pray either in the ritualized prayer or in the more personalized *du'a'*. *Dhikr* also came to be applied to the particular form of worship developed by those who have been known as Sufis, followers of the mystical path of Islam. As such, it became specialized according to the different *tariqas* or orders, often associated with the repetition of certain ritual formulae based on the verses of the Qur'an, particularly those that contain some of the beautiful names of God.[74]

S. H. Nasr has done a study on the similarities between Sufi remembrance of God and the prayer of the heart in Christian Hesychasm. He attributes the resemblance between these forms of worship, not to any historical interaction or borrowing, but rather to the nature of spirituality in the two traditions and to what he calls "the constitution of the human microcosm."[75] The resemblance is seen most closely in the meaning of the prayer of the heart, which, for the Sufi, is precisely the *dhikr* or constant remembering of God through the invoking of His name. The two traditions share the understanding that remembrance of God is not an occasional thing, but, in its deepest meaning, implies an invocation of God's presence with every breath. This involves not only good intention, but the necessity of careful spiritual training under the guidance of an experienced teacher. When practiced in this way, *dhikr* is both meditation on God and the accomplishment of the concomitant spiritual virtues and practices.[76]

Many who have written about the importance of *dhikr* in the devotional life of Islam have stressed its function in bringing together the different strands of one's life, of providing an integrating experience in which, through contemplation of the oneness of God, one realizes a kind of spiritual unity. "It is in prayer and in what, in Islam, is called *dhikr* — the constant remembrance of God — that the different threads are brought together, multiplicity is absorbed into unity, and dreaming gives way to full wakefulness," says Gai Eaton.[77] In the process of *dhikr*, we see again the bidimensional aspect of prayer in Islam. *Dhikr* is reciprocal insofar as it acknowledges God's mindfulness of humanity. In the remembering and realization of God, the worshipper not only draws the connection between himself and God and brings together the elements of his or her own life, but he also understands his relationship to, and therefore he prays for, all of creation. The worshipper is thus alone with himself, with God, with the rest of the world of humanity and, indeed, of all creation. And, in this experience, this centeredness through remembrance of one's Lord, time and space coalesce, and one enters into the sacred arena of God's presence. This is the fullest expression of *tawhid* — recognizing, acknowledging, and responding to the reality of the oneness of God.

Dhikr, as it came to be understood and developed in many of the Sufi orders, while not negating the importance of the formal prayers, in one sense served to open up the requirement so that it could be more flexibly interpreted. The formalities of the *salat* sometimes could be set aside for the more immediate task of engaging in constant *dhikr*. When this was carried to the extent that it could be called antinomianism, it not surprisingly raised serious concerns among others in the community. For the Sufi, however, *dhikr* could be a way of avoiding the rigidity of scholastic theology and of breathing life and richness into the worship experience. In a kind of parallel to the physical prostrations that accompany the formal prayer or *salat*, Sufis have developed specialized techniques of breathing and crying out to God, sometimes accompanied by chanting and/or the use of musical instruments. And, as the *salat* is carried out with one's fellow worshippers, emphasizing the communal nature of Islam, so the *dhikr* rituals performed with other members of the order serve to solidify the sense of belonging, with one's fellows, to a community of worshippers. The rigid structure of the *salat*, in which specific formulae are repeated by all worshippers, is modified in the *dhirk* in which believers are free to interject their own invocations or personal prayers.

Common to almost all Sufi orders is the repetition of the first phrase of the *shahada* or profession of faith, that which testifies to the oneness of God *(la ilaha illa' Llah)*. It is considered to be particularly efficacious because it incorporates the absolute negation of anything other than God with the absolute affirmation of the reality and being of God. These negative and positive poles then reflect the experience of annihilation of self, *fana'*, experienced by the mystic in the highest stages of contemplation, followed by the experience of *baqa'*, abiding or existence, in which one finds oneself infused with the being of God. These poles, incidentally, also reflect the experience anticipated at the end of time, at the coming of the day of resurrection, when God will first annihilate all that exists save Himself and then revive all of creation to experience the judgment and consignment to the abodes of punishment or reward.[78]

While the term "saint" is not really applicable in Islam, nonetheless certain persons throughout history, and continuing today, have been understood by many to be invested with special qualities or characteristics by virtue of their own experiences with God. Such a person is often called a *wali*, or friend of God, because he or she has attained a nearness to God by virtue of having achieved the highest of the states and stages of mystical contemplation of God or simply having lived a particularly virtuous life. Particularly after death, these *wali*s are considered by many in the Islamic world to have special qualities that, in fact, may be called upon in assistance of those who are still living. Often, a saint is revered by having his or her body placed in a special coffin *(tabut)* and displayed inside a shrine. The size and decoration of such a shrine vary greatly according to the importance of the one who is buried, the resources available to those who remember this person, et cetera. Shrines are in evidence across the Muslim world, and, while they and the practices that accrue to them have been regularly denigrated by those who fear that they impugn the purity of Islam, they have remained an important element in the private religious lives of many Muslims.

As we observed above, intercession *(shafa'a)* is a problematic concept in Islam and, if accepted at all, is generally attributed only to the Prophet on behalf of the believers. Nonetheless, for many Muslims, often, but not exclusively, those of lower economic and educational levels, the practice of visiting a saint's shrine does involve what can be understood only as the request for a certain kind of intercession. And, although devotion in the full sense of the word technically can apply only to the response of the individual believer to God, there is also an aspect of devotion that operates in the response of the visitor to a *wali*'s tomb that cannot be denied. The understanding is that the "friend of God" became so close to God, and continues in that relationship even after death, that he or she is able to bestow blessings on the one who comes to pay respect and also is able, in some senses, to intervene in the affairs of that person's life. A visitor to a shrine may perform both *salat* and *du'a'* in the presence of the saint (who, incidentally, is believed to be not only continuingly alive, but active in a life of prayer to God), may listen to religious songs performed by live musicians or recorded on tape, may speak privately with the saint requesting his or her assistance/intervention to help solve some particular problem the visitor is experiencing, or may simply sit quietly in the presence of one considered to have achieved this closeness to God. At the shrine of Imam al-Shafi'I in Cairo, I watched one afternoon while a young boy with his school book in hand asked the saint for assistance in the classroom, a mother requested that the Imam find a husband for her daughter, and an elderly woman wanted to be assured that she would have a place in the Garden of Paradise after death. Often, the petitioner will "repay" the saint for his or her hoped for assistance by tying ribbons or flags around the covering of the coffin, rubbing the brass or silver fittings with the edge of a garment to make them shine, or putting money on the *tabut* to assist the caretaker of the shrine.

Sometimes, the interaction between the believer and the saint amounts almost to a kind of contract, with the petitioner offering to provide some sort of reward to the one considered to have spiritual powers or making a vow as to what he or she will do if the requested help is provided. Vows are often written out and placed either on the *tabut* or in what is called a vow box.[79] The more formal rites of vow making often include praying, reciting of some Qur'an verses, lighting of candles, et cetera. In one case recorded in contemporary Egypt, a woman who promised to perform some meritorious act in relation to a saint found that her petition had not been answered and, instead, rubbed the tomb with garlic to "punish" its occupant. The faithful may go individually or in large numbers to a shrine. For women, the experience of spending time at a shrine has been particularly important, especially when it represents one of the few sanctioned occasions for them to leave the confines of the home.

Are such practices part of orthodox Islam? For the most part, they cannot be considered such, although sometimes they do get official approval, as in the 1971 statement of the Council of Islamic Affairs in Egypt acknowledging the special abilities of saints.[80] "The great tradition of world Islam stoops to conquer in Egypt," says Frederick Denny, "by allowing and even embracing otherwise deviant or at least idiosyncratic local saint cults, which in turn have their analogues throughout much of the rest of the Islamic world."[81] To some extent, there have been efforts to "legitimize" such visits to saints' shrines, as Philippe Marçais notes: "Il importe cependant de souligner que le formulaire des demandes est nourri d'invocations religieuses, d'eulogies rituelles, et, pour celles des femmes qui en savent un peu, de citations coraniques. Ainsi l'Islam recouvre de son voile d'orthodoxie un visage que déparent bien des verrues de la superstition."[82] More to the point of this essay is the question of whether or not the petitions made to saints constitute a form of prayer. Insofar as prayer involves a direct relationship between the believer and God, the answer must be no. A bit more obliquely, however, to the extent to which such petitions represent the attempts of the believer to mitigate the circumstances of his or her life, to solve problems that might seem too trivial to present before the Lord of the Worlds, and to find solace in the face of difficult circumstances, it probably can be said to be a particular form of petitionary prayer. This kind of activity allows the individual to experience a sense of power and control over his or her own life. It is also, I would argue, an acknowledgment of the fact that certain pious individuals have indeed been able to find great favor with, and closeness to, God and that, as an expression of God's mercy, they are able to provide a means of bringing closer the human and the divine for others, of allowing the humble servant who is less advanced in piety or in spirituality to transcend the mundane and to participate in some sense in the world of the spiritual.

*   *   *

What, then, might the Christian observer of the various forms of Islamic prayer ritual "take away to ponder," so to speak, of that experience? Let me propose six characteristics of Muslim prayer that I think might be instructive to Christian thinking about this activity, recognizing that many of these characteristics or qualities may also be true of, or applicable to, certain varieties of Christian prayer.

1. Prayer as comprehensive. As I have pondered the different types and purposes of prayer and worship as it is understood in the Islamic tradition, I have been particularly struck with the variety of ways in which it is comprehensive. Worship is prescribed by God, not only for humans, but for all of the other members of God's creation, including the angels, as well as for that interesting class of beings known as the *jinn* who are created, not of clay, as are humans, but of fire and who, nonetheless, also will be subject to judgment on the Day of Resurrection. Prayer is comprehensive to the degree that it infuses all the other prescribed religious duties. It is inconceivable that one would perform the pilgrimage without prayer, or that one would undergo the rigors of the monthly fast without recourse to direct communication with the divine for succor and nourishment, or that one would give of one's goods through the paying of the alms tax without prayerful contemplation of the relationship of piety to charitable support of the community. And, prayer is comprehensive in that it occurs at regularly prescribed intervals, carefully spaced and timed, and yet, in another dimension, it can and should happen as the constant activity of the human soul and heart in response to, and praise of, God.

2. Prayer as bidimensional or, perhaps, even multidimensional. Prayer in Islam might be described as a "reaching out" which involves God, the individual worshipper, the community of all of those who worship together, and all of creation itself. God, through His word in the Qur'an commanding prayer and directing the Prophet and his followers as to the particulars of the way prayer should be performed, has reached out to His creatures and extended to them the means whereby they can express praise and invite guidance. Humans in their prayerful response to God as individual submitters, *Muslims*, in turn reach out to their Lord in praise, supplication, and devotion. As we have explored above, in the recognition of God's oneness articulated in the prayer of the

shahada, humans take upon themselves the responsibility to live with integrity. Acting out this integrity, then, constitutes the reaching out of the believer to his or her fellows through acts of kindness, mercy, and justice as a reflection of those same qualities of the divine. As Muslims join together in praise of, and supplication to, God, they reach out and acknowledge each other as members of the community of Islam. *Du'a'* allows for the prayer of petition whereby one calls to God on behalf of one's fellows, and the related *da'wa* or call to others to submit to God is a reaching out in mercy to those who have not yet accepted the call to Islam and thus are in danger of consignment to eternal punishment.

3. Prayer as connectedness. As the opening quotation from the Islamic prayer manual indicates, *salat* forms the *sila* or connection with God, and whoever prays makes this connection directly and selfconsciously. Likewise, whoever refuses to pray, or does not accept the absolutely essential nature of prayer, cuts himself off, disconnects himself, from God to the point where, by some interpreters, he may even be considered an apostate. Individual worshippers are connected not only to God, but also to each other through the repetition of the same prayer formulae in the *salat*, through the undergoing of the same *raka*'s, and through attention to the same *qibla* or prayer direction. While worship is individual through one's own *niyya* or intention, one's own attitude toward God while in prayer, and one's own private prayer, in the course of the *salat* one is nonetheless together with God, with one's fellow worshippers, and with all creation in the realization that all creatures are God's servants.

4. Prayer as equalizer. Or, perhaps, I should say prayer as an illustration of the basic affirmation of Islam that all of humanity is on an equal plane in the eyes of God. Muhammad's appointment of the freed African slave Bilal to be the first to give the all important call to prayer underscored for succeeding generations the understanding that all races are equal in Islam. All Muslims are asked to adopt the same dress when undertaking the pilgrimage, in the course of which prayer is an essential ingredient. Any Muslim male who is morally upright, regardless of his training or knowledge, is qualified to serve as *imam* or one who calls to prayer. (It is beyond the scope of this essay to debate whether or not inequality between the sexes can be construed by the fact that, to date, women have very rarely been able to serve in this function.) The same prayers are prescribed for everyone, and everyone is expected to recite, indeed, participate in them from early youth through old age. And, the same opportunity is available for everyone to evoke the prayer of the heart. Even the advanced stages of the *dhirk* as the prayer discipline of those who are mystically

oriented are at least theoretically available to anyone who is able to move toward their achievement through the directed processes of spiritual discipline.

5. Prayer as preparation. As we have examined in detail, outside of particular, extenuating circumstances, one does not simply begin to pray in Islam, whether it be *salat* or *du'a'*, without making specific and clear preparation. This involves the preparation of the heart and mind through hearing the call and declaring one's intention, and the preparation of the body through the ablutions and putting on proper clothing. By the time the Muslim actually begins the prayer, he or she is *ready* and also, in one sense, has already begun to pray. While it is obvious, and perhaps natural, that any ritual has the possibility of becoming rote, the variety and comprehensiveness of the modes of preparation almost guarantee that, at some point, the worshipper will be snapped to attention, so to speak, and fully readied for the prayer experience to follow.

6. Prayer as physical response. From the moment that the call of the human voice of the *mu'adhdhin* strikes the human ear, the physical body is fully involved in the performance of prayer. The ritual washings are of the physical body; the turning toward the *qibla* or prayer direction is physical as well as spiritual; the whole body takes part in the movements of the prayer from the time the hands are placed on the sides of the head to the moment when the worshipper places his or her head on the ground in absolute obeisance. The Muslim worshipper is not seated quietly in a chair or pew, but quite literally throws him or herself fully into the act of prayer. Even the most elderly or infirm, whose physical movements may be severely limited, use whatever flexibility is left to them to enter, as fully as it is possible, into the experience of bowing, in the most literal sense of the word, before their Lord.

My teaching over the years has been almost exclusively in the context of a Christian seminary. I have taken it as my task to help students understand, as fully as it is possible, what the different elements of the faith of Islam mean to those who believe in and practice them. To that end, I have had them read as many different Muslim writers as it is possible and have invited Muslims to speak to my classes about their faith and the way it is expressed. With increasing numbers of Muslims in our schools and universities, as well as in our local communities, the opportunities for students, church members, and others to get more of this firsthand explanation are constantly being enhanced. Muslims are not only responding to invitations to talk about their faith, but, in many places, are taking the initiative to invite classes and church groups to visit their local mosques and Islamic centers in order to better understand the essentials of the religion "in context."

For the most part, my experiences, both in inviting Muslims to my classes and taking groups of students to the mosque, have been highly successful. Of course, there have been exceptions. One time I took a class for its last session on Islam to the local mosque, at the invitation of the members of the Islamic community there, to witness and, in some sense, participate in the service of prayer. (It is probably important to note here that not all mosques feel that it is appropriate to have nonMuslims observe, to say nothing of share in, the observance of prayer.) We had spent some time trying to understand the meaning of prayer for Muslims, and I believe I had succeeded in inculcating in these liberal Protestant students a fair level of appreciation for the different elements of the ritual. Then, the women discovered that they needed to be fully covered except for their hands and faces. I managed to persuade them of the importance of doing this, not to say courtesy in the face of Muslim hospitality. But, when we arrived at the mosque and these women, many of whom were preparing for ordination and positions of leadership in the church, discovered that they had to sit in a room well above the worship hall in which they could barely see and hear, while their male colleagues joined the Muslim men in rows directly in front of the *imam*, their patience gave way completely. I felt frustrated and sad that my efforts to instill appreciation and understanding were vitiated by this experience that was so offensive to my very politically correct Master of Divinity students, but was made aware again of the deep, cultural presuppositions that, along with theological considerations, underlie some of the most basic of the religious practices of any community.

While I believe that it is essential for those of us who study other religious traditions to try to share our best understanding of what seems to us meaningful and, even, potentially instructive to Christians about the faith of others, in this case about the prayer practices of Muslims, I also think that it is crucial to present as full a picture of what underlies those practices as it is possible. Sometimes this can be very difficult and, like the mosque experience for the women cited above, can end up being rather counterproductive. For example, it is difficult for anyone who is not Muslim to grasp fully what the Muslim understands as the absolute requirement of the five pillars of Islam. The very prayer manual cited at the beginning of this essay follows a traditional pattern by completing its lovely description of the fullness of the *salat* experience with the dire warning that the one who rejects the duty of prayer, i.e., rejects God by refusing His command, can be declared an apostate. By some interpretations of Islamic law, as the Salmon Rushdie affair illustrates, an apostate deserves the penalty of death. Obviously, Muslims do not normally go around killing those who refuse to pray; nonetheless, not surprisingly do students find the possibility of such a drastic consequence for apostasy, and perhaps even the concept of apostasy itself, very hard to comprehend. It is, of course, much easier to appreciate those elements of other faiths that we can appreciate than those that offend our sensibilities, and the temptation to avoid discussing this reality with students whom I want to persuade of the beauties of Islam is always great. Generally, I try to explain it in the context of the absolute Muslim conviction of the necessity of following God's commandments as a way of attesting to His reality and oneness. Nonetheless, the very concept of punishment as in any way related to prayer is virtually inconceivable to most Christian students and sometimes leads to their concluding that the whole exercise of required prayers is coercive and undercuts the beauty and value of spontaneous prayer done out of personal conviction and desire.

All of which points to the obvious fact that, while there surely is much to learn personally by studying and attempting to experience some of the elements of other faith traditions, some things simply cannot be fully grasped from outside of the faith. Be that as it may, however, there is another dimension of the task of thinking about Christians and the Islamic experience of prayer that needs to be addressed in light of increasing efforts at Christian-Muslim dialogue across the country. That is whether Christians and Muslims can, or should, actually attempt to pray together. While not without interesting historical precedent, especially in the context of North America, this is relatively new territory, and we have few guidelines. Again, let me offer a few examples from my own experience that illustrate possible pitfalls.

After the Oklahoma bombing when Muslims were immediately and incorrectly assumed to be culpable, the Colorado Council of Churches organized an "interfaith" worship service to express solidarity with the Muslim community. The service, in which Muslims and Jews participated, though somewhat minimally, was well attended and generally appreciated. Nonetheless, it was absolutely clear that it was not really an interfaith service at all, but a Christian one in which a few members of other traditions were asked to contribute a small piece. In any case, it does provide one model, though some would argue an inadequate one, for common worship.

Another model is suggested by the attempt of members of an interfaith group in Hartford, Connecticut, last fall to put together what was deemed by most of the participants to be a successful interfaith worship service. It included not only Christians and Muslims, but members of several other traditions. After great effort and much discussion, the planners were able to develop a service, including a series of prayers, that were not offensive to anyone. That it was judged to be successful, I think, had to do more with appreciation of the fact of having accomplished that difficult task than it did with the spiritual content of the service or of the prayers. As I have talked with Christian friends and students since then, they have revealed no small sense of frustration at having had to compromise so much that there was little left of the richness of their own particular tradition. To date, there have been no efforts to replicate the experience.

These examples have to do with experiments in common worship in which prayer is understood to be shared either in the sense of mutual participation or in the sense of one tradition sharing its prayer with another. An incident that took place recently at Hartford Seminary has led to some serious institutional conversation about prayer in an interfaith classroom context. A young Muslim woman enrolled for a class taught, not in the curriculum of interfaith studies, but through the regular academic programming of the school. She was the only student in the class who was not Christian. On the first day, the professor followed his regular custom of asking a member of the class to open with prayer. That student, an African evangelical, concluded by asking for his petitions in the name of the Lord and Savior Jesus Christ. The Muslim woman took great offense, arguing that she had been engaged seriously in the prayer herself and was jolted by the phrase which, in light of her convictions, seemed blasphemous both in terms of intercession and in terms of salvation through Jesus. The student who gave the prayer responded that not to pray in the name of Jesus would be to take the very life out of the petition. A challenging set of discussions between the seminary and the local mosque to which the student belonged ensued. While these did not result in any clear conclusions as to what is appropriate in the context of a seminary trying to reach out to the Muslim community, they nonetheless engendered some significant consciousness raising on the part of seminary faculty.

What can we say or think, then, about the possibility of Christians and Muslims praying together? One answer, of course, is to continue to look for ways to foster conversation and better mutual understanding, but to keep prayer separate as the activity of each community respectively. In this way, particularities can be honored and offenses avoided. I think it is fair to say that this is the preference of most of the Muslims I know and probably of most Christians, too, if they think about it at all. Another possibility is to struggle to find our commonalities and to try to formulate prayer that can be both meaningful and acceptable to both parties. Such prayer would be engaged in "commonly" only on special occasions, with those elements particular to each community reserved for worship in their own congregations. The question that must be addressed by members of both communities, of course, is whether the experience of common sharing in the prayer experience is of sufficient value to offset the almost inevitable sense on everyone's part of a rather "watered down" prayer. Or, is the endeavor of common prayer so important, and so special, that it can take on a new life of its own, thus augmenting the traditional prayer of each community? For this to happen would obviously require a deep sense of commitment and willingness to struggle to some new understandings on the part of select members of each community. A third possibility is to share occasions in which Muslims offer the prayers that they feel are appropriate and Christians do the same, with the other parties open to better understanding while trying to keep their sensibilities under control. This has some obvious advantages, at the same time that it does seem to foster an atmosphere of observation and learning rather than of worship. The very fact of being "observed," some would argue, seriously mitigates against the possibility that one can be in a stance of real prayer.

Variations on these basic models could be developed, of course, to suggest other possibilities. The longstanding debate among people of faith, as well as historians of religion, about commonalities and particularities, about whether those things that distinguish different religions from each other are basic and not to be compromised, suggests that the answers are not easy. I would offer to the conversation only these reflections:

First, that whether prayer is held in common, separately, or "in tandem," in fact all of us can learn something from each other. I have never been an advocate of the dictum so dear to many participants in interfaith discussion that the experience of mutual exposure is not for the purpose of changing anyone's mind or heart. The value in interfaith exchange is greatly enhanced, I believe, if we at least hold open the possibility that we can be personally engaged and that our own faith can be deepened (i.e., changed).

Second, that attempts to try to develop some kind of shared prayer experience inevitably are going to run into deep difficulties. If made in frankness and candor, they may well bring out responses from both Christians and Muslims that feel rather mean spirited. Rather than leading to deeper understanding of the riches of our respective traditions, we may find such discussion, and attempts at commonality, frustrating and even hurtful. That does not suggest to me that at least engaging in the effort may not be of some value, though I would also argue that it is certainly not essential for, and perhaps not even very useful for, understanding the faith of the other. Kenneth Cragg, in his collection of Muslim and Christian prayers entitled *Alive to God*, quotes Shylock in Shakespeare's *The Merchant of Venice* saying, "I will buy with you, sell with you, walk with you, talk with you . . . but I will not pray with you."[83] Cragg laments this reality; while in the long run of things I cannot help agree with him, I have some appreciation for Shylock's reservation.

Third, that while I personally am deeply devoted to the exercise of knowing more about other people's religious beliefs and practices and argue regularly that, not only students, but church people and others should attend to this kind of interfaith understanding with diligence and enthusiasm, I know that it is not for everyone. A former professor of mine used to insist that "the serious study of the faith of other people is a very dangerous business." Having devoted the better part of my life to that activity, I am quite persuaded that he is right. While it may be true that a little knowledge is a dangerous thing, for many, I expect, that it is all that they can or should be asked to cope with. The serious student of other religions must be willing to face serious consequences, and these can be challenging and disturbing as well as exciting and enriching.

All of this said, however, I nonetheless invite the Christian reader to reflect, to whatever degree possible, on the various dimensions of Muslim prayer activity and its capacity to frame, as it were, the entire life experience of the individual believer in his or her relation to God, to other Muslims, and to humanity. If we are not able to comprehend, to say nothing of appreciate, the full context of what prayer means as a divinely commanded responsibility, perhaps there can be at least moments in which the richness of that experience intrudes into our own understanding of prayer and its possibilities for moving us beyond the comfort of familiar patterns into new dimensions of divine-human interchange. I offer in conclusion a prayer from a disciple of the thirteenth century, 'Ali Abu'l-Hasan al-Shadhili, that has been particularly important in challenging my students to broaden their own understanding of prayer:

> Allahumma! We ask of Thee fear of Thee, hope in Thee, love for Thee, intimacy with Thee, contentment with Thee, obedience to the command from Thee, on the carpet of contemplation of Thee, looking from Thee toward Thee, making utterance of Thee from Thee — There is no god beside Thee! Glory be to Thee.[84]

NOTES

[1]Ahmad 'Isa 'Ashur, *Hukm Tarik al-Salat wa Kayfa Tusalli* (Cairo: Dar al-I'tisam, n.d.), 9.

[2]Abu Hamid al-Ghazali, *Inner Dimensions of Islamic Worship*, trans. Muhtar Holland (Leister, UK: The Islamic Foundation, 1983).

[3]According to the classical exegete of the Qur'an, al-Tabari, different terms are used for the worship of humans and that of other of God's creatures, namely, *salat* for the former and *tasbih* for the latter. See Mohamed A. Dollah, "Al-Tabari's Interpretation of Salat in the Qur'an: A Psychological Examination," *Hamdard Islamicus* 17 (Spring, 1994), 54.

[4]Goolam Mohamed Karim, "The Symbolism of Prayer in Islam," *Dialogue & Alliance* 3/4 (Winter, 1989-90), 32.

[5]Mahmoud Ayoub, "Thanksgiving and Praise in the Qur'an and in Muslim Piety," *Islamochristiana* 15 (1989), 2.

[6]Kenneth Cragg, *Alive to God. Muslim and Christian Prayer* (London: Oxford University Press, 1970), 38.

[7]Elmer H. Douglas, "The Art of Worship," *Bulletin of the Henry Martyn Institute of Islamic Studies* 8/3 (July-September, 1978), 36-37.

[8]All translations of the Qur'an are from Muhammad Marmaduke Pickthall's *The Glorious Qur'an* (Des Plaines, IL: KAZI Publications, Inc., 1994).

[9]See J. I. Smith, *An Historical and Semantic Study of the Term 'Islam' as Seen in a Sequence of Qur'an Commentaries* (Missoula, MT: Scholars Press, 1975), chapter one.

[10]Bill A. Musk, "Muslim Qiblah Orientation: Toward and Beyond 'Mecca,'" *Bulletin of the Henry Martyn Institute of Islamic Studies* 9/36-53 (January-June, 1986), 36.

[11]Cited by Syed Ali Ashraf, "The Inner Meaning of the Islamic Rites: Prayer, Pilgrimage, Fasting, Jihad," in *Islamic Spirituality: Foundations*, ed. S. H. Nasr (New York: Crossroad, 1987), 118.

[12]"One way to be in tune with the Infinite," says Allahbakhsh Brohi, "is to stay in a prolonged state of prayer and be receptive to the finer forces that descend from above to lift man to a higher plane of existence" (*Islamic Spirituality*, 143).

[13]Elmer H. Douglas, "Prayers of al-Shadhili," in *Medieval and Middle Eastern Studies*, ed. Sami A. Hanna (Leiden: E. J. Brill, 1972), 107.

[14]Joseph Feghali, "La prière dans le Coran," in *L'Expérience de la Prière*, ed. Henri Limet and Julien Ries (Louvain-la-Neuve: Centre d'Histoire des Religions, 1980), 399.

[15]William A. Chittick, *Faith and Practice of Islam* (Albany: State University of New York Press, 1992), 134, citing the 13th century writer, Sayf al-Din Tughril.

[16]The phrase, *al-asthma' al-husna*, most beautiful names, comes from S. 7:180. Most of the names themselves are Qur'anic, although some are found only in the *hadith* or traditions of and from the Prophet. The two most important describe God as the merciful (*al-rahman*) and the compassionate (*al-rahim*), the terms used in the verses which open all of the chapters of the Qur'an save one. See Martin Forward, "Islam," in *Worship*, ed. Jean Holm with John Bowker (London: Pinter Publishers LTD, 1994), 112.

¹⁷Dollah, 47-48.

¹⁸Ayoub, 2.

¹⁹Clinton Bennett, "Islam," in *Rites of Passage*, ed. Jean Holm with John Bowker (New York: Pinter Publishers, 1994), 94.

²⁰See, e.g., 2:33, 2:177, 17:78. The verses connecting prayer with alms-giving were revealed in Mecca.

²¹Ibn Hisham, *The Life of Muhammad* (Eng. transl. A. Guillaume), 186-87, as cited by Ilai Alon, "Interpretation as Compromise: The Case of the Five Daily Islamic Prayers," in *Interpretation in Religion*, ed. S. Biderman and B. Scharfstein (Leiden: E. J. Brill, 1992), 208.

²²See Yoram Erder, "Daily Prayer Times in Karaite Halakha in Light of the Times of Islamic Prayer," *Revue des Études Juives* 153/5-27 (January-June, 1994), 19-22, who cites arguments for a Jewish influence on Islam both in the earlier number of two or three prayers and in the establishment of five prayers later.

²³Feghali, 394.

²⁴Alon, 211-15.

²⁵Karim, 35.

²⁶As cited in Ashraf, 114.

²⁷Thus, the *imam* coordinates the activities of the mosque, often serves as a pastoral counselor to members of the congregation, represents the mosque in public community events, and, in other ways, plays a role unlike that traditionally ascribed to an *imam.*

²⁸From al-Bukhari, as cited by Maulana Muhammad Ali, *The Religion of Islam* (U.A.R.: National Publication and Printing House, n.d.), 380-81.

²⁹African American Muslims in America, taking this appointment of a black African to occupy such an important position in the Prophet's community as a clear indication of the principle of racial equality in Islam, often call themselves by the name Bilalian.

³⁰Goolam Karim goes so far as to assert, "The pealing of mournful bells or the fear-instilling blast of the trumpet represent a wrathful divinity compared to the beneficent and merciful God of Islam, calling people to progress and prosperity both in this world and the next!" (32).

³¹Al-Ghazali, 20-21.

³²*Forty Hadith Qudsi*, trans. Ezzeddin Ibrahim (Beirut: Dar al-Koran al-Kareem, 1980), 56.

³³"Though ethnomusicologists might consider the call to prayer, and the chanted prayers which the gathered group performs, music, because of sustained and rhythmically patterned tones, the Arabs separate these two forms from the *musiqa* (music) that contains texts which comment on things of the secular world" [Ruth M. Stone, "Sound and Rhythm in Corporate Ritual in Arabia," in *Music and the Experience of God*, ed. Mary Collins, David Power, and Melonee Burnim (Edinburgh: T&T Clark, 1989), 73-75].

³⁴". . . *falah*, whether relating to this life or to the next, carries with it the idea of the complete development of the inner faculties of man, the attaining to both material and moral greatness. . ." (Ali, 356).

³⁵Forward, 98.

[36]Spoken directly to the Prophet, encouraging him to perform his duty as a warner and magnifier of the Lord early in his mission.

[37]From the *Discourses* of Jalal al-Din Rumi, as cited by Kenneth Cragg, 60.

[38]Karim, 34. Karim also notes that this symbolizes the freeing of the worshipper from the chains of poverty, ignorance, and subservience.

[39]For a more detailed discussion of *wudu'*, see John Burton, "The Qur'an and the Islamic Practice of Wudu'," *Bulletin of the School of Oriental and African Studies* 51/1 (1988), 21 sq.

[40]Musk, 37.

[41]See David J. Zucker and Jane I. Smith, "Jerusalem, the Sacred City: Perspectives from Judaism and Islam," *Journal of Ecumenical Studies* 32/2 (Spring, 1995).

[42]Sulayman Bashir, "Qiblah Musharriqa and Early Muslim Prayer in Churches," *The Muslim World* 81 (1991), 268, describes the discovery of a mosque in the Negev which has two *qiblas*, an original one facing east and a later one facing south, and Joseph Feghali refers to a little mosque in Medina which, in memory of the change of direction, is called the mosque of the two *qiblas* ("La prière," 397).

[43]Ashraf, 115.

[44]Al-Ghazali, 45.

[45]Ali, 366.

[46]Feghali, 397-98.

[47]*Forty Hadith Qudsi*, 58.

[48]Ayoub, 3.

[49]Ibid., 4.

[50]Brohi, 133.

[51]Karim, 38.

[52]Al-Ghazali, 26.

[53]Douglas, *Art of Worship*, 34.

[54]See, e.g., Saadia Khawar Khan Chisti, "Female Spirituality in Islam," in *Islamic Spirituality: Foundations*, 212.

[55]Al-Ghazali, 24-25.

[56]Yann Richard, "La Fonction Parenétique du 'Alem: La Prière du Vendredi en Iran Depuis la Révolution," *Welt des Islams* 29 (1989), 61-82, discusses the institution of Friday prayer in postrevolution Iran and the impact of new forms of media on its constitution and delivery.

[57]Ali, 435.

[58]Constance Padwick, in her classic work, entitled *Muslim Devotions* (London: S.P.C.K., 1961), 12-13, cites the verbs related to *da'a'*, such as *su'l* (to ask) and *tadarru'* (make petition).

[59]Annemarie Schimmel, "Some Aspects of Mystical Prayer in Islam," *Welt des Islams* 2/2 (1952), 112. Schimmel notes that it was only the stern pietistic mystics who questioned the appropriateness of any form of prayer.

[60]For a rich listing of these many prayers, see the classic translation of Abdul Hamid Farid, *Prayers of Muhammad* (Karachi: Karkhana Tijarat Kutub, 1959).

[61]Dollah, 48.

[62]Cragg, 30-31.

[63]Anonymous, "Du'a'," in *Shorter Encyclopedia of Islam*, H.A.R. Gibb and J. H. Kramers, eds. (Ithaca, NY: Cornell University Press, 1952), 95.

[64]See Ahmad Kamal, *The Sacred Journey* (New York: Duell, Sloan and Pearce), entire.

[65]Philippe Marcais, "La prière de demande dans la pratique religieuse populaire de l'Afrique du Nord," in *L'Expérience de la Prière*, 401.

[66]Cited in Ayoub, 9.

[67]*Forty Hadith Qudsi*, 78.

[68]Annemarie Schimmel, *Mystical Dimensions of Islam* (Chapel Hill: University of North Carolina Press, 1975), 160.

[69]Farid, 250.

[70]Constance Padwick, "The Language of Muslim Devotion III," *The Muslim World* 47 (1957), 201.

[71]Ibid., 208.

[72]As cited in Schimmel, *Mystical Dimensions*, 40.

[73]Jean-Louis Michon, "The Spiritual Practices of Sufism," in *Islamic Spirituality: Foundations*, 275.

[74]Frederick M. Denny, *An Introduction to Islam* (New York: Macmillan, 1985), 285-87, provides a helpful explanation of the three main forms of Sufi *dhikr*, which he identifies as *dhikr al-awqat*, the set *dhikr*s following at least one of the two obligatory *salat*s, the *dhikr al-khafi*, a personal remembrance under the guidance of a leader, and the *dhikr al-hadra*, the communal remembrance in which the *hadra* or presence of God is invoked.

[75]S. H. Nasr, "The Prayer of the Heart in Hesychasm and Sufism," *Greek Orthodox Theological Review* 31/1-2 (1986), 196.

[76]Ibid., 198. Nasr describes what he calls "profound morphological resemblances between certain aspects of Christian and Islamic spirituality."

[77]Gai Eaton, "The Revolving Wall," *Parabola* 15/20-25 (Summer, 1990), 24.

[78]See Jane I. Smith and Yvonne Y. Haddad, *The Islamic Understanding of Death and Resurrection* (Albany: State University of New York Press, 1981), 70-72.

[79]"The vow box is an intrinsic part of the ordinary Muslim's diurnal round of life with its huge threats of disequilibrium. It stands as silent witness to the beliefs and activities of men and women in stress" [Bill A. Musk, "The Muslims' vow box and Christian mission," *Theologia Evangelica* 20/9-19 (June, 1987), 9.

[80]*Karamat al-Awliya'* (miracles of the saints), cited in Smith and Haddad, 185.

[81]Frederick M. Denny, "'God's Friends': The Sanctity of Persons in Islam," in *Sainthood*, ed. Richard Kieckhefer and George Bond (Berkeley: University of California Press, 1988), 76.

[82]Marcais, "La prière de demande," 405.

[83]Act I, Sc. E, line 32f., as cited in Cragg, 3.

[84]Douglas, "Prayers of al-Shadhili," 116.

The Sacred Work of Prayer: The Native American Christian Experience

Carol J. Gallagher

Introduction

We have come together to reflect on prayer and its global experience. I would like to begin with a brief reflection on the reality of prayer in the Native American experience. To begin with, I consider it essential, as one engaged in the study of theology as well as someone who tries, at every moment, to be a faithful representative of my people, the Cherokees, to share honestly with the reader my personal reasons for writing this essay. I have been invited to share my reflections on the nature of Christianity and the Native American Experience of prayer. The experience of being both Native and Christian, living, as it were, biculturally, is the focus of this particular experience which I will share.

Although I will reference some ancient tribal customs and their continued presence in modern Native Christianity, it is my goal to focus on the creative, powerful, and unique experiences found amidst the apparent ambiguity of prayer in this bicultural world of Native Christianity. I will also be using a style of presentation that might seem, at least at first, unfamiliar or inappropriate for this scholarly volume. James Treat, who received his doctorate from the University of California at Berkeley and who has done extensive research in the area of Native Americans and Liberation

183

Theologies, gives an important explanation of the unique process of Native Christian theological discourse:

> The contextual orientation of contemporary Native Christian literature points to other important methodological features of these writings. Most of these texts employ autobiographical narratives as primary methodological techniques for making (and not merely illustrating) theological points and many of them also make use of stories drawn from a more general, collective, cultural context . . . The prominence and centrality of narrative accounts in contemporary Native Christian testimony suggests that Native Christians consider personal and collective experience to play a central role in religious insight. While conventional Christian theology is typically doctrinal and rational, Native Christian reflection is experiential and performative; while conventional Christian theology is often dogmatic, Native Christian discourse is confessional.[1]

Treat provides us with a strong starting place and initial framework for undertaking a Native Christian perspective on prayer. Treat goes on to explain that "contemporary Native Christian writers have problematized and reconfigured the theological tradition, challenged the Christian establishment by articulating their demands through cross-cultural discourse, and used autobiographical and cultural narratives to express their own religious identities."[2] I apologize in advance for any discomfort this unique (often strange to the Western ear and eye) approach to theology might cause in this essay or in other Native Christian narrative discourse. In presenting this essay, I am attempting not only to present and construct an understanding of prayer that is radically different from the Western European and Judeo-Christian paradigm, but also to make that presentation in a manner consistent with a Native Christian approach to the theological task.

My personal commitment to the task of defining an understanding of Native Christian prayer comes from both my mixed heritage (Cherokee and European) and my Native heritage which has included almost six generations of Native Christians. At present, I am an Episcopal priest and serve on the Episcopal Council of Indian Ministries, a national body dedicated to finding authentic expressions of our Native Christianity within our Anglican tradition. This has led me to pursue a doctorate from Princeton Theological Seminary, focusing on the issues of training Native people for leadership roles in the Episcopal Church. The traditional seminary training that most of our present Native leaders experienced has not been reflective of what Treat has described as Native Christian narrative discourse. It is my hope to establish a new approach that would incorporate the traditionally Native, personal, confessional, and experiential aspects into the process of leadership training.

The questions that arose as I researched this work were formed from the problematic experiences of articulating prayer and all forms of religious experience in a Native Christian context. How can we talk about prayer that includes both a Native and a Christian context, when each offers contradictory approaches? What kind of images and insights might better form a Native Christian interpretation of prayer? In presenting this essay, I would like to suggest that the metaphor of prayer as daily *sacred work* is one way for Native Christians to dialogue with other Christians in order to gain better crosscultural understanding. As Native Christians, we stand in a confusing place that more often is defined by the Western understanding of work — that which provides identity through accomplishment, success, and station. It is this entangled dualism that I would like to attempt, first, to disentangle and, then, provide a new metaphor for one possible concept of the Native approach to prayer. The most helpful way to begin is by participation. By embedding this entire discussion in an experiential, performative exercise of prayer, we can begin to redefine our experience of prayer from a more Native context. I ask the reader to participate in the Call to Worship or the Prayer of the Four Directions. This prayer was originally written as an invocation for the *Celebration of Survival* on October 12, 1992, held in the Cathedral of Saints Peter and Paul in Washington, D.C., which included representatives from more than forty different tribes.[3] As chairperson of the worship design for this service, I had the pleasure and challenge of crafting a liturgy that would reflect and honor both our Christian and Native traditions. This experience of designing and implementing a worship service of this magnitude has directly informed my understanding of Native Christian prayer and has been a constant referent for my approach in this essay.

As a Native person, engaging in a theological undertaking, whether it might be prayer or study, I find it essential to physically participate or, in other words, to *work out* my experience of study and faith. I have learned this in a very visceral and personal way from the time of service preparation and from my work on a national board:

CALL TO WORSHIP

> **Leader:** Come, Great Spirit, as we gather in your name. We face EAST: To your symbol color — gold, for the morning star. To your animal sign — the Eagle which can soar ever upward in the praise of God and calls us to do the same. To your lessons calling us to balance of mind in the spirit of humility.

To invoke your spirit of Illumination and far-sighted vision.
Help us to love you and one another with our whole heart, our whole mind, and our whole soul, we pray:

People: Come, Holy Spirit, Come.

Leader: We turn to face SOUTH:
To your symbol color — white, of clarity and brightness.
To your animal symbol — the Quetzal which brings us in touch with earthiness and growing things.
To your lessons calling us to balance of our body in the spirit of a good sense of humor.
To invoke your spirit of innocence, trust and love.
Help us open our eyes to the sacredness of every living thing, we pray:

People: Come, Holy Spirit, Come.

Leader: We turn to face WEST:
To your symbol color — black, still and quiet.
To your symbol — the thunder mighty and purposeful.
To your lessons calling us to balance our emotions in the spirit of gentleness and honesty.
Give us your strength and the courage to endure, we pray:

People: Come, Holy Spirit, Come.

Leader: We turn to face NORTH:
To your symbol color — red, the hue of revelation.
To your animal symbol — the Buffalo strong and nurturing.
To your lessons calling us to the balance of our spirit in harmony with brothers and sisters.
To invoke your wisdom and grace and the goodness of the ages, we pray:

People: Come, Holy Spirit, Come.

Leader: We turn to complete the circle and look:
To God who cleanses our earth with snow, wind and rain.
To Jesus Christ who fills us with the wideness of mercy and lovingly embraces us all, and to the Holy Spirit who inspires us.

People: Come, Holy Spirit, Come.

Explanation of Terms

1. Prayer as Ceremony

Before I begin to lay out an argument for the way I perceive *sacred work* to be an appropriate metaphor for understanding Native Christian prayer, I would first like to clarify some terms I will be using throughout this presentation. First of all, when I speak of prayer, I will be referring to a variety of communally and personally performed experiences, involving such ritual and liminal elements as song, dance, vision, and what Christians would normally refer to as liturgy. Paula Gunn Allen, Laguna Pueblo/Sioux, professor of English at UCLA, explains:

> To say that ceremony contains songs and prayers is misleading, for prayers are one form of address and songs are another. It is more appropriate to say that songs, prayers, dances, drums, ritual movement, and dramatic address are compositional elements of a ceremony . . . The purpose of a ceremony is to integrate: to fuse the individual with his or her fellows, the community of the people with that of the other kingdoms, and this larger communal group with worlds beyond this one.[4]

So, when I refer to prayer in this essay, I am referring to her all inclusive understanding of *ceremony*. Without resorting to too many generalizations, for Native people, ceremony is life giving, integrating, and infused throughout all areas of life.

2. Native, Native American, American Indians, et cetera

When I speak of *Native, Native Americans,* or *American Indians,* I am referring to those peoples whose heritage is *indigenous* to the North American continent, including mixed race and full blood persons. There is incredible diversity among these five hundred thirty distinct tribes (more than four hundred fifty of these are recognized by the federal government and have official status with the Bureau of Indian Affairs). The differences in tribal governments, world views, and religious practices make generalizations and universalization impossible. Both terms are in essence misnomers, as Columbus was off course when he named us Indians, and all who are born in North America are Native Americans. Whenever possible, I will acknowledge the represented tribal context of the various different speakers and ceremonies.

The predominance of my particular and personal experience has been in an urban setting, where Native people come together in multitribal gatherings. In these gatherings, such as the service in the National Cathedral, multitribal expressions of prayer have been introduced to respond to the variety and diversity in our midst. There is (and should be) quite a bit of difference between local tribal celebrations and those that take place in an urban setting. Home, the blessed place of the people, is always remembered, brought forth, and recreated in new ways in strange and alien environments. No one tribal group or individual representative can, or should, make universal statements about all Native people. That said, one detects common themes or threads that seem to indicate comparability among the tribes of this hemisphere that will help us set up a framework for understanding the idea of Native Christian *prayer as sacred work.*

3. Power and Place; Particular and Personal

Vine Deloria, Jr. (Yankton Sioux), professor of history at the University of Colorado, highlights a common understanding among Native peoples, namely, *place and power* are revealed in the relatedness or unity of nature:

> The best description of the Indian metaphysics was the realization that the world, and all its possible experiences, constituted a social reality, a fabric of life in which everything has the possibility of inti- mate knowing relationships because, ultimately, everything was related. This world was a unified world, a far cry from the disjoint- ed and sterile world painted by western science. Even though we can translate the realities of that world into concepts familiar to us from the western scientific context, such as space, time and energy, the Indian world can be said to consist of two basic experiential dimensions, which, taken together, provided a sufficient means of making sense of the world. These two concepts were place and power, perhaps best defined as spiritual power of life force. Familiarity with the personality of objects and entities of the natur- al world enabled Indians to discern immediately where each living being had its proper place and what kinds of experiences that place allowed, encouraged and suggested.[5]

Professor Deloria further explains: "Power and place are domi- nant concepts — *power* being the living energy that inhabits and/or composes the universe, and *place* being the relationship of things to each other . . . power and place produce personality."[6] Like Deloria, I would have us pay close attention to the fact that Native people view themselves as existing in a dynamic, living uni- verse in which *power* (invested and available in all creation) and *place* (the locations of dynamic power) are always taken into consideration.

4. Relationality or All My Relations

Basic to understanding a Native Christian discourse on prayer is an underlying assumption of *relatedness*. Deloria emphasizes this very clearly in his brief book of essays on Indian education:

> The personal nature of the universe demands that each and every entity in it seek and sustain personal relationships. The broader idea of relationship, in a universe very personal and particular, sug- gests that all relationships have a moral content. The spiritual aspect of knowledge about the world taught the people that rela- tionships must not be left incomplete.[7]

Allen echoes these sentiments of Deloria, but pushes our under- standing further by encouraging us to see the way this *relationality* is played out in the enactment of a ritual in the Native context:

> The community is not made up of only members of the tribe but
> necessarily includes all beings that inhabit the tribe's universe.
> Within this context the dynamic characteristics of American Indian
> literature can be understood. The structures that embody
> expressed and implied relationships between human and beings, as
> well as the symbols that signify and articulate them, are designed to
> integrate the various orders of consciousness . . . Some tribes under-
> stand that the human participants include members of the tribe
> who are not physically present and that the community as a com-
> munity, not simply the separate persons in attendance, enact the
> ceremony.[8]

The significance of *relatedness* is highlighted even in texts from
outside of the Native educational and theological structures. From
a counseling perspective, Derald Wing Sue of California State
University and David Sue of Western Washington University have
carefully noted in their counseling research the significance of
relationality and personal identity: "Indians see themselves as an
extension of their tribe. This identity provides them with a sense
of belonging and security, with which they form an interdepen-
dent system."[9] Native persons, then, see themselves as extensions
of a tribe, which, in turn, sees itself related to all of creation. All of
creation is living and participating at fundamental levels in the
experience of Native life. This unique Native understanding of
relationality also integrates the personal and universal while at all
times promoting the expectation of moving towards the completion, or healing, of relationships.

5. Native Identity and Christianity

Since shortly after the arrival of Columbus, debate has been
waged over whether it is possible to be Native and Christian:

> The idea of Native Christian identity is both historically and cultur-
> ally problematic. The blatant opportunism and oppressive dog-
> matism of the missionization process, the open complicity of white
> religious leaders in the widespread land dispossession, and the
> growing strength of the Native traditionalist revival work together
> to challenge the legitimacy of the personal religious choices many
> Native Christians have made.[10]

The complexity of trying to integrate and resolve these seemingly
warring cultural and religious perspectives has extreme consequences, and some Native people have returned to their traditional worship practices, while others have abandoned all forms of
cultural-religious identification. There are those, like myself, who,
despite the incredible complexity of living "unresolved" at times,
strive to live faithfully and responsibly, informed by both traditions. For myself and others, it is a matter of survival, and, in

response to our *relatedness* to all of creation, we strive to articulate and practice that organic unity in which we find ourselves located, despite the sense dislocation in which both Western European and Indian society have, from time to time, placed us:

> To dismiss all Native Christians as acculturated, anachronistic traces of religious colonialism, is to miss innumerable demonstrations of their insightful historical and social analysis, their complex and sophisticated religious creativity, and their powerful devotion to personal and communal survival.[11]

To undertake the task of living as a Native Christian, one is often confronted by those who would question the adequacy of either one's Christian theology or one's tribal commitment. There are no adequate answers to these, but I hope to explore this issue further as I delve into the understanding of Native Christian *prayer as sacred work*.

The Present Cultural Situation

As we begin to reflect on an understanding of *prayer as sacred work*, I think that the best starting place is to describe the modern and postmodern understandings of *work* and the way they contrast to the concept of *prayer as sacred work* for Native people. Since the time of Marx, almost a hundred and fifty years ago, modern human beings have been affected by his proposition that one's work defines or brings identity to the individual in community. His exacting critique of capitalism brought clearly into focus the suffering caused when the worker was alienated from the product and means of production by an élite class:

> In estranging from man (1) nature, and (2) himself, his own active functions, his life-activity, estranged labour estranges the *species* from man. It turns for him *the life of the species* into a means of individual life. First, it estranges the life of the species and individual life, and secondly it makes individual life in its abstract form the purpose of the life of the species, likewise in its abstract and estranged form.[12]

The hallmark of the modern era has been the interminable and painful wrestling with the inherent alienation that is realized by many people throughout the world in their *daily work*. Marx attempted, in drawing a clear connection between *identity* and labor, to revolutionize the philosophical understanding of human endeavor. The long history of labor movements, socialist governments, and communist structures has not seemed to diminish the grim reality that, in many countries, a minority class still very much controls the means of production and, therefore, controls (or marginalizes) the *identity* of individuals and communities. For the modern period, which begins with the industrial and scientific revolutions, we have seen a radical divide between one's individual *identity* and the *work* one must do.

At present, *work* is conceived as merely a means of reaching personal goals, often with no integration whatsoever of the personal and public spheres. *Work* is seen, as is the *work place*, as something to be survived, not as an integrated expression of the gifts and skills of a particular person or community. Karl Rahner, in his reflection on prayer in everyday life, powerfully describes the dominant culture's perception of *work* in everyday living:

> How can prayer be an everyday business, compatible with the monotony, uniformity, depression and dullness of our hearts, so tired and desiccated? . . . Prayer in everyday life is difficult. It is easily forgotten, since our rushed and fevered age does not foster and promote it.[13]

Indeed, it seems as though this alienated and fractured existence, so clearly described by Marx, remains as the elemental paradigm of our present existence. Built into Marx's philosophy was the continuing forward progress of human productivity, acted out in class struggle and resulting in revolution. One hundred fifty years after Marx's writings, scholars are struggling to identify new ways to integrate the existential dilemmas that he detailed by their intentional move away from objectivity to a more locally focused subjectivity. Postmodern philosophers criticize Marx for his ideology and his positivistic expectation that social theory could or should encompass and adequately describe the human condition. The present postmodern move has helped us to focus on the local, the contextual, and the local narrative. Although thinkers like Lyotard and Foucault focus on the pragmatic and local constructs of *identity* and *power*, their inability and unwillingness to theorize (prescriptively) has merely exacerbated the condition of the average worker. Discarding overarching theory, they can leave the already alienated laborer unable to communicate beyond his/her local social boundaries:

> Thus, even as he argues explicitly against it, Lyotard posits the need for a genre of social criticism which transcends local mininarrative. Despite his strictures against large, totalizing stories, he narrates a fairly tall tale about a large-scale social trend . . . Lyotard's story presupposes the legitimacy and integrity of the scientific and political practices allegedly threatened by performativity.[14]

Fraser and Nicholson, in their critique of Lyotard and others, point out their continuing concern for male privilege within the academy and the inability of the postmodern paradigm to address the critical issues of alienation specifically experienced by women and other minorities because of what they see as continuing male privilege in the academy and in the economy. Their critiques and concerns have a crucial place in our discussion, as there seems to be no one presenting creative solutions in this postmodern conversation which strenuously avoids any positivistic activity whatsoever. And yet, we have seen that people who experience *work, drudgery and alienation to be synonymous beg for a transformative way to view and engage in daily life.* Many seek what Rahner announces as a "pious folksong, full of good intentions and straight from the heart"[15] that will transform and rename the toil of their daily living.

Alienation and *dislocation,* as described in both the modern and postmodern context, would appear to be a common theme for both Native and nonNative people alike. Very little in the modern or postmodern paradigms of philosophy has helped Native people and other groups to reckon with a nonrelational, isolating sense of *identity* within the dominant cultural framework. Such critics as Charlene Spretnak clearly articulate the further *dislocation* caused by the "death of subject" in postmodern thought:

> In the Western, patriarchal societies where deconstructive postmodern flourishes, deeply ingrained cultural norms of separateness, reactive autonomy and self-absorption have devoured the sense of grounded, responsible being at the very moment we have finally realized that the destruction of our habitat may have passed the point of no return . . . In the deconstructive-postmodern play of disintegration and impossibility of reason, one can merely strike self-conscious postures as if one's responses had meaning.[16]

Native people, especially those who practice the Christian faith, live out in their daily existence a life of conflict. They experience painful times of being *alienated* from the tribe and from the Church, times when neither way is enough, many times when daily living is an incredible burden, *a labor of wrenching balancing acts* which often bring them criticism from both Native and Church traditionalists.

Many Native people have looked to Liberation theology for inspiration and insight in an attempt to better articulate their struggle in finding an *identity* within the Church. Many, like George Tinker (Osage/Cherokee), Professor of Crosscultural Ministries at Iliff School of Theology, have quickly recognized that there is a critical difference in the starting points of theological discourse between Native and Liberation theologians. He has concluded that Liberation theology's starting place can be inappropriate and unhelpful in a reintegration process for Native peoples:

In *The Power of the Poor in History* Gutierrez begins by expounding on God's revelation and proclamation in history, arguing that God reveals God's self in history. I want to argue that this is not only not a self-evident truth, but that a culturally integrous Native American theology must begin with the confession that is both dramatically disparate from and exclusive of Gutierrez's starting point. Essentially, a Native American theology must argue out of Native American spiritual experience and praxis that God reveals God's self in creation, in space or place and not in time . . . The problem from Las Casas to Marx, is the assumption of the hegemonic trajectory through history which fails to recognize cultural discreetness.[17]

Praying from a Native Paradigm

In *The Life of an Indian* there was only one inevitable duty — the duty of prayer — the daily recognition of the Unseen and Eternal. Daily devotions were more necessary than daily food. He wakes at daybreak, puts on his moccasins and steps down to the water's edge. Here he throws handfuls of clear, cold water into his face, or plunges in bodily. After the bath, he stands erect before the advancing dawn, facing the sun as it dances upon the horizon, and offers his unspoken orison. His mate may precede or follow him in his devotions, but never accompanies him. Each soul must meet the morning sun, the new earth and the Great Silence alone!

Whenever, in the course of the daily hunt the red hunter comes upon a scene that is strikingly beautiful or sublime — a black thundercloud with the rainbow's glowing arch above the mountain, a white waterfall in the heart of a green gorge; a vast prairie tinged with the blood-red of sunset — he pauses for an instant in the attitude of worship. He sees no need for setting apart one day in seven as a holy day, since to him all days are God's.[18]

These words from Charles Alexander Eastman, Santee Sioux physician, set the stage for beginning the discussion on *prayer as sacred work* for Native Christians. Eastman describes for us the singular daily *work of prayer*, that which is elemental to a Native sense of responsibility in relationship to all the created order. When ethnographers like James Mooney, who himself did extensive work on collecting the history and sacred formulas of my people, the Cherokees, encountered Native religious practices, many perceived (despite their own lack of awareness of their personal or cultural lens) Native people as religious by nature:

The Indian is essentially religious and contemplative, and it might almost be said that every act of his life is determined and regulated by his religious belief. It matters not that some may call this superstition. The difference is only relative. The religion of today has developed from the cruder superstitions and enlargement of the beliefs and ceremonies which have been preserved by the Indian in their more ancient form.[19]

From Mooney's data from more than a century ago, we can see two things. First, by the time of his work, there had already been much blending of traditional ritual practices and prayers with Christian practice among the Cherokees that he studied. He indicates that there was a secretive nature to the practices at the time, partially because of the scorn shown by Church leadership for the blending or commingling of these two worlds. Second, and more important for this part of our discussion, is the description of the Indian as religious in essence, religious as centering and at the core of one's being.

To begin understanding Native Christian *prayer as sacred work*, we must get a handle on how complicated and problematic an issue we are addressing. We are attempting to turn around almost two thousand years of practice and development, to approach prayer from a *Native world view that demands a radically different understanding of prayer and ritual* than has been the norm throughout the history of the Judeo-Christian narrative. Such present day cultural anthropologists as Clifford Geertz would challenge many of Mooney's presuppositions and his move to generalizations about the people he was observing:

> The religious perspective differs from the common-sensical in that it moves beyond the realities of everyday life to wider ones which correct and complete them, and its defining concern is not action upon those wider realities but acceptance of them, faith in them. It differs from the scientific perspective in that it presents realities of everyday life not out of an institutionalized skepticism which dissolves the world's givenness into a swirl of problematic hypotheses, but in terms of what it takes to be wider, nonhypothetical truths. Rather than detachments, its watchword is commitment; rather than analysis, encounter.[20]

What Mooney was observing and describing, that my people were fundamentally religious and contemplative, was something he was observing from what Geertz has described for us as *institutionalized skepticism*. One of the most difficult things for nonNative people to comprehend is that we look out on the world from a religious perspective, not from a postenlightenment scientific detachment. Understanding what and how Native Christians pray will require us to hear from inside what Geertz has called the *local web of meaning*. The complexity faced by nonNative peoples in attempting to approach and understand prayer is that their world view or *web* is constructed in a continuing duality, an ongoing separation between body and spirit, sacred and profane, public and private, objective and subjective. To look at the world from a Native point of view is to integrate the sacred in everything, to know by being subjected to experience rather than by analyzing it.

Integrating All the Pieces

> The "private soul at any public wall" is a concept alien to American
> Indian thought. The tribes do not celebrate the individual's ability
> to feel emotion, for they assume that all people are able to do so.
> One's emotions are one's own; to suggest that others should imitate
> them is to impose on the personal integrity of others. The tribes
> seek — through song, ceremony, legend, sacred stories (myths),
> and tales — to embody, articulate, and share reality, to bring the
> isolated, private self into harmony and balance with this reality, to
> verbalize the sense of majesty and reverent mystery of all things,
> and to actualize, in language, those truths that give to humanity its
> greatest significance and dignity.[21]

When we begin the discussion about Native Christians and prayer,
we need to begin from the Native perspective which honors the
primacy of *integrating*, the bringing into balance, as the work of all
ritual and prayer. The nonNative Christian experience of prayer is
often considered as one aspect of the individual's participation in
his/her own salvation:

> The goal of life is to win eternal life where followers receive imper-
> ishable bodies in which they can do exactly the same things that
> were punishable offenses in the present life. This condition is
> known as salvation. The Indian format is precisely the opposite. Not
> only the natural physical world is regarded as integral to human
> ambitions and activities, but also even the hypothetical geometrical
> structures of the world receive some form of religious acknowl-
> edgement. Thus, Indians pray to the "four directions," lay out
> elaborate sand paintings to represent the cosmos, and see in pipe
> bowls and sweat lodges a model of the larger cosmos as a whole.[22]

Our starting point, then, becomes a place where *integrating the
larger whole, the related universe, is seen as a primary task* rather than a
personal and/or single act of piety aiming towards fulfillment in
God. Stephen Bevans, professor of historical and doctrinal studies
at the Catholic Theological Union in Chicago, would refer to this
approach as an anthropological model of contextualizing
theology:

> These words express perhaps more clearly than any I know the cen-
> tral and guiding insight of the anthropological model: Human
> nature, and therefore human culture, is good, holy, and valuable. It
> is within human culture that we find God's revelation — not as a
> separate, supracultural method but in the very complexity of cul-
> ture itself, in the warp and woof of human relationships, which are
> constitutive of cultural existence.[23]

Although some might argue that anthropology as a science is
exclusively a Western European paradigm, Bevans' understanding

helps us to articulate the primary goodness (which has not been prevalent in the Western Scholastic understanding) of Native worldview and our practices. This methodological technique honors, as Native people do, the primary importance of the relationship of people to their culture context and to the life giving forces found in all of creation.

Remembering

The next step in approaching and understanding Native Christian prayer as *sacred work* is *remembering*:

> It begins with something as simple as remembering. To many of you, this may not seem a powerful way for God to act in the lives of God's people, but I can tell you from my own tradition that the power to remember and to pass on the story of the people, generation unto generation, is the heart of what it means to be a tribe, to be the people of God. We tell our children the tradition of our people. We tell our story in song and chant, in prophecy and in memory. We carry that one because it becomes for us the center of the tribe. There is a power, in doing that. There is a power that is released when we tell our story to one another, when we remember together. Our shared history makes us a people and what happened to us 500 years ago is our common story.[24]

This power of *remembering and sharing stories* is embedded in what we understand for us as Native people to be prayer. We *remember*, first of all, that we are *related and responsible* to one another and to all of creation:

> We return thanks to our mother, the earth, which sustains us. We return thanks to the rivers and streams, which supply us with water. We return thanks to all herbs, which furnish medicines for the cure of our diseases. We return thanks to the corn and to her sisters, the beans and squashes, which give us life. We return thanks to the bushes and the trees, which provide us with fruit. We return thanks to the wind, which, moving the air, has banished diseases. We return thanks to the moon and stars, which have given to us their light when the sun was gone. We return thanks to our grandfather He-no, that he has protected his grandchildren from witches and reptiles, and has given us his rain. We return thanks to the sun, that he has looked upon the earth with a beneficent eye. Lastly, we return thanks to the Great Spirit, in whom is embodied all goodness, and who directs all things for the good of his children. (Iroquois)[25]

The body of this prayer demonstrates the *power* of *remembering* our *place* and *relationship* to the whole created order. It also describes for us an understanding of the personalities and powers acknowledged in a variety of created beings, not only people, as might be the more common notion for those in a Western European paradigm.

Charleston pushes us further by challenging us to *remember*, not only our *relatedness* to all creation, but the fact that, for Native people, God has been present and teaching us throughout the history of our tribal peoples:

> I cannot write about the Jesus of the gospels or the letters of Paul if I don't interpret them through the truths as I see them. That means the truth of the original covenant that God maintained with Israel, the truth of the witness of Jesus Christ as upheld in the "new" covenant, and the truth of the covenant between God and the Native people as revealed in the ancient testimony of Native America. Like any theologian, I have to work with at least three primary sources; the Old Testament of Israel, the New Testament of the Christian scriptures, and the Old Testament of my people. The three are integral, they cannot be separated.[26]

Again, we come back to realizing that, for Native Christian people, the *sacred work of prayer* will require an ability to *remember* the ancient and powerful truths told and *remembered* by our culture and people, and the skill to integrate those sources as described by Charleston into a constructive and creative understanding and practice of prayer.

This process of integration and creation will require a critical hermeneutic that takes into consideration the painful and inappropriate aspects of the collected sources. Robert Warrior (Osage), professor of English at Stanford University, challenges the wholesale acceptance of the Exodus liberation narratives of the Old Testament by pointing out the people of Israel were liberated at the real expense of the indigenous Canaanites, who lost lives and culture in order for God's covenant to be fulfilled:

> No matter what we do, the conquest narratives remain. As long as people believe in the Yahweh of deliverance, the world will not be safe from Yahweh the conqueror. But perhaps, if they are true to their struggle, people will be able to achieve what Yahweh's chosen people in the past have not: a society of people delivered from oppression who are not so afraid of becoming victims again that they become oppressors themselves, a society where the original inhabitants can become something other than subjects to be converted to a better way of life or adversaries who provide cannon fodder for a nation's militaristic pride.[27]

So, *remembering* for Native Christian people is a prayerful *work* of balancing the *power* and goodness of our culturally *integrated* histories while maintaining a keen awareness of the ability of humanity to break the hoop, bend the circle, and distort the truth until it is no longer life giving, but death dealing. This *remembering* is not a romantic, looking back and sighing, but a grounded, sensitive partaking of the presence of God in both traditions. This participation in the sacred demands an openeyed and rigorous willingness to recognize the dangers accompanying claims for a one right way, the only way, or the best way, to pray. It recognizes and acknowledges the *relatedness* and responsibility that we have as Native people to all our relations. If one of creation is damaged, then the circle is broken, and healing is the correct response.

Words Never Enough

In framing an understanding of Native Christian *prayer as sacred work*, I must clarify that the *work* that we are doing is not simply a translation from one language into another. When we pray, as Native people, we sing, drum, dance. John S. Hascall (Ojibwa), a Capuchin priest and member of the Midewiwin (traditional religious society of the Ojibwas), describes the expression of *prayer as sacred work* as found in Ojibwa ceremonies and in many other tribes with whom he has worked:

> Native prayer comes from the heart of the one who prays, each in his or her own way. Such prayer expresses the fullness of heart of all the grandmothers and grandfathers who have gone before us. Its content consists of all that the individual, village, season and occasion conjures in the person who is praying. Yet the person prays on behalf of all the people who have requested prayer.[28]

Even though an individual who is offering a prayer might be very much concerned about the words chosen, and is including in those words all of the needs and experiences reflected in the gathered community, the emphasis of prayer is on the way it is performed. Paula Gunn Allen makes it clear that, for most Native people, the words are only part of what is going on when we pray:

> Ceremonial literature is sacred; it has power. It frequently uses language of its own; archaisms, "meaningless" words, or special words that are not used in everyday conversation . . . Each serves to hold the society together, create harmony, restore balance, ensure prosperity and unity, and establish right relations within the social and natural world.[29]

Also, when we pray, the praying is always done in a communal spirit, though it might be led by one singer offering up his/her gift of prayer. The act of prayer, in the Native Christian experience, is known both as gift given to community and community participation in the *work* of praying. The individual may offer, but the entire community is responsible for sharing in this *sacred work*. When we pray, all of who we are is offered up to the Creator in prayer. As Hascall goes on to explain, "Our songs, often sung by one person or group of singers, draw on the riches of the centuries; they hand on the good and the suffering our people have endured throughout the ages."[30]

Sacred Work and Liturgy

We move on to the place where, now that we have understood better the tribal and cultural framework of prayer for Native people, we can begin to articulate those places of common ground between the traditions of both the Christian Church and tribal religious practices. I am suggesting that, despite the grave differences in world views, there is the possibility of forming a bridge between cultures that does not ultimately destroy the Native context and which might even give new life to both the Native and Christian experiences when considered together. The original Greek understanding of *liturgy* is a combination of the words, people, and *work*, or, literally, the *work* of the people. The word's origin reflects an understanding of liturgy as "public work done at private cost."[31] Although the word has become synonymous with the term worship and has been thoroughly associated with services in the Temple since before the time of Christ, the definition of *liturgy that I will use here reflects this restored or reformed sense of liturgy*. As Charles Price and Louis Weil, both Anglican scholars, explain:

> But we should not allow ourselves to forget that in another equally important sense, liturgy is what we do with our lives. The liturgy which is Christ has an intensive form, enacted when Christians come together. It also has an extensive form, directly related to the intensive. The extensive liturgy begins when the gathered community scatters into the world to live obediently to the Christ whose one liturgy was encountered at prayer.[32]

Many scholars who have participated in liturgical reform and renewal, across several denominations, have reached back to the beginnings of the Church in order to better live out and express their worship. In this reaching back, scholars encountered a tribal people, a tribal way of worship. Although early Christianity was philosophically influenced by Greek thought and language, the *liturgy, the work of the people*, reflected a much more ancient tradition of Hebrew tribal life. The great feasts and occasions (and even daily life) demanded an authentic cultural context, active and honest *remembering*, an integration of faith in challenging circumstances, and a *relationality* that demonstrates each individual's participation in a corporate and sacred reality.

Modern day tribal people resonate with this interpretation of *liturgy*. As we acknowledge all our relations in *kairos* time, or non-linear transcendent time, we also recognize the living Creator as participant in all that we are and do. Liturgical scholars, like Aidan Kavanagh, professor of liturgics at Yale Divinity School, articulate, from a specifically Western Christian context, that which can be affirmed by Native Christians:

> Thus a church's worship does not merely reflect or express its repertoire of faith. It transacts the church's faith in God under the condition of God's real presence in both church and world. The liturgy does this to a degree of regular comprehensiveness which no other mode or level of faith-activity can equal. Therefore the liturgy is not merely one ecclesial "work" or one theological datum among others. It is simply the church living its "bread and butter" life of faith under grace, a life in which God in Christ is encountered regularly and dependably as in no other way for the life of the world.[33]

As Native Christians, we can affirm that *prayer* and *liturgy* are at the core of what we know to be our *sacred work*.

Price and Weil, like myself, are members of the Episcopal Church in the United States and the larger worldwide Anglican communion. What I am proposing is that Native Christian people, particularly those who share this tradition, are generally able to affirm this understanding of *liturgy which is the people's work*. As we delve more deeply into the specific parts of the Christian *liturgy* and the way *liturgy* might better express the Native Christian experience of *prayer*, let me remind the reader that I will be speaking out of my particular Anglican context and do not wish to imply or presume that the statements I make can, or should, be the norm for all Native Christian people. I do, though, want to push us beyond the problems of integration to a vision of what it might look like if Native people at *prayer* became fully recognized and fully welcomed and fullest expressions of our Christianity. James Treat reminds us about the work he has attempted, acknowledging the variety and diversity in the Native Christian experience:

> This collective voice represents a reasoned attempt to persuade the dominant culture and the religious establishment to acknowledge the undeniable veracity of Native Christian identities. This pluralistic voice expresses the intellectual acumen of an ongoing debate, crossing tribal borders and denominational boundaries, about the nature of Native Christian life. This intimate voice alludes to the intensely personal dimension of the struggle, the challenge to find faith in the midst of conflict, described so eloquently by Laverne Jacobs (Ojibwa) as a "lifelong dialogue with self," uncovering "different aspects of that reality like the many facets of a precious gem."[34]

As we acknowledge the possibility of a shared and useful understanding of *liturgy as the work of the people* and, therefore, *sacred work*,
let us not forget the tremendous personal and tribal effect of any
work that we do.

Sacred Work and *Sacred Symbols*

When we look at Christian *liturgy* and, specifically, the
Eucharist, we see a form of *praying that is communal, ceremonial, and
heavily symbolic.* All of the elements of the Eucharist come from the
good gifts found in creation — the bread, wine, and water.
Western Christians sometimes wish to separate *symbol* from actual
reality, but we can see in both (Native and Judeo-Christian) traditional understandings of *liturgy* as the *symbolic* enactment which
becomes a full participation in the then and living Christ. Leonel
Mitchell, professor of liturgics at Seabury-Western Theological
Seminary, explains this concept by referring to the words of the
Book of Common Prayer:

> By far the most important role for everyone is to be the celebrant
> community, the Body of Christ offering "the Church's sacrifice of
> praise and thanksgiving as the way by which the sacrifice of Christ
> is made present, and in which he unites us to his one offering of
> himself." We who are the Church assemble to do this "in Christ"
> and he is present to us and acts in us. We are united with him in the
> Paschal Mystery of his dying and rising.[35]

For the Native Christian, this present participant in ancient
mystery resonates with our sense of ritual and ceremony. Allen
confirms that:

> Not only are the "symbols" statements of perceived reality rather
> than metaphorical or poetic statements but the formulations that
> are characterized by brevity and repetition are also expressions of
> that perception. One sees life as part of oneself; a hint as to which
> particular part is all that is needed to convey meaning.[36]

I am taking care in this discussion not to present a syncretic
methodological understanding of Native Christian *prayer*, meaning a simplistic forcing together of meanings and *symbols*, declaring them to be one and the same. I am, rather, pointing out places
where there is the possibility of correspondent and mutually
acceptable understandings of the *work* of *prayer. The Eucharist, the
principal feast in Christian Churches, can be a place where the symbols, the
gifts from creation that Native people have special awareness of, can be
brought in and included, blessed by their presence, and become a blessing
to the community.* In the *Celebration of Survival,* we included the use
of drum, circle, cedar, sage, tobacco, sweetgrass, integrating our

traditional *symbols* from the earth with the traditional *symbols* and signs of the Church. This integrating is best demonstrated in the following prayer written by Cara Widrick (Cree/Ojibwa) for the Anglican Church of Canada:

A Prayer of Unity

The circle of life includes everything God our Creator has created. Nothing is excluded. No-one is excluded. The circle is a very important way of understanding our aboriginal sacred instructions. It is a symbol of our sacred teachings.

The Holy Bible contains teachings of God and Jesus his son, and the Holy Spirit. These teachings are also good for all nations and all creation.

Both teachings of my Native culture and the Bible will help me on my journey on the sacred path of life. Both teachings will assist our people on their journeys and will heal our people.

The black circle represents God our Creator, *Kitche Manitou.* Although we know him, he is still the Great Mystery and the one who gives all life.

The sweetgrass is one of our sacred healing plants and is also our sacred road. I saw a path in a dream and God said, "you shall walk the Sweetgrass Path."[37]

What Widrick and others, like myself, are articulating when we pray is this vision of the richness of our faith in the full complexity of our Native Christianity, nestling our *symbols* side-by-side, honoring both, and reducing neither. We look to do the hard *sacred work* of honoring God as revealed in and through both cultures.

John Hascall explains that the integration of the *symbols* of both traditions helps us as Native Christian people to be personally and publicly integrated and in harmony with all of creation:

In all these ways, the liturgy of Native Americans mirrors the ways of our culture. In effect, as Native Catholics our sacramental life must reflect our Native ways so that we can grow to wholeness as a people of God to help build the body of Christ. As I go among the different tribes, I go to draw forth the Christ who has always been with our people. My prayer is that we Native Catholic people will continue to grow in greater harmony with our creator, with others, with the world and with ourselves through the many gifts we have been given as Native people.[38]

Much more research and practice need to be done on the integration of *sacred symbols* in our *sacred work.* The work will best be done when Native Christians take bold steps to *introduce and integrate the profound transformative truths of our cultures into the transfor-*

mative work of Christian liturgy and ritual. As we pray together, from our tribal understandings, we can bridge out across territory previously navigated by missionaries who, faithful and well intentioned as they were, remained ignorant of the profound and unique gifts that Native people have brought to the table of faith. The offerings of our prayers, our *sacred work*, from the good of all creation, can be lifegiving and transformative in a new and powerful way. Our *work* is very much about bringing ourselves, all that we are, as an offering to our churches and our people. I want to turn to the words of Laverne Jacobs (Ojibwa), who passionately and profoundly details his Christian *journey* from renunciation of Native spirituality to a recognition of God's real presence in the midst of his people and in the *liturgy*:

> On this occasion, I attended a service of the Native community in my home diocese. This service, held in the Cathedral, began with Father Hascall praying with the Pipe in the Four Directions. He began his ceremony with a brief explanation saying that certain people would be invited to share the Pipe with him. His assistant called me to come forward. Time stood still. I struggled with the implications of this request . . . In my turmoil and anxiety I placed the Pipe to my lips and drew upon the sacred substance not knowing what would follow, but trusting and hoping that somehow God was present in this action and praying that I would be protected from that which I did not know or understand. I returned to my seat and watched as the ceremony continued . . . As I pondered the whole experience, I had a sensation of One saying "This is you."[39]

Conclusion

Sacred Work as Journey

Finally, common to many Native traditions is the prominence of life as a *journey*, life that is a pathway to be taken in a prayerful, harmonious way. Many of the traditional prayers, songs, and dances request safety on life's *journey*, recognizing both the basic needs of the traveler and the reality that the road ahead is uncertain. We travel in a circle of seasons and weather changes, of storms and cool, gentle winds, while at each turn aiming to come home with more wisdom and insight than we had when we departed. *Journey as sacred work* acknowledges the going out to seek wisdom and particularly new *vision*, while becoming more and more integrated, *coming home* related and sensitive to all our relations. *Journey* recognizes the fragility of our existence and exactly how little control we have over the created order. This Eskimo song-prayer shows us the very real and tangible importance, to Native people, of themselves and their *prayer* as integral participants in the *journey*:

Song

And I think over again
My small adventures
When with a shore wind I drifted out
In my kayak
And thought I was in danger.
My fears,
those I thought so big,
For all the vital things
I had to get and to reach.
And yet, there is only
One great thing,
The only thing:
To live to see in huts and on journeys
The great day that dawns,
And the light that fills the world.[40]

This Native concept of the *journey* intertwined with *coming home*, with healing, with all of nature, with the completion of the circle, is reflected in all of our *sacred work* of *prayer.* Juanita Little (Mescalero Apache) sees her *journey* as a catechist embedded both in the story of her people and the story of Jesus:

> Our people are a wandering people. Their history is one of wander-ing all over the southwest and into Mexico. So the Chief, the Leader, the Guide, is a very important person among the people. This guide has to clear the way. I see Jesus as One who has, first of all, won us a freedom through His suffering and death. He has cleared the way for us but He still walks with us on this journey. He walks with us as a guide, a provider, as protector, and healer. Being one of us and sharing the joy and the sufferings of this journey. As I look at my own personal journey with Jesus, I am impressed. I can see that He has sent certain people, has put me in certain places at certain times to keep me on the way.[41]

The way of *Native prayer* is a way of walking, talking, singing, dancing, and struggling in and through our daily experiences. It is not any less than *all that we are.* For Native Christians, to pray is to be Native and to live. Jesus, in our experience, comes to us and with us, *working* the *sacred* along with us.

I wish to close where we began: we will act out our *prayer* together, as a community, as the people of God. In the course of this essay I have tried to demonstrate the unique understanding of Native Christian *prayer as sacred work.* This *sacred work* is all encom-passing and elemental to who we are as Native Christians. *Prayer as sacred work is integrating, remembering, more than words, and found in liturgy, symbol, and journey.* It is acted out in every moment of our existence. This is the gift that Native people can bring to the present dialogue on *prayer*. Our *prayer*, our *sacred work*, is not private, but communal, not only still or contemplative, but active. And, it is this activity of our *sacred work* that we offer to all other Christians as we together face the end of the millennium:

Community Prayer

Creator God, you are with us in bright sunshine — in the sparkle on winter trees.

All: Creator, come to us.

As we stand alone at the side of a river, struggling with direction in our lives.

All: Creator, come to us.

As we witness pain in the lives of our people, as we wait for change founded on respect and gentleness, a healing place.

All: Creator, come to us.

In our humility as we struggle with our self-esteem.

All: Creator, come to us.

In a blizzard, touch and uplift us, in the gushing wind, bring us healing.

All: Creator, come to us.

In Christian ways and in traditional ways, in wind and grass, in birds that fly and in our places of *prayer*.

All: Creator, come to us.

In our quiet places, in the longing of a child for the love of a parent.

All: Creator, come to us.

We see you in the pain of peoples in prison, caught in structures of injustice. Help us bring healing.

All: Creator, come to us as our hearts and minds are joined in the circle.[42]

NOTES

[1]James Treat, ed., *Native and Christian: Indigenous Voices on Religious Identity in the United States and Canada* (New York: Routledge, 1996), 13.

[2]Ibid.

[3]Washington National Cathedral, *A Celebration of Native American Survival Pamphlet* (Washington: National Cathedral, 1992), 3.

[4]Paula Gunn Allen, *The Sacred Hoop: Recovering the Feminine in American Indian Traditions* (Boston: Beacon Press, 1986), 62.

[5]Vine Deloria, Jr., *Indian Education in America* (Boulder, CO: American Indian Science & Engineering Society, 1991), 10.

[6]Ibid., 14.

[7]Ibid., 15.

[8]Allen, 63.

[9]Derald Wing Sue and David Sue, *Counseling the Culturally Different: Theory and Practice*, 2nd ed. (New York: John Wiley & Sons, 1990), 176.

[10]Treat, 9.

[11]Ibid., 10.

[12]Robert C. Tucker, ed., *The Marx-Engels Reader*, 2nd edition (New York: W.W. Norton & Company, Inc., 1978), 75.

[13]Karl Rahner, *On Prayer* (Collegeville, MN: The Liturgical Press, 1993), 52-53. Rahner continues by challenging the reader, despite the frenzied and alienated age in which we live, that there is tremendous transformative power in the culturally embedded, daily enacted "pious folksong."

[14]Nancy Fraser and Linda J. Nicholson, "Social Criticism without Philosophy: An Encounter between Feminism and Postmodernism," in *Feminism/Postmodernism*, ed. Linda J. Nicholson (New York: Routledge, 1990), 25.

[15]Rahner, 58.

[16]Charlene Spretnak, *States of Grace: The Recovery of Meaning in the Postmodern Age* (New York: HarperCollins, 1991), 15. Spretnak suggests that the recovery of wisdom traditions and a willing participation in mystery are the remedy for the radical sense of dislocation in this disjointed and continuously isolating age.

[17]George Tinker, "Spirituality, Native American Sovereignty and Solidarity," in Treat, 119.

[18]T. C. McLuhan, *Touch the Earth: A Self-Portrait of Indian Existence* (New York: Outerbridge & Lazard, 1971), 36.

[19]James Mooney, *Myths of the Cherokee and Sacred Formulas of the Cherokees*, reproduction (Nashville: Elders-Booksellers Publishers, 1982), 319. This reproduction of Mooney's original manuscript for the Bureau of American Ethnography (#19 and #7) was compiled in 1900 and 1887-88 respectively. They are a rich source of both ancient tribal ritual and the influence and interweaving of Native Christian understanding from more than a century ago.

[20]Clifford Geertz, *The Interpretation of Cultures* (New York: Basic Books, 1973), 112.

[21]Allen, 55.

[22]Vine Deloria, Jr., *God Is Red: A Native View of Religion*, 2nd edition (Golden, CO: North American Press, 1992), 154. This book was originally written in 1972 at the height of the American Indian Movement. Deloria, who is the son of an Episcopal priest, has great criticism of the cultural ignorance of Christian missionaries as a whole.

[23]Stephen B. Bevans, *Models of Contextual Theology* (Maryknoll, NY: Orbis Books, 1992), 49. In choosing this methodological approach to understanding prayer, I am acknowledging that Bevans' categories are limited by complexities of model-making in itself. The push towards an anthropological approach comes out of my conviction that the Native world view must be inserted into this discussion in a primary position in order to highlight the unique characteristics of the Native concept of prayer.

[24]Steven Charleston, *Good News for Native America* (New York: Church Center, 1994), 37. This excerpt is taken from the sermon preached on the occasion of the *Celebration of Survival* on October 12, 1992. Charleston has repeatedly encouraged Native and nonNative people in the Americas to understand the commonality of their shared history, their shared stories, the relationship and responsibility we have for each other.

[25]John Bierhorst, ed., *In the Trail of the Wind: American Indian Poems and Ritual Orations* (New York: Farrar, Straus and Giroux, 1971), 38.

[26]Steven Charleston, "The Old Testament of Native America," in Treat, 75.

[27]Robert Warrior, "Canaanites, Cowboys and Liberation: Deliverance, Conquest and Liberation Theology Today," in Treat, 99.

[28]John S. Hascall, "The Sacred Circle," in Treat, 181.

[29]Allen, 73.

[30]Hascall, "The Sacred Circle," in Treat, 181.

[31]Charles P. Price and Louis Weil, *Liturgy for Living* (New York: Seabury Press, 1979), 21.

[32]Ibid., 24.

[33]Aidan Kavanagh, *On Liturgical Theology* (New York: Pueblo Press, 1981), 8.

[34]Treat, 22.

[35]Leonel L. Mitchell, *Praying Shapes Believing: A Theological Commentary on the Book of Common Prayer* (Minneapolis: Winston Press, 1985), 129.

[36]Allen, 70. Although Allen is referring to Native literary works, this sense of symbols making real one's part of the whole correlates with the Body of Christ made participant in the Eucharist.

[37]Cara Widrick, "Unity Prayer," in *The Dancing Sun* (Toronto: First Nations Ecumenical Liturgical Resources & History and Publications Board & The Division of Missions, 1992), 10.

[38]Hascall, "The Sacred Circle," in Treat, 183.

[39]Laverne Jacobs, "The Native Church," in Treat, 239.

[40]Bierhorst, 164.

[41]Juanita Little, "The Story and Faith Journey," in Treat, 215.

[42]"Community Prayer," in *The Dancing Sun*, 17.

Index of Persons

Al-Ghazali, Abu Hamid, 145, 156, 161, 178, 179, 180
Allen, Paula Gunn, 187, 188, 198, 201, 205, 206, 207
Allport, Gordon, 122, 144
Al-Shadhili, 'Ali Abu'l-Hasan, 147, 177
Amalorpavadass, D. S., 55, 56, 57, 76
Andrews, Charles Freer, 60, 61, 62, 63, 77
Ashraf, Syed Ali, 178, 179, 180
Ayoub, Mahmoud, 148, 158, 178, 180, 181

Berry, Thomas, 6, 42
Bevans, Stephen B., 47, 74, 195, 206
Buddha, 1, 110, 111, 112, 115, 120, 121, 123, 127, 128, 129, 131, 132, 134, 135, 137, 140

Cenkner, William, 47, 74, 77, 78
Chung, Hyun Kyung, 28, 29, 30, 31
Collins, Mary, 179
Congar, Yves, O.P., 21, 44
Cousins, Ewert H., 42, 74, 79
Cragg, Kenneth, 145, 163, 177, 178, 180, 181

de Chardin, Pierre-Teilhard, 1, 2, 6, 41, 42
de Mello, Anthony, S. J., 4, 5, 42, 52, 53, 75
Deloria, Vine, Jr., 188, 205, 206
Dollah, Mohamed A., 178, 179, 180
Douglas, Elmer H., 146, 178, 180, 181
Dunne, John S., 50, 74
Dupuis, Jacques, S.J., 69, 78

Eck, Diana L., 4, 5, 42
Eckhart, Meister, 143, 144

Feghali, Joseph, 178, 179, 180

Gallagher, Carol J., 27, 183
Gandhi, Mahatma, 49, 60, 61, 62, 63, 77
Greeley, Dolores Lee, R.S.M., 1, 45
Griffiths, Bede, 63, 64, 65, 66, 67, 68, 69, 70, 71, 78

Hascall, John S., 198, 199, 202, 207
Hays, Edward, 6, 41, 42
Heschel, Abraham, 104
Hoffman, Rabbi Lawrence A., 100, 107, 108

Idelsohn, A. Z., 83, 106

Jacobs, Father Laverne, 200, 203, 207
James, William, 135, 143, 144
Jaspers, Karl, 1, 2, 41
John XXIII, Pope (Angelo Roncalli), 17, 18, 19, 22, 43
John of the Cross, Saint, 117, 119, 120, 131, 134, 136, 137, 138, 143, 144
John Paul II, Pope, 36, 37, 38, 39, 40, 46
Joyce, Kevin Patrick, 54, 55, 76
Julian of Norwich, 34, 45
Jung, Carl, 132, 144

Karim, Goolam Mohamed, 159, 178, 179, 180
Kavanagh, Aidan, 200, 207
Knitter, Paul F., 44
Kohler, Kaufmann, 90, 105, 106
Küng, Hans, 37, 41, 45